Madam 90210

ALEX ADAMS AND
WILLIAM STADIEM

Madam
90210

MY LIFE AS MADAM TO THE RICH AND FAMOUS

VILLARD BOOKS • NEW YORK • 1993

This a true account. Except for incidental
references to public figures, the names and identifying
characteristics of the participants have been changed
to protect their privacy.

Library of Congress Cataloguing information is available.
ISBN 0-679-42065-7

Manufactured in the United States of America on acid-free paper
98765432
First Edition

Author's Note

I met Alex Adams in the spring of 1992 and from that time have been immersed in the world of Hollywood deluxe prostitution. While Alex has been the central resource for *Madam 90210*, well over a hundred others have contributed to the book's authenticity. Among these are over fifty clients, some rich and famous, others merely rich; an equal number of call girls; a dozen or so other madams; a sampling of psychiatrists, psychologists, and plastic surgeons, representing the medical support system of the call-girl universe; their cosmetic counterparts: *boutiquiers*, beauticians, manicurists, and masseuses; and, finally, law-enforcement officers.

Because the use of call girls is so prevalent within the film community, in which I work as a screenwriter, I myself knew quite a few clients who were willing to share their experiences with me. Alex was instrumental in introducing me to the highest end of this market, asking some of her closest friends, the major "Players," to talk to me. They graciously accommodated her.

The most difficult task in embarking upon this project was finding high-level call girls, past and present, to speak openly about their profession. Here Alex's participation was essential in convincing ex–call girls who had gone on to success—maritally, professionally, or both—to talk freely about the darkest secret of their past, as well as in persuading current call girls, often earning annual six-figure incomes, to talk freely about the darkest secret of their present. It is a tribute to the esteem in which Alex is held in this unique community that these women trusted her enough to trust me.

In Hollywood, everything revolves around validation and credibility. Selling a script to one studio makes all the others vie for your next one. Call girls and madams operate on the same principle. Once word was out that I was writing a book with Alex, gaining access to other women in the business proved much simpler. They assumed that if Alex, Hollywood's "Super Madam" for the last twenty years, was collaborating with me, then *Madam 90210* was going to be the definitive statement on the subject, and they wanted to be part of it.

My quid pro quo for all this remarkable access was nothing more than to adhere to the cardinal rule of a long and ascendant career: "Discretion, discretion, discretion." Where the clients were concerned, patronizing a prostitute is the misdemeanor whose public opprobrium is most disproportionate to its legal censure. Careers, marriages, entire lives, have been wrecked by the revelation of this technically minor offense. For women, the wages of justice are higher, particularly for the madams, for whom a pandering conviction in California is a felony with a mandatory three-year prison sentence. The wages of society are sternest of all: A prostitution accusation, to say nothing of an arrest, even for being a call girl to the stars, is a scarlet letter that is almost impossible to expunge. While it is the mission of this book to present as complete, candid, and unexpurgated a portrait of this heretofore uncharted territory as possible, I could not and would not name names, nor reveal true identities. Nevertheless, every character in this book is drawn from a true occurrence, as recounted to me by one or more of the participants therein. To protect true identities, I have scrupulously avoided reporting any salient characteristics or behavior that would enable a reader to say, "Aha, that can only be ————." I have also added certain other aspects drawn from different real people to effectuate the disguises, along with fabricating names of movies, agencies, and other business entities. Aside from this, the people are real, the stories are real, the sex is real.

I have been asked how I can ascertain that what I have been told is true. Sex is the murkiest of all areas in this regard. Short of being in the bedroom with a video camera, absolute certainty is impossible. Again, I am fortunate in having a depth of sources and in having Alex Adams, whose decades of experience have made her a shrewd judge of character and veracity, as well as a captivating raconteuse. In any event, in this netherworld of shadows and candlelight, sighs and whispers, all I could ultimately rely on was the investigative and interrogatory skills I learned in my past life as a lawyer, tact, taste, and my own best judgment to pierce the veil of mystery surrounding Hollywood's most tightly guarded secret and tell it like it is.

—WILLIAM STADIEM
Santa Monica, California
August 1993

Contents

MADAM 90210

CHAPTER ONE

MADAM 90210

*T*here were so many Ferraris, Bentleys, and Aston Martins jammed into the chaparral-and-bougainvillea-covered shoulders of Tower Grove Drive that the steep road leading to one of the highest and most exclusive estates of the Beverly Hills resembled the parking lot of Mortons on a hot Monday night. It was thus with some discomfiture that Jack Nicholson emerged from his long black stretch limousine when it was unable to negotiate the first of Tower Grove's several hairpin turns and faced the prospect of a long trek uphill. Tucking his Evian bottle under the arm of his black parachute-silk jacket, Nicholson took a deep breath and began his ascent. This was one party he wasn't about to miss.

The road was peppered with fellow travelers in Armani wools and Maxfield leathers, whose bodies had been primed by their personal trainers for these sorts of climbs up Hollywood's stairways to heaven. These were men who didn't park their own cars, but word had come down from the top that there was no valet parking. This was unusual for a fete in these hallowed precincts, but this was an unusual fete.

Several of the climbers nodded hello to Jack Nicholson, who nodded back. Several others passed misery-loves-company remarks about the arduousness of the trek. Nicholson swigged his Evian, caught his breath, and panted upward. That such a star was making the trip with them made the other men feel good. Nicholson was here, and that, by definition, was sufficient to make this an "A" event.

Actually, it was a scarlet A. Red and hot. Oddly enough, that the party was being given for Mick Jagger accounted for only part of the heat. Jagger was in Los Angeles to record a new album. He had just broken up with Jerry Hall and had rented the Mulholland Drive villa of Bettina Bancroft, the Dow Jones heiress, for fifty thousand dollars a month, as the love nest for himself and his new inamorata, Italian megamodel Carla Bruni. But Bruni had decamped for Milan, and Jagger was a bachelor in paradise. Which led to the other, and more important, reason why this party was the hot ticket of the season: The hostess of the event was none other than Heidi Fleiss, who had just bought the estate from Michael Douglas.

Heidi Fleiss was not some lady who lunched at the Bistro Garden, whose husband had made big bucks in Omaha pork bellies and gone west. Heidi Fleiss was twenty-six years old, sleekly attractive, and entirely self-made. She had bought the Douglas house with nearly two million dollars of her own earnings, and those earnings didn't come from such get-rich-quick Southern California venues as wrinkle creams, chocolate chip cookies, or neoprene bikinis. Heidi Fleiss sold sex. Three hundred of Hollywood's most beautiful call girls would be her guests tonight.

Heidi Fleiss was a madam. She wanted to be *the* madam. The legendary Madam Alex, for whom Heidi had worked and whose acolyte she had become, had retired. A group of about ten lesser madams, of whom Heidi was one, were carving up Alex's golden pie, a multimillion-dollar business of erotica for the rich and famous. Every one of them was deeply avaricious. Every one wanted it all. Every one wanted to cut the others out. Tonight's bacchanal was much more than a tribute to a king of rock and roll. It was Heidi's own housewarming, her coming-out party, a brazen, in-your-face challenge to her rivals: Look at my house, look at my girls, see who I can get. With Alex gone, Heidi Fleiss wanted more than anything in the world to be the new Madam 90210.

Heidi's house was just below the intersection of Tower Grove and, appropriately enough, a road called Shangri-La. At least fifteen huge pro-football-size black men in blue blazers and headsets stood sentry at the gates, while two 5' 10" brunet bundles of skintight Azzedine Alaia mini-dresses and Charles Jourdan high heels checked guests off against a computerized list the length of a small telephone book. As gracious as Disneyland guides could be when one was on the list, these sirens became foaming, nightshade-sprouting Cerberuses when confronted with a crasher wearing a T-shirt and a tuxedo jacket who said he was here to meet Bruce Willis. That a Don Johnson look-alike would take the name of Bruce Willis in vain was considered the height of effrontery. "Bruce Willis is *not* on the list," one of the brunettes snorted venomously, cutting a backward glance to one of the headsetted guards, who took only one menacing step toward the interloper. "You'd better move on," the bouncer said. The uninvited man cursed under his breath, and was gone. There was none of the old Studio 54 "You look right so you can come in" doorman discretion. You were either on the list, or you were off the list.

"I'm here with Alan Finkelstein," Jack Nicholson said, vaguely out of breath. Alan Finkelstein was one of Nicholson's closest friends, the co-producer of his film *The Two Jakes* and the majordomo of the Monkey Bar, Hollywood's current boîte of the moment. He also had a reputation, even a renown, for being surrounded by beautiful women. The hostesses checked the list as Nicholson arched a brow. "Oh, yes, Mr. Nicholson." The giant bouncers stepped aside and welcomed the Joker into the party.

The white, sprawling ranch house was one of those expensively anonymous mansions often seen on the front page of the Metro section of the *L.A. Times* as the site of a multiple murder or suicide. In fact, it was just across Benedict Canyon from the Cielo Drive residence where Sharon

Tate and her companions had been mutilated by the Manson family. Tonight, few of the women were old enough to remember who Sharon Tate was, but many looked like her, the perfect tall blond natural beach goddess, the type the Beach Boys immortalized in "California Girls." The sea of blondes was staggering. Even Jack Nicholson seemed impressed. Here were hundreds of blondes in black leather, in blue denim, in miniskirts; endless taut, Malibu-tanned, Sports Connection–toned flesh and fantasy. It was like stumbling into the ultimate MTV rock video. Hollywood Babe-ylon. Heidi Fleiss had outdone herself this time.

At midnight, when most Los Angeles parties were beginning to wind down, this one was starting up. Mick Jagger had not yet arrived. He was on rock time, still at the recording studio. Heidi Fleiss had not yet been seen, either. With no one around to make introductions, men and women seemed to group together in gender clusters, waiting for the right time to make a move. There was a lot of staring. The steady stream of new females pouring in was evocative of a Miss World pageant. Each was more stunning than the last. Men seemed reluctant to commit, if only for a chat, for fear of missing someone even better who hadn't yet arrived. So men talked deals among themselves, and women simply waited, beautiful wallflowers at this super-prom.

Most of the women outside were sitting on the grass around the hurricane lamp–lit Olympic-size pool. Soft, warm Santa Ana winds rustled the jacaranda as the lights of the towers of Century City twinkled in the distance. There were two outside bars serving a surprisingly meager selection of cheap vodka and California Coolers. The San Pellegrino water had already run out, as had the ice. The deafening rap music blasting from the giant speakers inside the living room made the interior of Heidi's house off limits to all except those whose eardrums had already been wrecked by an adolescence spent in the front rows of all the best rock concerts. Many of the girls here fit that category. A few of these disco princesses danced with each other on the bare hardwood floors, while others sat together on the cheap Haitian-cotton couches and IKEA chairs that constituted the house's only furnishings. There were no paintings on the walls, no books on the library shelves. The main decor consisted of four giant-screen televisions, one in every living area.

The real action inside the house was at the two main bathrooms, where lines of mixed couples and triples perhaps thirty people long waited to get in. The wait was endless. Each ménage lasted anywhere from five to fifteen minutes, after which the door would open and the line would cheer as the glazed and smiling revelers emerged. The house rule was BYOD (Bring Your Own Drugs). The preferences for the evening were coke, crack, Ecstasy, crystal meth (a synthetic cocaine substitute), and Mandrax, the English equivalent of quaaludes. The selection of narcotics was greater than the choice of liquor at the bar.

If the women at the party tended to look like Sharon Tate, a goodly number of the men bore some resemblance to Charles Manson, or Jesus, or a combination of the two. There was a lot of long, wild hair, leather vests over naked, muscled, hairless chests, jeans, sandals. Like the women, these men were young, in their early twenties, and they didn't look as if they could afford a meal at Fatburger, much less the thousand dollars for an hour of pleasure that was the asking rate for one of Heidi's women. Why, then, were they on the list? The reason was that they were the rock-and-roll and/or drug-dealer contingent, the dudes these blond "creatures" actually hung out with. Some had gone to high school with the girls, some got them backstage passes, some sold them crack, some had been in drug rehab or A.A. or C.A. or N.A. with them, and some were just simply Their Type. The attraction between cover girl and grunge rocker was ineluctable.

Peering across this generation gap with a mix of revulsion and envy, the older men at the party, i.e., everyone over thirty, constituted an entirely different constituency. Jack Nicholson said hello to actor Timothy Hutton, who had just finished shooting the horror film *The Temp*, about a secretary from hell, and to comedian Pauly Shore, son of the owner of the Comedy Store, fresh from his own success in *Encino Man*. He nodded to Prince Rupert Loewenstein, who managed Mick Jagger's high finances. He had a warm greeting for Richard Perry, one of the town's leading record producers, who had done big albums for everyone from Barbra Streisand to the Pointer Sisters and was a legendary party giver himself. Perry even had a discotheque in his home, which was just across the road from a great party house of another era, where George Cukor had entertained Greta Garbo and Cary Grant. Nicholson greeted Nick Wechsler, the lawyer turned film producer, who was flush from his hip successes with *Drugstore Cowboy, sex, lies, and videotape,* and *The Player.*

Tonight, if you were over thirty, you had to be a major Player or you wouldn't be here. This party was the sexual equivalent of a front table at Mortons, courtside seats at Laker games, donors' treatment at Cedars-Sinai. It was also hard evidence that the legend of the Hollywood playboy, which had come into its fullest flower with the Sinatra–Martin–Davis, Jr.–Lawford Rat Pack in the Marilyn Monroe 1950s, had not died with the recent marriage of Hugh Hefner, but rather had evolved. AIDS and Family Values notwithstanding, Hollywood gentlemen still preferred blondes. There was an elite corps of these men, a number of whom were at this party, who spent many of their non-deal-making hours in pursuit of the most beautiful women in a city that undoubtedly had more professionally good-looking women than any other. These Hollywood pashas could be called the Beauty Bunch.

From Jack Nicholson on down, members of the Beauty Bunch were often famous, were always wildly successful, and typically had endless patronage to dispense. Arguably, they could have any woman they fancied. Truffle hounds of pulchritude, these men could always be found Where the Girls Were: art galleries, club openings, fashion shows, "A" parties, "A" whatever, but always "A." The women they were with were invariably gorgeous, though what really distinguished these Players from all others in Hollywood was that they went out, as opposed to cocooning in their million-dollar mansions in Malibu and Montana.

What kind of men made up the Beauty Bunch? Brat Packers like Kiefer Sutherland, who was once engaged to Julia Roberts; Sean Penn, who had been married to Madonna and was now with Robin Wright; Rob Lowe, whose X-rated home video actually helped his career; Charlie Sheen, who was on the cover of *Penthouse;* and Judd Nelson, the token preppy from St. Paul's and Haverford. They might currently be married, or in love, but they still liked to go out. There were older actors like Nicholson, Joe Pesci, Harry Dean Stanton, Peter Weller, Dennis Hopper, and Warren Beatty, before they went domestic. There were rock stars like Don Henley and Glenn Frey, late of the Eagles. There were foreign producers like Victor Drai, the former jeans manufacturer from Morocco who had married both Jacqueline Bisset and Kelly LeBrock and produced the American remakes of French comedies like *Cousin, Cousine* (*Cousins*) and *Pardon Mon Affaire* (*The Woman in Red*). There were American producers like Steve Tisch, the Loew's heir and the man who gave Tom Cruise to the world in *Risky Business*. There were agents like Bill Block, whose short-lived Inter-Talent Agency had taken on the colossus Creative Artists Agency only to be reabsorbed by ICM, and who had posed in *Vanity Fair* in what amounted to a fashion statement. When it came to beautiful women, no producer could even come close to Robert Evans, except perhaps hairdresser turned studio head Jon Peters, but Evans was entertaining at home these days, and Peters was blissfully ensconced with supermodel Vendela, who had a development deal at Sony-Columbia, where Peters himself had a huge producing deal after bailing out, with a platinum parachute, as co-chairman. Their domesticity notwithstanding, if Evans and Peters had materialized on this or any other "A"-list beauty night, no one would have been surprised.

Anyone trying to spot stars like Kevin Costner, Harrison Ford, or Mel Gibson at parties where the Beauty Bunch was out in force would be sorely disappointed. Nor would they ever see a mogul like Michael Eisner or Mike Ovitz, or even one of the shoguns of Sony or Matsushita, who owned the town, surveying their domain on the L.A. equivalent of a Tokyo boys' night out. These were all family men. Aside from paying their respects at a charity event at the Beverly Hilton, like Marvin Davis's Carousel Ball, they stayed home.

But why would pashas consort with call girls? What did call girls have that these men couldn't get at home, or at least at the Monkey Bar? To begin with, what interested the pashas was the girls, not the call. They were ladies' men, not guidance counselors. If the girl were divinely right, the pashas couldn't have cared less what she did for a living. The notion of the Hollywood call girl was a very fluid concept; today's call girl could be tomorrow's movie star, and vice versa. By the same token, today's model, or accountant, or salesgirl, or development girl, could also be today's call girl. Furthermore, these men were rich; a thousand-dollar happy hour was nothing to someone making a million a week. Then again, no one was saying that these men were in fact paying for sex. Getting a call girl to sleep with you for free was one of Tinseltown's major ego trips, the equivalent of big-game hunting. It should be stressed that not every woman at Heidi's party, however she looked, was or would ever be a call girl. That all were worth buying did not mean that all were for sale. The guessing game was a great deal of fun. The main point here was that this was a sexy, wild party with hundreds of the prettiest girls in the world. What red-blooded man, much less movie star or mogul, would want to miss it? Just because many of the women would occasionally take money for their favors—in the most discreet manner, of course— did not in any way tarnish them or the event, nor diminish their desirability. Heidi herself did not get upset if the girls who worked for her "gave it away" to the movie stars. The attention of the stars validated the girls to the real people, assuming you could call *Fortune* 500 business leaders or Arab princes or Texas oil millionaires, who constituted the bread and butter of Heidi's business, real people. The stars were loss leaders; they let Heidi justify her Bijan prices.

This was Beverly Hills, where the fact that a house had previously been owned by Cher, or even Sonny, could add hundreds of thousands to the price tag. Being a madam in Beverly Hills was all about marketing, and the best way to market anything in Beverly Hills, whether it was pizza by Spago or Body by Jake, was to invite the stars. It was the closest thing America had to England's "By Appointment to Her Majesty." Alex had truly been madam to the stars. Heidi and the others were desperate wanna-bes. That Heidi could get the likes of Mick and Jack in her house made her high as a kite. Who needed the crystal meth?

Many of the ladies of Heidi's evening were familiar faces at show-business-frequented nightclubs. They were queens of the night whose lovely presence was essential to make a club "hot," for a club's heat was directly proportional to the beauty of its distaff patrons. The club owners courted these night birds; they needed them as much as Heidi and the other madams of Beverly Hills did. These girls' beauty was the clubs' reward. And so they danced at Roxbury on the Sunset Strip, which used to be Preston Sturges's Players Club. They danced at Ava's in the bowels of the Beverly Center, which used to be Tramp, owned by the Italian mystery man who bought and lost MGM, Giancarlo Parretti (Tramp itself had begun as an offshoot of London's Jermyn Street night spot, a favorite of Mick Jagger's). They danced at Bar One on Sunset at Doheny, which used to belong to Johnny Scotto, who now owned Ava's, which he had named for his girlfriend, Ava Fabian, a 1989 *Playboy* centerfold. They danced at downtown's Vertigo, which was run by Mario Oliver, the former boyfriend of Princess Stephanie of Monaco, and was soon to be taken over by the rock star Prince and converted into an outpost of his hometown Minneapolis disco, Glam Slam. They danced at the Gate on La Cienega, which had replaced the transvestite cabaret La Cage aux Folles. They danced at Tatou in Beverly Hills, which had been opened by two New York clubmeisters, Studio 54 impresario Mark Fleischman and Danceteria impresario Rudolf, who sensed there was gold after dark in the once somnolent Beverly and Hollywood hills. Los Angeles was, at last, becoming a nightlife town, but the key was getting the blondes out at night. The California Girl fantasy was what kept these places open.

When the typical denizen of these clubs—the ravishing twenty-three-year-old who had just moved here from Dallas—drove a new BMW with a car phone, lived in an expensive rented condo in the Wilshire corridor, and did not hold a job or come from a wealthy family, there were only a limited number of conclusions about the means of her financial support to which one could jump. The club girls were members of that unique local species known as the MAW, or Model-Actress-Whatever. Working models and actresses had very-early-morning calls that precluded night crawls, so the girls packing the clubs presumably either had an occasional night off or, more likely, were not practicing their chosen profession. Because of Los Angeles's position as the movie, television, and video capital of the world, every prom queen from Rapid City, sweetheart of Sigma Chi from Chapel Hill, and head cheerleader from Phoenix seemed to be drawn here to try her luck in the media sweepstakes. The competition was devastating. The overwhelming majority failed to make it, but not everyone went back home. The big question was what happened to those who stayed.

Some got lucky and married either strategically, or happily, or sometimes both, and became Brentwood wives. There were lots of pretty salesgirls in the Rodeo Drive boutiques and the La Brea emporia. No city had more good-looking waitresses. Yet even allowing for the host of aerobics instructresses and personal trainers, this still left thousands of would-be and never-were starlets unaccounted for. This was where the "whatever" came in, that great unmentionable whatever, Hollywood's ultimate dirty secret. Turning a trick or two was not without a certain honor. Marilyn Monroe was not above it, when she was still Norma Jean Baker, nor were many other stars, including a number of Madam Alex's finest. In a way, a stint as a call girl could be regarded as a Hollywood actress's rite of passage. Still, it was the one rite that was never discussed.

Not that all the call girls at Heidi's party were failed actresses. Many were actresses who had not failed, but were struggling to stay afloat. These women were less concerned with sleeping their way to the top than simply paying their rent. All they wanted was enough to survive a little longer so that they could keep waiting for that big call from their agent. In Hollywood, where appearances are everything, waitress tips and temp wages weren't enough to let a girl keep up with the Winona Ryders, eat at Chianti Cucina, dress at Maxfield, and hang on with the style that might get her that break.

Others of Heidi's girls that night weren't actresses or models at all. They were local sun-kissed beauties who had spent their teen years at the Roxy and the Rainbow, giving backstage blow jobs at the Greek, girls whose most memorable achievement may have been a one-night stand with some doped-out rock star. These post-teenyboppers had always gotten free rides based on their looks, and wanted to keep riding. Sex meant nothing to them, especially if they were anesthetized on drugs and needed more drugs to keep their pain from seeping in. These beauties may have had occasional jobs as studio receptionists or nightclub hostesses. They were face women, front women, but, in the end, women who could never seem to earn enough.

Oddly enough, many of the quintessential California Girls at Heidi's were actually recent arrivals from Florida. Perhaps it was that there was a glut of blondes in the new American Côte d'Azur centering on Miami's super-hip South Beach that the exodus west had resulted. Whatever the reason, the Florida sunshine and beaches were, if anything, an even better crucible than those of the Golden State in producing fantasy girls for the Hollywood pashas. These special Sunshine State transplants were called "hurricane hookers" after the tropical winds that had blown them west. There were entire colonies of them in the nothing-down apartment complexes of West Hollywood and Marina del Rey. It was definitely a matter of supply following demand, a demand that was apparently so high that a sort of sexual gold rush was taking place.

These, then, were the sorts of women whom Madam Alex had sought, had "discovered" the way Lana Turner had, according to legend, been discovered at Schwab's, and had groomed into her fabled "creatures," who not only made hundreds of thousands a year, but met, through Alex, the real power players who not only made them rich but sometimes made them stars and sometimes made them their wives. This was Hollywood's forbidden fantasy, and this was the void that Alex had left that Heidi Fleiss was making her big play to fill. Heidi was the serpent in this tinseled Eden, the Middlewoman of Chaillot, who was trying to broker a Faustian deal of love for money by making the money so big that it would sugarcoat Faust out of the transaction altogether.

At two A.M., Heidi finally made her grand entrance. Twenty-six, 5′ 8″, and rail thin, she was a specter in ebony, with her jet-black straight hair and live-by-night pallor, very Morticia Addams. Heidi was wearing black heels, black tights, a black miniskirt, and an unbuttoned black silk shirt. Heidi looked like a rich, spoiled L.A. woman, and she was. The daughter of a successful pediatrician, she had grown up in affluent Los Feliz near the home of Cecil B. DeMille. Although her mother taught gifted children, Heidi had no interest in education. She flunked out of Immaculate Heart, then dropped out of John Marshall High. Like many other local Jewish American Princesses who wanted it all but weren't willing to work for it, Heidi found her way to Madam Alex, the patron saint of these decorative lost causes. And like a number of the more successful of Alex's girls, Heidi had graduated from call girl to madam.

These days, Heidi didn't see clients. Some were so intrigued by her unavailability that they would offer her an unconscionable sum, like five thousand for a single orgasm. These clients were like those amateur boxers who would fork out a small fortune to go a round with the champ. But Heidi would say no. Heidi preferred madaming. She loved the volume, she loved playing general, she loved negotiating.

Rushing through the party, Heidi didn't even bother to say hello to Jack Nicholson, who, with his protégé Alan Finkelstein, was deeply engrossed in conversation with a towering Australian redhead. Heidi wasn't concerned that the two bars had run out of liquor, or that enough drugs were being consumed in her two guest bathrooms to run several hospitals or support a new regime in Medellín, or that the police might raid her over the cataclysmic noise, or that the guest of honor, Mick Jagger, had still not shown up. What she was worried about was what the motorcycle boots and spike heels would do to her floors. "I just had them sanded!" she shrieked, though not loudly enough to be heard by her guests.

With Heidi was her best friend of the moment, Victoria Sellers. Victoria Sellers, dressed in hot pants and Chanel combat boots, was Hollywood royalty. Her father was Peter Sellers, her mother Britt Ekland, and her stepfathers had included both Rod Stewart and Lou Adler, the rock impresario who produced the great albums of the Mamas and the Papas and other 1960s rock legends. Adler also owned the Roxy on Sunset, which had been for years the city's greatest showcase for cutting-edge musical acts, and the private club above the Roxy called On the Rox. For three nights a week, Adler's stepdaughter would turn the club into her local salon, bringing her own disc jockey, creating her own guest list, and presumably taking a percentage of the bar receipts. Victoria's nights at

On the Rox had become the hottest nights in Los Angeles, and not because of her disc jockeys. What gave these nights their zing was the presence of Heidi and anywhere from ten to thirty of her slinky charges, arriving in black Sevilles with Nevada license plates. The girls would sip cheap Freixenet champagne, smoke endless numbers of cigarettes, talk zodiac and workouts and manicures, drive the old studs crazy and dance with the young studs, and the next morning Heidi would have more telephone calls than she could humanly handle asking her who the girls were and begging her to set up introductions.

These On the Rox nights were not only bringing prostitution out of the closet, they were starting to make it chic. While Madam Alex had been so discreet and exclusive that only her clients knew about her, *everyone*, and not just everyone who mattered, seemed to know who Heidi was. She certainly wasn't trying to hide anything. Not only were stars and top executives and agents hanging out with her and her girls in the clubs, they had begun dropping by her house and turning it into a kind of salon.

Heidi was running a twenty-four-hour-a-day open house. The Players would come by, unannounced, and they would bring their friends. Since there would always be pretty girls around, and anything could happen, an impromptu visit inspired a special frisson that everyone was talking, not even whispering, about. Even if the stars paid nothing, they were great for free publicity, just the way they might be comped in restaurants and hotels. Their association with Heidi was making Hollywood's dirtiest secret seem a lot cleaner. Lots of women, normal women with normal jobs, jobs now jeopardized by the recession, women who might once have been appalled by the idea of prostitution, were now saying, "Maybe that's not such a bad idea." The Los Angeles real estate market that had made paper millionaires of so many people had come to a grinding halt and was threatening to collapse. No longer as rich as they thought they were, their portfolios as shaky as the fault lines that crisscrossed the earth under their now deflating homes, Hollywood wives and Hollywood divorcees were suddenly thinking about being Hollywood hookers.

Tonight's party, which would only serve as more p.r. for Heidi's burgeoning love machine, was a massive domestic version of an On the Rox night. Aside from some poolside making-out and an occasional blow job in one of the cocaine bathrooms, no real sex took place chez Heidi. It was Look now, leap later. The party was nothing but a giant mixer, Hollywood-style. Unfortunately, Heidi was a terrible hostess. She was too obsessed with her scuffed floors to bother introducing anyone to anyone else, the way Alex would have. Heidi operated on the scatter theory. People would find each other. She did a volume business. She knew her phone would be ringing off the hook for the next week. When Mick Jagger finally arrived at three A.M., Heidi locked herself in her bedroom, took a Halcion, and went to sleep. She was assured the party was a smash. *Tout* Hollywood would be talking. She had the buzz, and this sort of buzz could only make her richer and richer. Heidi wasn't worried about being busted. She already had too many friends who were judges, cops, politicos, big-shot lawyers. Nor was she worried about the recession. "My people are bulletproof," she said. She felt invulnerable. She just wanted to get bigger and bigger, until one day she could be as big as Alex had been.

Like all her rival madams, Heidi was obsessed with Alex. She blamed and hated Alex for turning her into what she was, yet on the other hand, what Heidi was was everything she had ever dreamed of being, even before Alex came into her life. Moreover, given how much she detested Alex, Heidi used to speak to her every day, five, ten times a day, as did a number of the other pretenders to the vacant throne of Madam 90210. They all wanted to be Alex; they all hated what they wanted to be. Yet Alex never cut them off. In retirement, she would still talk to them when they called. Alex was one of the most generous and forgiving of women. She had to be to have not only survived but triumphed in this most vicious of all universes, this galaxy of beautiful, mercurial, fickle, cutthroat, desperate women. More than a Buddha or a Sibyl, Alex was, quite simply, the mother of all madams.

CHAPTER TWO

Roots

*M*ost of your worst fears never come true. It's worry for
nothing. But sometimes if you worry *too* much, you can worry
your worst fears into existence. My mother was worried about sex.

I can't say I came over on the *Mayflower*, but then again, the *Mayflower* didn't sail from Manila, where I was born in 1933. I did come
from a very good family and I did have a very privileged, though overly
sheltered, childhood. My father was, you might say, the meat king of
the Philippines. He owned the Superior Provision Company, which
put the finest beef on the best tables in Makati, the Beverly Hills of
Manila, the suburb of walled estates and lovely gardens where I grew
up.

My father, whose name was August Hugo Kuntze, was actually an

American citizen of German parentage. He had been born in Connecticut and moved to the Philippines as a young man. My mother was an Adriano, one of the old Spanish families of the country. The Philippines were a real melting pot. Aside from all the different Asian strains in the islands, the Spanish *conquistadores* had taken over the country in the sixteenth century, only to lose it to the Americans when Admiral Dewey sank the Spanish fleet in 1898. I grew up in what was basically an American colony, and we Filipinos always loved Americans, especially General MacArthur, who *did* return to save us. Before the war, Manila was a beautiful, gracious city, with ancient Spanish churches and convents and an amazing bay where we took *paseos* to see the most dramatic sunsets in the world. My brother, Carl, who was a year older, and I had nannies and cooks and servants and went to Catholic church and Catholic schools. Mine was called Holy Ghost. My mother was terribly strict, and, of course, we were terribly well mannered. Or else.

The great life we had was shattered when the Japanese invaded in 1941. My father could have used his German name to protect us, pretending he was part of the Axis. But he was fiercely patriotic. He joined the resistance and ended up in a concentration camp. Oddly enough, my mother was less concerned with the Japanese, who destroyed our lovely city, than with the American troops who liberated us in 1944, just as I was approaching my teenage years. Worried that I might lose my virginity, or something like that, to one of the thousands of American G.I.s, my mother had the brilliant idea in 1945 to send me to live with an uncle in, of all places, Japan. It was one of life's little ironies that Mother didn't stop to think that the U.S. Army was in Japan as well. So early on I developed a taste for Americans, and Mother's plan to keep me away from men backfired. I was back in Manila and at the Holy Ghost convent in a year.

At fifteen I went on to Maryknoll College. I was very good with languages. You had to be in the Philippines. I spoke English, Spanish, German, Tagalog, and a little Chinese. The Chinese were big shots in Manila. The Spanish were the aristocrats, the Americans the heroes, and the Chinese owned all the big businesses. Everyone intermarried. That's why the mixed-blood women, the *mestizas,* were so beautiful.

I wasn't bad as a girl. I was thin, with a pretty complexion, and the boys seemed to like me, enough to make Mother very nervous. She always wanted me chaperoned everywhere. The first time she let me go out on my own, it was only because I was going with this nice older girl whom I met with Mother at the beauty parlor. Well, this nice girl turned out to be a hooker who was going to set me up on what was going to be a trick with none other than the Manila chief of police. The chief was a family friend. Was he embarrassed!

After the war, after my father got out of the concentration camp, he resumed his business but not his marriage. My mother sometimes blamed me and my brother for our father's leaving her. I mean, it wasn't *our* fault, but we both ended up feeling guilty anyhow. Maybe that's why Mother was so strict with us. The older I got, the worse we got along. I'm not sure if it was to keep me out of trouble in Manila or just for her to start a new life, but in 1951, when I was seventeen, my mother decided to move with me to San Francisco. I would miss Manila and my friends, but to all Filipinos, America was the Promised Land. I was excited. We sailed on the *President Wilson,* via Honolulu. Mother was seasick the entire voyage. I was on my own, and had a great time. On board I met Howard Strickling, the head of publicity at MGM, who had worked on all their great movies, including *Gone With the Wind, The Philadelphia Story,* and *National Velvet,* which I loved. He told me stories about Clark Gable, and Greta Garbo, and Cary Grant. This was my first encounter with Hollywood. Mr. Strickling bought me a Pink Lady and told me that "a wolf is a man who will protect a woman from everyone except himself." I'd never forget that.

When we got to San Francisco, I realized that I had to get away from Mother, or I would never have a life of my own. So I ran away, and where did I end up but back with the Catholic church. I could run but I couldn't hide. The church was great to me, especially because I didn't have to go back home. I got a job as a housekeeper at the parish priest's residence at Our Lady of Lourdes Chapel over in Oakland. I stayed there for two years, and really grew up. All my life, I had been waited on and pampered, and now I got to wait on other people. I learned all about flower arranging and cooking and generally making a man happy. After all, this was a priest, and I thought that if I did anything wrong I could be excommunicated. I tried very hard, and he couldn't have been kinder.

In 1953, I moved by myself down to Los Angeles, I'm not sure why, perhaps to be even farther away from my mother. I certainly didn't come to break into pictures. My father sent me money, so I could be on my own, though it was never enough. My first job was as a receptionist at Veloz and Yolanda's Dance Studio, next to the Hollywood Roosevelt. Soon, however, I was enlisted to teach gentlemen how to tango. It would have been Last Tango in Hollywood, because I sure had no idea how to dance, but I learned fast—quick, quick, slow—in front of the mirror, and soon I was a regular Arthur Murray.

In 1955, I got married to a physicist who worked in the aerospace industry. It was a typical Eisenhower fifties marriage, with a big house in Los Feliz near where Cecil B. DeMille lived, and a Cadillac with tail fins and two wonderful sons.

Although I was living in Los Angeles, Hollywood couldn't have been farther away than if I was still living in Manila. All the glamorous nightclubs like Ciro's and Mocambo, where the stars had gone out at night, had closed. The McCarthy Communist witch-hunts of the early fifties seemed to have taken all the joy out of Hollywood. The nightlife was nothing compared to what we had in Manila, which was a total party town. Not that a physicist was a party animal, all caged up with nowhere to go. Most nights we stayed home with Ed Sullivan or Lawrence Welk. After eight years we found we had nothing to say to each other and got divorced.

In 1963, after my divorce, I started going out again. I also took a job working at the flower shop at the Ambassador Hotel, home of the Cocoanut Grove, one of the few places where L.A. people went when they wanted to put on black tie and dance to Guy Lombardo or some other big band. In the early sixties, the hotel was considered just as exclusive as the Beverly Hills Hotel or the Beverly Wilshire. Through the flower world, I made a lot of gay friends and started going to their parties, at one of which I met my very straight second husband. He was an Austrian businessman, and he told me I looked like Joan Crawford, which was a big compliment in those days long before *Mommie Dearest* made her such a caricature. He somehow got into a big fistfight at that party and ended up in the hospital, and I went with him. The next day he sent me a whole orchid tree, and I guess that was that. We got married and moved to a nice house on Catalina Street, near Hancock Park. Although we eventually had a son of our own, I decided that I wanted to continue my life as a working mother, so I kept my job at the Ambassador.

I loved the flower business. Every day was like opening night. With all the big events, there was a lot of excitement. I had great customers: Liza Minnelli; Roger Vadim and Jane Fonda (when she was still a sex kitten and not an antiwar activist); the famous producer Charlie Feldman and his girlfriend, the elegant Capucine. I was still such a good Catholic, I worried that doing flowers for Jewish weddings at Temple Beth Am would get me excommunicated. Little did I know what the flower business would lead me to.

One of my customers was an English realtor whose sister, a woman named Arabella Carlton, called me one day in 1971, asking me if I would be interested in buying her business. I told her I knew nothing at all about dogs, and she just laughed. You see, she had all these Yorkshire terriers, and I thought she ran a kennel. Then she told me something that really knocked me out. She told me that she wanted to do the Yorkshire kennel full-time, but that she had another business that she wanted to sell. And that business was her madam business.

I was totally shocked, not only that this very classy, very refined, very proper English lady in her early forties would be a madam, but even more thinking she could sell the business to me. Arabella explained that she had heard that my husband had been quite ill with a heart condition, and that she thought that I was very charming and good on the phone and had run the flower shop so well for so long that I could be a natural as a madam. She really sold me on it. She said this was a great opportunity to make a ton of money and stay home and look after my husband at the same time.

And I said, "Come on, I know nothing about this," and in her wonderful, assuring English voice, she said, "I'll train you," and she made me believe I could do it. I thought, Wow, I can get rich with this. It wasn't even that dangerous. Today if you're convicted of pandering, it's a minimum sentence of three years. Then, it was only ninety days in jail. To be honest, I wasn't even thinking about jail. In the Philippines, prostitution was wide open. Roxas Boulevard along the Manila harbor was a Miracle Mile of brothels. No one cared. It was part of our social life, even among all the good Catholics. No, I wasn't thinking about the law at all. I was thinking about money.

I went to meet Arabella, and she showed me the ropes. I did a thirty-day apprenticeship with her, watching her work the phones. I was shocked at the prices Arabella was quoting, two hundred dollars an hour and up for something the boys might have paid at most twenty dollars for with the sexiest bar hostess on Roxas Boulevard back home. I was even more shocked at Arabella's language. Here was this regal woman, who looked like she should be having tea with Queen Elizabeth, saying things like "How would you like to come over here and eat my box?" Apparently, Arabella saw clients as well as arranging dates for her girls, but she assured me I'd never have to see anyone.

There had been a huge earthquake in 1971 that had damaged our house. At the time I met Arabella Carlton, the insurance company came across with a check for five thousand dollars, which is precisely the amount Arabella wanted for her business. So I endorsed the check over to her, and out of nowhere I had a brand-new career, as a madam. Now, five thousand dollars may seem pretty cheap for a going business, but once I actually took things over, I saw that I had gotten pretty much what I had paid for. Arabella may have even oversold me. Her business consisted of a list of twenty-five men, most of whom were retired gentlemen, and I'm not talking about old stars like Tom Mix or Lon Chaney or Buster Keaton, or old moguls like Sam Goldwyn or Adolph Zukor. These were just plain old men, most of whom couldn't get it up. They had one foot in the grave and the other on a banana peel. From all the phone calls and talk about eating Arabella's box and all that, I expected Maurice Chevalier, someone very suave, but that was not to be.

The girls Arabella sold me—all five of them—weren't a lot better than her johns. Maybe they were fine for the old geezers, because these guys probably would have been inert if Sophia Loren offered herself to them. But they were hardly starlets. They all had day jobs—a bank teller, a secretary, two salesgirls, and a waitress—and they did this, as I was doing, to supplement their incomes. I quickly saw, however, that I wasn't going to supplement mine by much unless I got some business. I was pretty depressed the first month or so. My big break came when I was talking to an old flower client friend of mine, and I confessed to him that I had gone from the flower business to the deflower business. His name was Roger, and he had a big construction company that had built a lot of the postwar-boom houses not only in Beverly Hills but around the country. Roger knew everyone, from the White House to Little Italy, and he seemed highly amused at what I was doing.

Certainly more amused than I was, because I was a madam without any johns. Roger said he could help. He gave me the names of about fifty of his friends, mostly Hollywood executives, agents, and producers. But he strictly forbade me to use his name. "Cold-call them," he told me. "You're one of the best salespeople I've ever met. Just say, 'I'm in the entertainment business, and I'd like you to call me if you have any friends who need entertaining.' " And that was it. Roger told me that all of the names he gave me were "players," that is, that they used call girls, and they were always eager for something new. So I called them. And Roger was completely right. I owe him my business.

When I started as a madam, the movie business was in the toilet, at its lowest ebb. Television was killing the movies. Everyone was staying home. The studios were dying. Twentieth Century–Fox lost eighty million dollars in 1970 and had sold much of its back lot to the high-rise speculators who built Century City. MGM was concentrating more on the Grand Hotel in Las Vegas than on films. Columbia retreated from Hollywood to the Warner Bros. back lot in Burbank. The big epics that had made Hollywood what it was, movies like *Cleopatra* and *Lawrence of Arabia*, were albatrosses. What people wanted now was weird things like *Easy Rider*. The glamour of the business was over. But Roger's contacts were hornier than ever. Maybe they were so depressed by the business that they wanted to lose themselves in sex. Maybe it was an "Eat, drink, and be merry because tomorrow the studio goes into Chapter 11" attitude. *Klute* had just come out, with Jane Fonda as a fancy hooker. The movie had everyone talking about call girls, and there just weren't enough of them, not the fancy New

York kind, in Los Angeles, where the flower children and rock groupies were giving it away. Though not to the players on Roger's list. In their forties and fifties, these men were not from the love-child generation. But they did want a piece of the wild sixties action that was still going on in the early seventies. These guys couldn't relate to *Hair* and *Woodstock*, but they liked the bare breasts and underlying attitude. Sex was definitely in the air and on Hollywood's mind. Roger's friends were dying to buy pussy, although I would have never put it that way back then. Virtually every one of them wanted to meet whomever I could send them. I had to get cracking and find some new talent.

I met a lot of my girls at my beauty parlor, Pagano's, near Wilshire and Doheny. I used to be so impressed with all the beautiful women there when I was just a housewife. But now I looked at them with totally different eyes, and noticed that very few of the best-looking of them were wearing wedding rings. So I'd start chatting and invite them back to my house for tea. And my house was always furnished in a way, that, well, with the art and antiques, the girls were always impressed. The more impressed they were, the more I could see that they'd like more money than they had. Eventually I'd bring up what I did, and they all went for it, especially when I told them some of the names on my list. I wasn't the threatening type. I was just a housewife, with three boys, and this little cottage industry on the side.

So one thing led to another, girls to guys, who sent other guys, who introduced me to nice girls. Before long I had almost twenty girls on my list, which let me make my list of guys even longer, and I had met my first star johns, which never ceased to amaze me, celebrities *paying* for sex. Yet here they were, so I felt under pressure to give them something very special. They were gods, and they deserved goddesses. Actually they were, under it all, just horny guys who would have settled for a lot less, but I was too starstruck not to want to wow them. Most of the first stars I got called me because they didn't want to cheat on their wives. In fact, most of my initial clients were happily married. They simply wanted some variety without all the baggage of a long affair. My favorite definition of alimony is that it's the fucking you get for the fucking you got. Under California community-property laws, that fucking could be intense. No wonder men wanted call girls. My task was to find them girls as pretty as the ones they had seen in the movies or magazines or malls, who had gotten their hormones going, so they wouldn't go and get into real trouble on their own. I'm no messiah, but my goal was to save marriages, not wreck them.

The new girls usually needed makeovers. A lot of them were hippies, girls who looked like they hung out at the Source or the Aware Inn down on Sunset and had gone to one too many Doors concerts. My guys were pretty much the coat-and-tie variety, the kind the girls might call "uptight," and I'd have to explain to them that the customer is always right, if not always hip and cool. There was a culture clash here between one generation of free spirits who burned their bras and another who wanted to pay them to wear garter belts. But money talked.

Despite Watergate and despite the oil crisis, 1972, my first full year in my new business, was shaping up to be a good one. I quit the Ambassador flower shop and became a full-time madam. I didn't tell my husband what I was doing. By the same token, he didn't tell me what *he* was doing. I never knew for sure exactly what it was, although I had my suspicions that it might have been mob-related. But business was business, and we didn't discuss it. We had a family without any money problems, and that was good enough for both of us. Then disaster struck. I had a friend who was a bartender in the Palm Court of the Ambassador. I told him about my new business, and he would send me clients in return for kickbacks. In February of that year, one of these referrals turned out to be a cop. My case for pandering went to court in June. I got a suspended sentence of sixty days, a one-year unsupervised probation, and a fifty-dollar fine. I thought I was lucky. Then a week later, on June 20, both my husband and my father died of heart attacks. On the same day!

I thought God was sending me a message: Get out of this crazy business! But I had three young boys to support, and send to Catholic school, and no one to help me anymore. I had given up the flower business. I didn't believe in turning back. I thought I had gotten pretty good at madaming, and was getting better all the time. Plus, at the top end of L.A., I didn't really have much competition. If I had, these rich guys wouldn't have kept calling as often as they did. So I said prayers for the two men I had lost, and crossed my heart and my fingers, and prayed I'd never get caught again. In addition to holding on to my superstitions, I took out a more practical insurance policy by beginning a relationship with the Administrative Vice Division of the L.A.P.D., the people who arrested me. It was a get-to-know-your-sheriff kind of community-outreach thing, where I would show them what a good citizen I was. I helped them, they helped me, and we all became great friends. It lasted nearly two decades, and when the cops turned on me again, I never felt more betrayed in my life.

What about other relationships? Even though I had now been married twice, I still felt guilty about sex. My mother had beaten it into me that being and looking sexy was sinful. I tried my hardest always to look demure and refined, the same way I decorated my house. Despite all this, I couldn't go out on the street without some guy propositioning me, so when my second husband died I started putting on weight so the guys would leave me alone. My clients never bothered me. For the first few years, they never saw me. I was just a voice on the phone. Only after I got much more successful did I begin entertaining at home.

I did fall in love—what a stupid mistake!—with a married man, a very big wig at one of the networks. It lasted seven years. He spent hundreds of thousands of dollars on me in gifts and jewels and trips, and I spent about at least as much on psychiatrists trying to break my addiction to him. I finally did, and that's when I took up with my cats, who are better in every conceivable way.

My other real pleasure was my business, my business of pleasure, and watching it take off. Why did it take off? Supply and demand. There was a large demand for call girls, fancy call girls, that was about to explode, and I was the only one there to grab this market. It seems amazing, but when it came to sex for sale on a high level, L.A. was a completely hick town. In the early seventies, its best whores were about as sophisticated as its best food, which was a prime rib at Lawry's or chili at Chasen's or maybe the gloppy veal Oscar at Scandia. In the old days, the glory days of Hollywood in the thirties and forties, there had been glorious brothels, like the one where all the girls were look-alikes of Rita Hayworth and Greta Garbo and Jean Harlow, where black waiters in white tie and tails poured champagne, and a small orchestra played while the gentlemen danced with their star substitutes.

Places like that had gone the way of Mocambo and the Players Club. In the early seventies, aside from the Whisky a Go-Go and other druggie, hippie, psychedelic rock scenes on the Sunset Strip, L.A. was as dead as Omaha. There were a few small-scale madams, each with at most twenty girls. If Arabella Carlton was supposedly the crème de la crème, the rest of the crème was more like skim milk. There were a lot of cheap street hookers down on Sunset toward Hollywood, and some really scary street hookers on Western Avenue, a few strip clubs, a massage parlor on La Cienega called the Circus Maximus, with about ten middling girls, and a place on Santa Monica Boulevard called the Paris Revue that issued you box cameras so you could take nude pictures for a half hour of the three so-called models they had working there. The area soon became Boys' Town, and I could see why. And that was it. That was the swinging seventies sex scene in Los Angeles, movie capital of the world.

My first client list, Roger's list, were mostly older men who remembered the glory days. They were downright nostalgic for them. It was up to me to bring them back. Surely there were more gorgeous women here than anywhere, all the hopefuls who came from around the world to make it. Most of them weren't going to make it. Most of them were lost. But that didn't make them any less gorgeous. I could help these girls. They needed me. I was going to rescue them. That was my challenge. Besides, a new era of glory days was right ahead of me, and I didn't even know it.

I forged ahead, recruiting, remaking, and living on the phones. I started getting rich. Really rich. Beverly Hills rich. All for being in the right place, with the right business, at the right time. I loved being an entrepreneur. I loved not being dependent on anyone. Sometimes I felt like a Virginia Slims ad. I'd come a long way, baby. But I couldn't have done it all by myself. I feel like it's Oscar night, because there are a number of people I have to thank for helping me to get where I got.

Steven Spielberg. George Lucas. Michael Eisner. Jimmy Carter. John Travolta. Donald Trump. Mike Milken. The Ayatollah Khomeini. Madame Claude. And the Red Brigade.

What? What kind of list is this? Well, I thank Spielberg for *Jaws* in 1975, and Lucas for *Star Wars* in 1977, for creating a new genre of techno-blockbuster films that got Americans out to the movies once again and gave Hollywood a desperately needed shot in the arm. And I thank Michael Eisner for being the best of all the studio executives riding this wave of money and for not being shy about getting paid not seven but eight figures. He *earned* it. The point is, their box office was great for my *box* office, if you know what I mean. By 1975, Hollywood was starting to roll in it once again. The town was hot, with money to burn and hits to celebrate, deals, deals, deals, and I could provide the ultimate celebration. I introduced the whole new generation of "baby moguls" to my creatures, which is exactly what those girls were. As the money rolled in, I began grooming the girls in the classic style, creating ladies out of groupies. Just like an MGM musical had a "look" and an Indiana Jones movie had a "look," my girls had a "look"—and a "hook"—and I got a reputation for it, the Henry Higgins of call girls, running the Neiman-Marcus of sex. The rest were K mart.

I thank John Travolta for *Saturday Night Fever*, the film that kicked off the entire disco era in 1977 and got America partying again. It all led more revelers to me. And I thank President Carter on two counts. First was his wonderful southern hospitality to the Arab oil sheikhs, making them feel welcome in the country whose economy they had wrecked at the gas pumps. The Arabs, now the richest men on earth, discovered how much they liked the richest place on earth, which was Beverly Hills. One of the reasons that they liked it so much was me. The other reason I'm so grateful to Jimmy Carter is that the fiscal failures of his presidency led to President Reagan and the Greed Era of the eighties. If you weren't a millionaire, something was wrong with you. And all these millionaires had to spend their new money on *something* besides horse ranches and sports franchises and corporate jets. So I must thank Michael Milken, who like Michael Eisner made so much money, and Donald Trump, who spent so much, so flashily, and became a role model for high rollers and conspicuous consumers. The Donald was the role model, and I became a status symbol.

In a backhanded way, I also have to thank the Ayatollah, for driving the Shah and his ruling class out of Iran, and the Red Brigade, whose relentless acts of terrorism drove the capitalistic ruling class out of Europe. The Persians adored Beverly Hills, which became Tehran-on-the-Pacific. It also became a last resort for what the locals jealously called Eurotrash, who finally gave some real class and style to a city that never really had anything but money and movie stars.

By the early eighties, this new international jet set of Arabs, Persians, and Europeans had become the core of my business, more important than the stars and the studios, who were cheapskates by comparison. My normal rates, $300 an hour, $500 for two, $1,000 a night, $2,000 a day on trips, were almost an insulting giveaway to these rich foreigners. They *insisted* on paying more, and who was I to argue? They saw me as a global, not a local, madam, and told me that if the Bel Air could charge the same rates as the Ritz, I should be charging the same as Madame Claude. You should have heard some of the stars and producers squeal and shriek when I told them that they had to accept our global economy. They squawked, but I never lost a customer over price. As I always said, "A hard cock has no price sensitivity." (Boy, did I develop a nasty mouth the longer I did this.)

I must thank Madame Claude, too. As I got bigger and better, everyone used to compare the two of us, Claude in Paris, Alex in L.A. I was totally flattered to be in such fast company, even though I was in the business five years before I was doing well enough to even know who she was. And then, about 1980, because of political changes in France, Madame Claude moved to Los Angeles. And everyone told me I was finished. Here comes Madame Claude, who's so chic and who has all these countesses and supermodels working for her and they speak all these languages, and everyone told me to pack it in and yield the crown and the town to her.

And you know what? It was just like with Jewish delis. When the Stage and the Carnegie decided to open in Beverly Hills, everyone said Nate 'n' Al's was finished, *kaput,* hang up the salamis. And what happened? People are still lining up at Nate 'n' Al's, and the Stage and the Carnegie are half-empty. Madame Claude didn't last two years in L.A. It wasn't that the men here had anything against getting blow jobs in French or getting it on with countesses, but L.A. is a peculiar town, a tough town, and you have to sell L.A. sex in L.A., not snobby Paris sex, but fun, sunny, beachy L.A. sex. And you have to give a warm welcome and make people feel at home. So I was very honored when Madame Claude threw it in and went back to France. It felt as good as when the Lakers beat the Celtics. I had gone head-to-head, as it were, with my archrival (whom I never met), and won the War of the Madams.

That's when I got my biggest business, the early eighties. I got all the heads—heads of state, heads of corporations, heads of universities, heads of studios, heads of record companies. I had been making great money. I might well have been one of the highest-earning self-made women in the country, up there with Mrs. Fields and Donna Karan and Diane von Furstenberg. I was really proud of myself, and sorry they couldn't write up my success story in *Fortune*. I looked at all kinds of ventures to invest in, from selling steel to the Gulf States to starting a fat farm up in Washington State. I also supported my mother, my brother, who had become a successful *Life* magazine photographer and then suffered a stroke, and my sons.

I also caught the L.A. real estate fever, trading up from one house to another. When you service heads of state, you want to be able to entertain, and since I was a great cook and had wonderful antiques and art, I wanted to meet some of these famous clients and not just be a voice on the phone. My first serious house was in the hills of Malibu, with a wonderful pool and gardens and views of the Pacific. I had a party every lunch and every dinner, though I usually kept my constituencies separate. I'd keep the Arabs together, and the movie people together, and the politicians I'd have one at a time. And if I had a new customer I didn't like, I'd send him back to Beverly Hills the long way around on Sunset Boulevard, which would take forever and scare him away from ever wanting to make this endless drive back. But I liked most of my clients. That's why I called them my friends, because I got to know them, and got to know all about their lives and their problems. I probably knew more about them than their shrinks did, because they were trusting me, especially the hung-up Americans, with one of their biggest, most vulnerable, and potentially most embarrassing secrets.

Now, the entire AIDS crisis began around 1982. A lot of people thought hookers would quickly become extinct. People became terrified of sex, and America, which was *always* terrified of and fascinated by hookers, branded them as the Typhoid Marys of this awful plague. Nevertheless, in the face of all this paranoia, my business boomed. I think it was because my clients trusted me. I made every girl get an AIDS test and I insisted on condoms. I warned my clients not to break the rules, or else, and they knew what that "or else" meant, that I would cut them right off. Everybody behaved. Because they did, both the clients and the creatures knew they were a lot safer with me than playing Russian roulette with their lives with some beautiful stranger in the night at Flaming Colossus or Vertigo, or whatever the club of the week happened to be. My business was founded on sex. You can't stop sex. All I could do was make it as risk free as I could. Most guys said they'd *die* to have one of my creatures. God forbid!

So the party, now wrapped in latex, went on. My Malibu place was a great summer house, but it was bad in the winter, when mud slides would close the Pacific Coast Highway and make me inaccessible. I sold it and got a real mansion in Bel Air, on Stone Canyon Road next to the Bel Air Hotel. That was the ultimate party house: Casa Pussy, as everyone called it. The only reason I moved was because I found an amazing deal up above the George Cukor estate on Doheny, which is where the notorious bust took place that ended all the fun.

It was great while it lasted. Everybody had a great time, and it was as much about good food and good conversation as about good sex. *Tout le monde,* as Madame Claude might have said, came to my house. I remember a very famous actress being brought up for tea by one of my favorite producers. She was preparing to play a prostitute and didn't have a clue. I would give her some pointers. I had some of my creatures there for her, and the superstar asked them what a rim job was. None of the creatures had a clue, either. And I laughed and I told the star, "My creatures are *spoiled*. They don't have to do that." That was the way it was. I spoiled my creatures, and I spoiled my friends, and it gave me the most pleasure you can imagine. If Xaviera Hollander was the Happy Hooker, I was the Merry Madam. I had a blast, a twenty-year blast, and I don't think we'll see anything like it ever again.

CHAPTER THREE

THE LIFE IN A DAY, 1987

| Family Night

*I*t seemed like a very civilized Hollywood evening at home—the superstar, his current girlfriend (the unwed mother of his child), and his former girlfriend. The only thing that was odd—and it was only slightly odd, because, after all, this was Hollywood—was that the former girlfriend, who had been the former girlfriend of a lot of stars and the former wife of another, was being paid for the pleasure of her civilized company. Swept up in the tidal wave of 1980s paternity mania, the superstar had done the right thing and let his girlfriend carry an heir, but the superstar was getting bored. So he called Alex, who titillated him with the information that one of the hottest of his old flames was in financial straits.

The superstar leapt at the bait, and the old girlfriend was dispatched to add some spice—two-thousand-dollar spice, to be exact—to the superstar's tenuous domestic tranquillity.

Call girls don't usually pick up a pizza on their way to an assignation, but this was going to be a family outing. Lynn Armstrong stopped at Santo Pietro in the Glen Centre at the top of Beverly Glen, where Clint Eastwood was at one table and Steven Spielberg at another. Though superficially like any other aging strip mall, the Glen Centre was the number one star-watching venue in all Los Angeles because so many of the biggest stars had homes nearby on Mulholland Drive, where they could have spectacular vistas of the San Fernando Valley on one side and the L.A. basin on the other. Jack Nicholson lived up here, as did Warren Beatty, whom Lynn spotted in the parking lot getting out of his Mercedes with Gary Hart. Lynn knew Warren, and she had met Donna Rice, but she ducked out of sight to avoid making eye contact. She didn't want to start lying about what she was doing.

In her high heels and sinuous new black mini–cocktail dress she had bought on sale that afternoon at a French boutique run by Persians in the Beverly Center, Lynn could feel the guys in the Glen staring at her. This wasn't a stay-at-home, pizza-buying outfit. Yet at this pizza joint and at the sushi place and the dim sum place and the deli, gorgeous girls like Lynn, dressed for Cockatoo and for Vertigo, were the rule, not the exception, except that Lynn was exceptionally gorgeous, a brunet rarity in the blond world of rock trophies. In the Los Angeles pecking order of Men Who Get Babes, rock stars were at the very pinnacle. The game of Hollywood Pickup was a bit like bridge; just as spades beat hearts, music beat movies. The wildest dream of an MAW was not to win an Oscar but to be a backup singer for Axl Rose. Lynn, who looked like the Platonic ideal of an MTV bombshell, had gone way beyond that, beyond Axl Rose, beyond Keith Richards, beyond the Boss and Duran Duran. She had actually married one of the Big Ones, which took her out of the Who's Who of groupies and put her into the pantheon of rock wives. Her affair with the movie superstar, whom we'll call Jed Reville, and who was now about to become her client, was viewed by her girlfriends as a step down, and as somehow "uncool," not just because he was older but because he was on screen rather than on stage.

The superstar and his girlfriend, Ellie, greeted Lynn at the door. They had given the servants the night off. They showed Lynn the new Ed Ruscha (he was the hip L.A. artist who made his name painting gas stations) and the new baby, in that order. Ellie was a rangy mountain girl from Utah who had dabbled in modeling and dated a few of Jed's friends before landing The Prize. She was pretty, but she had no discernible personality other than her awestruck silent devotion to Jed. Lynn was overcome by a wave of jealousy and self-loathing, feeling that she had missed the boat and that hers was sinking. Knowing that Jed and Ellie were both in A.A., she didn't wait for him to bring out the coke, as he would have in the old days. Even if he hadn't been in the program, Lynn couldn't have waited. She excused herself to go to the bathroom, popped a Valium, did two quick lines of coke, and came out as positive as if she had just left a Course in Miracles meeting.

Lynn didn't talk shop. She didn't dare ask Jed about what he was up to, for fear he'd ask her. Besides, she didn't have to ask. *Calendar* and *People* and *Vanity Fair* kept her up on Jed, whom she would have never wanted to see this way if she hadn't needed the money so badly. Still, Jed didn't put her on the spot. He didn't talk about their time together. Maybe he was being discreet out of respect to Ellie, but if he was, why did he send for Lynn to begin with? Whatever, there was no hint of sex. Or movies or rock and roll. What they talked about was pizza. Jed castigated himself for not telling Lynn to get the pizza at Pericoloso, a whimsical Spago-like restaurant in the celebrity shopping center that at lunch buzzed with agents from Beverly Hills and studio executives from Burbank. Pericoloso was an ideal halfway house whose vegetarian cheeseless pizza appealed to Jed, who had recently gotten a high cholesterol reading. Who could blame him for trying to eat healthily? Here was a man with everything to live for.

Even though she admitted she preferred the grease, Ellie dutifully volunteered to go down to Pericoloso for the health pie, but Jed decided he was too hungry to wait. So he went to the gleaming hotel-size kitchen and got out a six-pack of diet Coke for him and Ellie and a bottle of Roederer Cristal champagne for Lynn and they went into the screening room to eat the pizza and watch a tape of one of Hollywood's great unseen disasters, the unreleased *Hearts of Fire*, which starred Bob Dylan and Rupert Everett as dueling rock stars in a love triangle. The film's director, Richard Marquand, had died of a heart attack in London in the course of the troubled production.

"What was it like to fuck Bob Dylan?" Jed asked Lynn when the film was over.

Lynn was taken completely aback. She had gotten so comfortable with the pizza and the champagne and the movie and the creamy leather couches that she had completely forgotten why she was there. Even though Lynn had spent her entire post-adolescent life backstage and on tour buses and in trashed motel rooms with profane music men, now that she had become a call girl she was having trouble with the "f" word and others like it. As if in denial, Lynn was finding herself acting much more demurely, cringing at the very thought of things she had made other people cringe at. Now that she was getting paid to do the things she had always done for free, these things seemed much harder. It was a job. She had to force herself. "Who said I fucked Bob Dylan?"

" 'Cause you're famous for fucking rock stars and Jewish intellectuals," Jed said. "And he's both."

"Then where did you fit in?" Lynn taunted Jed. She remembered his style and gave it right back to him.

"Right between those tight Calvins you were wearing, and I haven't stopped thinking about it," Jed said with a devilish grin. Ellie, who had been shy and quiet and impassive, if not uncomfortable, all evening, started to giggle. The ice had been broken.

"I would have loved to fuck Bob," Lynn said, getting into the dialogue. "But Bob never wanted to fuck me."

"Everybody wanted to fuck you," Jed said.

"Wanted? Do I belong in the sex museum?" Lynn said, half meaning it. She was twenty-eight. These days she was feeling much older.

"Yeah. I'd like to see that," Jed said, leaning across the couch and squeezing her derriere. "You're museum quality. Tell us about Bob."

"Bob went with a friend of mine. They met at that acupuncture college in Santa Monica. When they broke up, every time she would see a black crow she believed it was him following her," Lynn said.

"Was that when he was a born-again Jew or a born-again Christian?" Jed asked.

"I think Christian, but I'm not sure," Lynn said. "She also said he was into black girls."

"What about Woody Allen?" Jed pressed.

"Where'd you get this Jewish intellectual thing?" Lynn replied. "Norman Mailer, too? Philip Roth? Come on. David Lee Roth, maybe. I'm a rocker. The guys I went for carried either guns or guitars."

"Or a big stick," Jed said, laughing. Ellie giggled some more.

"What about Prince?" Ellie queried softly.

"Hey, *that's* what you want?" Jed feigned outrage and stood up.

"Jed, you've got nothing to worry about," Lynn said with a wink. "But Axl Rose, well, that's a different story."

"What does he do that I don't?"

"He makes love like a woman," Lynn said.

"So why don't you just get a woman?" Jed challenged her.

"I can't always find what I'm looking for," Lynn said, turning her gaze on Ellie, who nervously cut her eyes downward.

"What do you look for in a woman?" Jed prodded her.

Lynn was rolling now. She felt in control. She was taking this exactly where Alex had told her to go. "I look for myself. I'm very narcissistic. I'm into bodies like mine. Small, firm, upturned tits. A tiny waist. A black girl's ass. Long, strong dancer's legs." She crossed these legs provocatively, deliberately, looking square at Ellie, whom she caught staring at her. "I love my body. Ellie, you've got a body like mine."

"Sort of. Before Jonah was born," Ellie said.

"Don't be so modest," Lynn encouraged her. "You're beautiful."

"You're making me hot," Jed said, getting up. "I need another diet Coke."

"Me, too," Ellie said, making a move to go to the kitchen.

"I'll get it, babe. Lynn?"

"I'm fine," Lynn said. "Maybe some Evian."

"You've got it." Jed left for the kitchen.

"You've got a great life here," Lynn said.

"I know," Ellie said, a bit wistfully, and Lynn knew why. Ellie wasn't married. Despite the child, she could be cut loose at any time, and everyone knew that Jed was a star of infinite whims. Sure, she would get a house, probably in the Valley, and a car, probably a Wagoneer, and some money, but it wouldn't be the same as being Jed's wife. Even *that* wasn't a sure thing. Lynn had been a rock wife to one of the biggest stars in the business, and the cool million he had given her as a divorce settlement was gone in barely two years. Granted, they were two great years, but now she was paying the price. By charging a price.

"You have incredible hair," Lynn said, running her fingers through Ellie's thick, tawny, leonine mane. On a physical basis, she could see what Jed saw. But Lynn thought that she herself was better. That she was here tonight was proof of that, wasn't it? But she knew she had to stifle these recurrent stabs of jealousy if she was going to do her job effectively.

"No wonder you were a big model," Lynn flattered her.

"I was big all right," Ellie said. "They sent me back from Paris because all I did was eat."

Lynn started asking Ellie about her life, getting familiar. Ellie told her how Johnny Casablancas, the playboy chairman of Elite Model Management, had found her as a teenager at a shopping mall and tried to groom her into the next Cheryl Tiegs, and how it didn't happen. Lynn told Ellie how at 5′ 7″ she was an inch too short to be a model, but that she hadn't really worried about it all that much since she had started doing heroin at fourteen in her affluent Chevy Chase, Maryland, high school. She fucked a senator at fifteen, her first rock star at sixteen, and was on tour with the Cars before she got her driver's license. The more Lynn talked, the more Ellie wanted to hear. Did they really drain Keith Richards's blood every year in a Swiss clinic? Was Simon Le Bon everything all the girls said? The more animated Ellie became, the more convinced Lynn was that Ellie would have preferred to be a rock widow than a celluloid mother. Speaking of which, Lynn was aware that Jed had still not returned from the kitchen. She knew he was listening, watching, waiting.

Jed didn't like to be kept waiting. That might have been what ruined it for her years ago. Lynn was always late and often never turned up at all. It drove the normally cool Jed into a snit, which would become a rage. If she ever showed up. She wouldn't keep him waiting tonight. The customer was always right. Goddamn him. Lynn leaned over, took Ellie's American beauty head in her hands, and plunged her tongue into Ellie's mouth.

Ellie responded immediately. It was as if she had been waiting for this all evening, which indeed she had. But half the game was the foreplay, which in this and other Hollywood cases was celebrity name-dropping. Ellie ceded to Lynn the role of the aggressor. After making out with Ellie, probing her ears, nuzzling her neck, sucking on the small of her throat vampirically, Lynn pulled Ellie's UCLA T-shirt over her head and began to work on her breasts. Ellie was still slightly plump from her delivery. Lynn saw herself as physically superior, sleeker, leaner, meaner, which, again, evoked that "Why her?" jealousy that Lynn suppressed by losing herself in Ellie's body.

"I love your big tits," Lynn lied. "You're so lush. You're so beautiful." And Ellie moaned and writhed and bought every word of it. Lynn untied the drawstring of Ellie's sweatpants. She began the final approach. But then she began to laugh.

"Am I too fat?" Ellie asked, stricken and vulnerable.

"No, no," Lynn said. "You won't believe this."

"Believe what?"

"Unzip my dress. You'll see."

Ellie did as she was told. The minidress slipped off Lynn's white shoulders. Ellie let her fingers glide over Lynn's hard nipples as the dress went down. It was just a split-second hold, but it was clearly intentional. Ellie liked what she saw. And then she saw what Lynn was talking about and gasped in surprise. Both women were wearing the identical black silk G-string bikini panties from Janet Reger in London that only Neiman-Marcus carried.

"Did he buy those for you too?" Ellie wondered, in a mounting panic.

"Oh, no. I bought them for myself today. I thought I remembered his taste, but I didn't realize how much," Lynn said.

"Gee. I was worried he was cheating on me," Ellie said.

It was a kick in Lynn's gut. *This* wasn't cheating, because it was out-front. It was a service, like the lawn man and the personal trainer. It didn't count, hence Lynn didn't count. She felt like a nonperson, a performer, a chattel. She needed another line. "I hope you don't mind," Lynn apologized, as she went into her bag for her vial of medicinal white. She offered it to Ellie.

Ellie shook her head. "We're in the program."

Lynn's head opened up. The shred of self-loathing dissipated. She was the queen of the moment. This was her show. She flaunted her body to Ellie, stretched the top of her panties with her thumbs, spun around slowly to reveal the perfect round ass that a couple of her rockers had written private songs about. She watched Ellie's eyes glued to her body, but she was putting on this show as much for Jed, who she knew was watching somewhere. "I'll show you mine if you show me yours," Lynn said with a wink, sinking to her knees and kissing Ellie again. Lynn worked her way down the length of Ellie's body, sliding her finger inside Ellie's black panties and finding herself gloating at how incredibly wet Ellie was.

The two women had sunk to the floor in a long and languid *soixante-neuf*. Ellie had come several times and Lynn had pretended to match each of Ellie's orgasms. It had been harder and harder for Lynn to come since she had started working for Alex. She could only get aroused if she truly desired someone, and all she really desired these days was money. Not that Ellie wasn't trying. Lynn could see the lingual skills that must have endeared Ellie to Jed; however, Lynn had never really been into women.

Having closed her eyes and trying to get into the soft rhythms of

Ellie's relentless, gentle tongue-lapping, Lynn was jarred by an awful prodding behind her. It was Jed, now completely naked, trying to penetrate her from behind. "Exit only," Lynn snapped, shoving him aside.

Ellie looked up. Lynn expected her to be in deep pain seeing the father of her child trying to have another woman that way, yet her eyes betrayed no emotion. She looked up, smiled at Jed, then proceeded to continue performing cunnilingus on Lynn. Jed settled for vaginal sex, with a rear entry, but neither that, nor endless fellatio by Lynn, could get him off.

After an hour of copulation, a spent Ellie took a break and went to the bathroom. Jed pouted like a spoiled child. "I can't believe you wouldn't let me," he complained to Lynn, his penis still erect.

"I don't do that."

"You did it then."

"That was then. Do it with Ellie. Do it with someone you love," Lynn said.

"I want to do it with you," Jed persisted.

"Forget it."

"I'm clean. I'm negative. There's no risk."

Lynn cut him a dirty look. "How do you know *I'm* safe? You have a child to raise."

"Don't give me that shit. You're torturing me."

"You love it, Jed. I didn't realize you were so anal compulsive."

"Funny girl." He put his hand on Lynn's rear and started massaging it. "*You* love it," Jed said. Lynn slapped him away.

"I said no."

"How much more?"

"What?"

"How much more? Three hundred? Four? Five?"

"No way, Jed. I'm not going to do it. It's not negotiable."

Here was Mr. Superstar, begging her for sex. She felt like she was in the power spot, but she knew deep inside that she was simply in a spot.

"Seven fifty," Jed upped the ante.

Lynn lowered her head onto Jed's crotch. She wanted to get him off so she wouldn't have to deal with his compulsion. She wanted to hold something back. She wanted to keep something of herself for herself. It didn't work.

"I don't want head. I don't want pussy," Jed insisted.

"It's enough for any man."

"Not for me."

"It's not for sale, Jed."

"Goddamnit. A thousand. That's it. A fucking grand."

Lynn groaned and turned over on her stomach and spread her legs. She pressed her face against the leather couch so Jed couldn't see the tears falling from her eyes.

| The Mother of All Madams

The Doheny Estates house of Alex Adams, the Madam Alex of Beverly Hills, was so elegant, so refined, so tasteful, so totally un-L.A., that a visiting Turkish prince, whose imperial Ottoman forebears knew a thing or two about elegance and taste, averred before meeting Alex that he should forgo seeing her girls and just marry her. Doheny Drive was the borderline where the ostentation of Beverly Hills gave way to the flash of West Hollywood. It was where the twin towers of legal and agent babble of 9255 and 9200 Sunset that were the pulse of the film business yielded to the Sunset Strip, which was the pounding heartbeat of the music world. It was a sexually charged area, with the aspiring starlets carrying their glossies to the towers by day, then changing into their black Lycra and spandex by night to hang out at the Roxy and the Rainbow and the Central and even the old Whisky a Go-Go. The Gil Turner's liquor store on the corner of Sunset and Doheny was where the two worlds collided, the brown suede producers and their blond models en route to their Coldwater Canyon domains, and the black leather rockers and *their* blond models en route to On the Rox. The blondes were the common denominator, and if you didn't have one, and you were very lucky and very privileged and very much an insider, the pay phones in front of Gil

Turner's were where you could call Alex and try to arrange a visit up the hill to her sexual Land of Oz.

Alex lived in the upper reaches of Doheny, past the streets with names like Wetherly and St. Ives that evoked the wilder shores of Devon and Cornwall. The streets up near Alex's, in the area called Birdland, were named Robin and Thrasher and Oriole and Blue Jay Way, which was where the Beatles had once stayed on a visit to the Coast and had written a drug-evocative song devoted to it. Alex's three-story Spanish-style house with a pool and grounds had a spectacular view of the city spread out below. It had been constructed in the Roaring Twenties. This gave it a venerability, if not landmark status, in a city where anything built before the fifties was considered an ancient monument. Alex had paid a half million for the house, which she had bought upon moving from her prior digs on Stone Canyon Road. L.A. real estate was still booming, and the house was now worth three or four times what she had paid, well into the seven figures. Even though Birdland was slightly less chic than Bel Air, she preferred the new house for its green gardens, for its grand views, and for its cleaner mountain air. Alex hated to go out. She liked the world to come to her. She knew it would.

Even though Alex lived in Birdland, her house may well have been called Catland. She had a dozen of them. What you first noticed upon entering was not the English Georgian antiques or the walls of Picassos and Dalís, or the huge staff of three Filipino maids, a pool man, a houseboy, and a driver, but rather the smell of cat urine. Alex didn't care. The cats came first, even before the clients. There was her favorite, Georgie, the love of Alex's life. Then there was Georgie, Jr., Georgina, Harry Handsome, Fatima, So Sweet and Sexy, and the others. These were Alex's family. The husbands were gone and the sons were grown. Alex's maternal instincts had thus been redirected to her felines, who were so much sweeter and more grateful than humans. Alex loved her cats, and she loved her business. Her business was all-consuming; she was as careerist as any Madison Avenue yuppie and as proud of her success as any Silicon Valley microchip entrepreneur. Not only was she the biggest madam in Beverly Hills, she could lay claim to being the biggest in America, in the world class of France's Madame Claude in her glory days. And even Claude wasn't Claude anymore. In exile from France, she had come to the American Riviera of Southern California and tried to re-create herself on Alex's turf. And failed.

It was a measure of Alex's global reach that her first call of the morning came from the megapound English conglomerator Sir John Ponsonby.

"How's my fairy godmother?" Sir John greeted her.

"Are you in London?" Alex asked him.

"No. I'm in New York, at the Carlyle, and I'm horny as hell, love."

"Who are you buying this time, General Motors?" Alex asked.

"Who wants them?" Sir John said, laughing. "Some tractor company. I won't bore you."

"You should buy a lingerie company," Alex cackled, referring to the august, 6' 6", burly big businessman's penchant for cross-dressing in garter belts and silk stockings that had to be made to his very large measure by a very discreet Parisian corsetiere on the Boulevard de la Madeleine who outfitted some of the world's kinkiest rich men.

"Alex, Alex, I'm dying," Sir John importuned her. "I can't even think about business."

What Sir John was thinking about was the California-born trophy wife of one of his lawyers at Rhoden, Kirts whom he had met at a party at Henry Kravis's. She was a sun-kissed Malibu Christie Brinkley type, tempered with the hauteur of a San Marino Junior Leaguer.

"Was she as pretty as Kravis's wife?" Alex asked him.

"My dear Alex, it's not even close. Carolyne's a vampire. This girl was pure sunshine."

"So take her. He's *your* lawyer." Alex knew how ruthless Sir John was. He was capable of trying to take Henry Kravis's wife, just to prove who was the bigger master of the universe. But Sir John didn't want Kravis's wife. He wanted his lawyer's wife. Alas, even he, the Lord of Threadneedle Street, couldn't exercise his *droit du seigneur*. The lawyer was one of the whiz kids of Rhoden, Kirts. He had designed the intricate takeover, and was its legal point man. Sir John wouldn't risk blowing the deal. He simply wanted a look-alike.

"Did you call Jackie?" Jackie was Alex's correspondent madam in New York. She lived on Sutton Place. Alex knew that Jackie had access to a few moonlighting Social Registrants who would turn the occasional trick if the price was right.

"All Jackie has are vampires," Sir John carped. "Whores who shop. I want beach. I want surf. I want sun. I want California. I'm counting on you, Alex."

Alex thought about the strapping, ruggedly masculine Sir John dressing up in a giant string bikini, or maybe a mammoth maillot, and gamboling with Miss California in the huge Jacuzzi he had installed in his permanent suite. Inside this most he-manly of all the world's financial leaders was a sylph dying to get out.

Sir John's kinks were his business, a business Alex was delighted to have. Sir John's price was more than right, and only Alex would have the supply to meet his demand. He would fly the girl out, first-class, of course, put her up across Madison Avenue at the Mark, and pay her ten thousand dollars for the weekend. Alex's 40 percent cut would yield her four thousand dollars, which seemed an inordinate take for a few phone calls. Nevertheless, Hollywood talent agents got far more for even less. What they, and Alex, were being paid for was their connections, not their time, though it had taken endless time to forge those connections.

Before Alex could attend to Sir John's request, she had to attend to the cats. She was out of the giant Ecuadoran shrimp Georgie was so fond of. She dispatched one of her maids with her driver in the new black BMW sedan, which an Arab oil emir had given her, to an old Japanese fish store in the Little Tokyo of West Los Angeles. It was the only market in striking distance that carried the huge crustaceans live in fish tanks. Warren Beatty doesn't eat as well as Georgie, Alex thought to herself, beaming that there was no expense she would have to spare for those she loved.

Alex loved to do all her work in her vast antique Dutch bed, her four telephones arrayed in front of her. Dressed in one of her trademark muu-muus, Alex looked a bit like a darker, plumper Marlene Dietrich. But despite her priceless antiques and paintings, and despite the standard of beauty she expected of her charges, Alex had no interest whatsoever in her own stylishness. She wore her hair very short, which would have given her a gamine look if she were thinner. She wasn't at all concerned about being too thin (too rich was another matter). Her bare legs and arms were covered with cat scratches, which she cherished as red badges of affection. Otherwise, her skin was flawless, as clear as a young girl's. It made her look far less than her own fifty-something. She also had a young, lilting voice, whether speaking in English, German, Spanish, or Tagalog. There was also a girlish grace that befitted one of Alex's earlier means of survival, as a tango teacher in Raymond Chandler–era Los Angeles. Now, however, she was dancing to her own drum. Once she got into high gear, giving orders like a field marshal, one knew that this was no girl but a woman, a woman of affairs and a woman to reckon with.

Sir John called again. It was seven-thirty in L.A., ten-thirty in New York, and he wanted to give Alex his whereabouts for the day—Salomon Brothers, Merrill Lynch, lunch at the Brook Club.

"Do you really expect me to call you at the Brook with David Rockefeller on one side and Henry Kissinger on the other and tell you your whore is being FedExed to you?" Alex teased the British mogul, who insisted that he did. Here he was in the middle of one of the biggest deals in the annals of high finance, and what was fueling him was not the deal but the fantasy of a girl who would not exist until Alex created her. That gave Alex a great deal of power, a power she was reluctant to exert.

"How can I come up with anyone as elegant as your wife?" Alex pressed him. Because Alex read all the magazines—literally, from *Hola* to the *Economist* to *Palm Beach Celebrity Society* to *Variety*—to stay *au courant* with her clientele, she knew that what was gnawing at Sir John was that his dear friend and rival Sir Gwaine Byrne had just married a beyond-beautiful Southern Californian named Betsy Martin, a trophy of trophies. Even though Sir John's own wife was lovely and in *Burke's Peer-*

age, she was of a certain age and the great sex was long gone. Sir Gwaine Byrne was having a better life, on Sir John's terms, than Sir John was, and Sir John was corrosively competitive. Hence all the aggression. Hence the call to Alex.

Alex had about three hundred girls on her mental Rolodex. With her prodigious memory she kept most of their vital statistics and phone numbers in her head. There was no black book, despite what the journalists and the gossips always said. At best, there were a lot of slips of paper that were perpetually being misplaced. Even if they were, and even if Alex forgot, which was rare, everyone would call back. Of the three hundred, Alex kept a "hot file" of fifty that included her superstars, her workhorses (or "racehorses," as she preferred to call them), and the new girls (or "discoveries"). Just as Hollywood preferred a new kid with no track record fresh out of USC Film School over a forty-year-old with lots of credits but no hits and no Oscars, to Alex's clientele newness was everything. This cult of novelty was what gave any madam her reputation, and Alex was famous for her pipeline to the playing fields that were as fecund with beauty as the Alaskan tundra was with oil.

During Alex's nearly two decades in the business, several thousand girls had worked for her. Of those thousands, all but a few hundred had vanished from Alex's awareness. That was prostitution. It might have been a profession, but it was rarely a career. Some girls would turn a trick and give up, some would last a month, some would work once a week, once a month, whenever they needed money. The life span of a call girl's career rarely exceeded a year. For most, it was the rare telephone number that wasn't disconnected after six months, and the turnover in apartments was equally rapid. Yet somehow in this ephemeral world, where the girls would disappear even more quickly than their looks, Alex always managed to find new talent—or, rather, new talent managed to find her. The men of Hollywood, and the world, could count on Alex's steady "three hundred." That was the same size as one of the major modeling agencies, Ford or Elite, except that here you could have sex with the beauties, not merely look at them. Girls would come and go, but the number of top-level working girls in Beverly Hills remained the same. The men were lucky they wanted novelty; they didn't have any choice in the matter.

The roster of Alex's clients, on the other hand, featured very few dropouts. Once an Alex man, always an Alex man. All in all, there were probably a thousand VIPs in Alex's mental Rolodex, an international Who's Who. The average client would see one creature every three months, but Alex had many men who would see someone every week, and a hard core of about twenty superjohns who would see someone every few days. Of her clientele, about four hundred lived in Los Angeles; the rest came from around the world. The Beverly Hills four hundred was, in its way, as exclusive as Mrs. Astor's Four Hundred, the number she could fit into her ballroom and what defined New York society in the Gilded Age. And to think Alex did it without the ballroom.

Alex was drawing a blank. She thought immediately of her two Pasadena debs, who had come out at the Los Madrilenos Ball and had been sorority sisters at UCSB (the University of California, Santa Barbara), which had the reputation of having the best-looking coeds in the nation. They would have been perfect. But one had just gotten engaged to a movie star and another was being kept by a Tokyo land developer who had bought and was now trying to unload a large chunk of downtown L.A. There was Marin from one of Fort Worth's finest River Oaks families, but she was too short, and there was Allie from Lake Forest and Miss Porter's, but she had gone to Sarah Lawrence and was too artsy bohemian, and there were a number of superb Jewish Princesses from Beverly Hills High School who had been bleached and lipoed and siliconed into Christie Brinkley Malibu girls, but Sir John was in too fragile a state of mind for ersatz pleasures. He wanted the Real Thing. He wanted a young Candice Bergen. He wouldn't settle for an older Candice Bergen, or even Candice Bergen herself.

The L.A. talent pool was short on class. Very long on looks, but short on the kind of girls you could bring to dinner at, say, Pamela Harriman's, which was where Sir John was supposed to go next week, but, no, he wouldn't *dare* bring her, not there. Madame Claude had Alex beat in that department, for she was in Europe, and that was the Old World, where her call girls had culture and spoke five languages. L.A. was a Teenage Wasteland, but most of Alex's men, including her many cultured men, loved and craved the sublime bimbos, the Marilyn Monroes of this new era, aerobicized and bikini-waxed and New Aged, but Monroes nonetheless. This was Hollywood, after all, and they wanted Hollywood. Sir John was different, and Alex prided herself on being able to meet all demands. Delivering the goods was more than sound business sense; it was a point of honor.

Alex got on the line to the other madams of Beverly Hills. Their shark-pond rivalry notwithstanding, as with Hollywood agents, if there was money to be made they would do a deal with anyone. Alex would split her commission with whoever could deliver her a San Marino deb-jock. But all the madams, Carole and Wendy and Brenda and Dixie, were fast asleep, their answering machines on, and they probably wouldn't even turn their phones on until after one in the afternoon. No wonder she ruled the business, Alex thought. Lazy sloths. By nine o'clock, Alex's own phone was ringing off the hook. Aside from Sir John, her top priority of the morning was to firm up plans for the bachelor party of the season, which was being held tonight. The honoree was Rex Fried, a Beverly Hills prince, who was soon to marry Sindee Cohen, a development princess. It was a match made in Burbank. Rex's father was a big television producer, his mother a Holmby Hills socialite. Sindee was straight out of Brooklyn, scholarship to Penn, beeline to Hollywood. If Dawn Steel had made her mark selling Gucci toilet paper, Sindee was determined to follow in Steel's footsteps, albeit more tonily, by going to Wharton and selling detergent at Procter & Gamble to figure out what America Really Wanted and then coming west and devoting herself to a career of working for the studios as a junior, and inevitably senior, executive making teen comedies and cyborg action movies. Sindee was on the fast track; Rex, who worked for another studio, was on the inside track. In a week they would be marrying at Temple Emanuel, where the pious moguls paid thousands for preferred seating during the High Holy Days. They would be Hollywood's new Fun Couple. But tonight, Rex's friends just wanted him to have fun.

The guest list for the party, which was to be held at a bungalow at the Beverly Hills Hotel, was a Who's Who of Young Male Hollywood, twenty clones of Rex—"hot" boys—agents from CAA, ICM, and William Morris; creative v.p.s at the majors, producers with at least one film released by a major, and lawyers with at least one "A" client. None of Rex's old friends from El Rodeo or UCLA were included, no matter how old, unless they had made it. No one was over thirty. In their eyes, if you hadn't scored big by thirty, you were an abject loser not worth returning calls to, much less allowing to party with the most exclusive call girls in Tinseltown. In short, a very arrogant group that no one except their own kind could stand to be with.

Of the twenty celebrants, fifteen were married and the other five had girlfriends, yet all of them were as excited as a kid going to Disneyland for the first time. For three thousand dollars, they were chipping in to see their friend Rex get royally screwed. Alex was sending, for Rex's delectation, Sarah from Montana, who looked disturbingly like Sean Young, and Liz from Richmond, who looked even more like Daryl Hannah. If the other moguls-in-training wanted to see the girls in one of the bungalow's three bedrooms, they could work that out with them. No one wanted to admit it, but all the young men were thinking about it. Even though each was an adept negotiator, this was one deal that they hadn't done before. The party was thus shaping up for these members of the *jeunesse dorée* as something of, as it were, a coming of age.

Jeff Rosenberg, a hot young Century City lawyer, was the designated arranger of the evening. He had gotten Alex's unlisted number through a client who was a close friend of industrialist Armand Hammer. Jeff must have called Alex fifty times. He was a nervous wreck. Now he was on the phone again in a new anxiety attack.

"What if the girls end up going on auditions with the guys?" Guys who were going to fuck girls for money tonight might feel uncomfortable facing then across a casting table tomorrow.

"Jeff, not everyone in this town's in show business," Alex told him. "Sarah's in real estate. Liz is in computers. They *look* like movie stars, but they're smart enough not to want to *be* them."

The phones kept ringing. A midwestern senator called from the Beverly Hilton, where he was in town to make the keynote speech at a charity function and then go out to Palm Springs to visit old friends and watch a polo match with Merv Griffin. He wanted a new girl—he'd leave it up to Alex to surprise him as long as the surprise was tall, blond, tan, and had large breasts. The one surprise he didn't want was to be seen by anyone. He couldn't entertain anyone at the hotel and he didn't dare go to an apartment building. When it came to misbehaving, fame was an enormous liability. That was why so many celebrities used Alex. To paraphrase the old Ban deodorant ad, she took the worry out of being close.

Alex had the perfect girl for the senator. Nonny had worked for Alex for two years while modeling for Eileen Ford and Nina Blanchard. She married the garment czar in whose ads she appeared, and three years later she had a divorce and the house on North Roxbury Drive, in the class part of Beverly Hills between Santa Monica and Sunset, and she was working for Alex again. The best part of the location, for Alex's purposes, was that it was a five-minute, unsuspicious, and unpopulated stroll from the Beverly Hilton. There were no curious pedestrians—nobody walked in L.A., and definitely not here. Nonny was thus geographically desirable for the senator. As for the rest, Alex had to check her out.

"How are your tits?" Alex asked, after she cajoled Nonny's maid, in Spanish, to wake up her mistress.

"I'm just looking at them," Nonny said in her throaty morning voice. "I always sleep in the nude."

"Well?"

"Outta sight. They're just spectacular. Silicone's the greatest thing since polyester."

The pert B-cup breasts that had served Nonny so well as a slinky fashion model were of considerably less utility now that she was in the market for a new husband in a city, not to mention a country, that had gone cleavage crazy. So Nonny had returned to the life, as had a number of transitional Brentwood and Beverly Hills wives. Nonny's alimony, ten thousand a month, simply wasn't enough, not in Candy Spelling land.

"A thousand?" Nonny sneered when Alex put the deal to her. "He's a fucking senator. Some bimbo could ruin his career. I'm covering his ass, for a thousand?"

"They're watching them like hawks now," Alex said. "It all has to be in cash. He doesn't have that big a discretionary fund."

"Except when he needs to bribe some Third World dictator. Come on, Alex, a thousand is bullshit."

"What else are you doing today?"

"There's a private sale at Chanel. Listen, it's just not worth it."

"For forty-five minutes?"

"It's the principle of the thing."

"He's a senator. He's sexy. He could be president. Aren't you curious?"

"Not for a thousand."

"You're not very patriotic," said Alex, who finally convinced Nonny to see the senator only by waiving her madam's cut.

Soon after Alex completed her slice of Nonny's fiscal humble pie, Lynn arrived with her white envelope. Part of the Alex ritual was for the girls to deliver Alex her cut the morning after if there was a night before, or the evening of, if the tryst in question was of an afternoon. In a baggy sweat suit, dark glasses, no makeup, and ratty hair, Lynn was the antithesis of the fantasy creature she had been mere hours before. The drill was to hand Alex the envelope, have a quick cup of fresh chamomile tea from Alex's herb garden, share a little gossip, and then depart quickly so that Alex could get back to the phones.

"You gave me too much," Alex said without even opening the envelope.

"I stayed longer."

"The deal was all night."

"I did extra." Lynn never tried to lie to Alex, to pocket any tips without telling her. The arrangement was 40 percent of a girl's gross, and everyone knew not to cross Alex or try to fool her. Alex was foolproof. In these matters, she was omniscient.

"Greek?" Alex asked.

"Greek," Lynn admitted abashedly, glad she still had her dark glasses to hide behind.

"Lynn, I want you to go to Betty Ford," Alex said, sorry that Lynn had not listened to her own better judgment and knowing what the culprit was.

"I'm not strung out," Lynn lied to her.

"I'll pay for it," Alex said. "You'll meet someone nice there. Look at Liz Taylor. It'll be fun." Alex was trying to make light of a heavy situation. Lynn had it all and she was hurling it away. Alex knew that maternal instincts were not only time-consuming but usually futile. Still, she couldn't stop herself.

"I really fucked up my life, didn't I?" Lynn started to cry. She took off the shades. Cocaine eyes.

Alex handed her some Kleenex. She almost felt guilty that she had sent Lynn on this date. But Alex knew how to avoid feeling guilty. Otherwise, she'd still be selling flowers. Lynn, all the girls, they thought they could handle it. Sometimes they could, though never with coke, which was a prime mover and a prime waste for so many of the rock goddesses like Lynn who worked for Alex and the other madams. It was a vicious circle. They needed the coke to fuck, and they needed to fuck for the coke. They could have all been rich and secure if they hadn't blown it all on the blow. Cocaine was the bedrock of the Los Angeles circus of glamour. It was a fact of life just like sex, and Alex, more than anyone else, lived in the real world. The best she could do was to provide a net when the girls fell.

Alex opened the envelope and gave Lynn the entire thousand-dollar "tip." "They'd probably call me—what is it?—an enabler, but they call me lots of things."

Lynn just stared at the money.

"Make me one promise," Alex added.

"What?"

"You'll spend it on anything but drugs. Anything. Go to Saks. Go be the JAP you always wanted to be."

"I promise," Lynn whispered like a little girl, unsure of whether she could resist the white temptation yet strangely hopeful and willing to try.

"Think about Betty Ford. Please. 'Cause I won't send you out anymore until you clean up," Alex threatened, walloping Lynn exactly where it hurt.

Lynn's only means of support, the younger woman realized, was her stunning body and her occasionally agile mind, which she had put to no use. She suddenly despised herself for doing nothing with her life other than collecting men. "Alex, really, I'm going to be better. I am."

Alex's next crisis was finding out that Fifi (short for Afifa), her six-foot-tall Jordanian ex-dancer, had been stabbed in the stomach by her five-foot-four estranged Israeli husband. Fifi had not shown up for an *après*-breakfast date with a visiting OPEC minister at the Beverly Wilshire, which was completely unlike her. A flurry of calls found her in intensive care at Cedars-Sinai. Contrary to popular belief, the free-spending Arab clients who constituted the bread and butter, or rather pita and sesame oil, of Alex's business did not necessarily prefer blondes. They were quite partial to Levantine call girls if they could ever find them, as Levantine call girls with Vegas bodies were in as short supply in Los Angeles as they were in the Middle East itself. Fifi was thus quite a find, and was one of Alex's great cash machines.

Again, drugs were a culprit. Fifi's husband was a member of the Tel Aviv counterpart of the Medellín cartel. Who else could have afforded such a showpiece? The relationship was as combustible as the West Bank. Alex was concerned for Fifi's present condition as well as her future. First, Alex called one of her doctor friends, a prominent physician at Cedars, to make sure Fifi would survive. Then she called the Parisian Florist, which had delivered Joe DiMaggio's flowers three times a week to Marilyn Monroe's crypt at Westwood Memorial Park, to make sure Fifi's private room was filled with orchids. Finally, she called one of her lawyer friends, an important member of the district attorney's office, to make sure charges would be pressed to the limit against the husband and that he would be deported to Israel as an undesirable alien.

| Pretender to the Throne

The doctor reported that Fifi would be back at "work" within a month. A plastic surgeon could erase the wound on her abdomen, though Alex mused that she could titillate the Arab princes by saying it was a battle scar Fifi got as a teenager in a commando raid on the Allenby Bridge or Hebron. Meanwhile, however, Alex had to find a replacement for the lubricious man from OPEC. Her first thought was Robin, who looked the most like Fifi. Robin's only liability, and it was a major one in this instance, was that she was Jewish. The lure of forbidden fruit notwithstanding, the Arab minister was too politically correct to cross the Jordan.

Robin was part of an entire group of young privileged hookers Alex had dubbed "the JAP Pack." They loved nightclubs, Porsches, Versace, and coke, mostly went to UCLA on and off, hated the idea of working at a *real* job, and could only soak their parents for so much. A member of the Pack had met Alex through her father, who bought and sold jewelry for Alex. This girl and her friends thought that working for Alex would be not only a kick but a gold mine, and a curious status symbol as well, and they were right.

Lissa Trapp, one of Alex's favorite girls, was a stepsister of the JAP Pack, a JAP wanna-be fringe member from south of Wilshire who was actually Italian and whose pre–Beverly Hills High name was Malizia Trapanzano. No high school in America could make you feel as bad about being poor as Beverly Hills High. Even Beverly Hills had a wrong side of the tracks, and that was where Lissa grew up, in a small apartment on Roxbury Drive off the drag strip that was Olympic Boulevard. Her father was the fish-department manager at the Safeway on Beverly Drive; her mother a secretary at the Wells Fargo Bank.

Lissa thus adolesced in a permanent pique of envy. Yet just as she was bitterly jealous of her classmates' baby Mercedeses and twenty pairs of Guccis and five-digit monthly bills at Neiman-Marcus and cool Moroccan coke dealers, her classmates were equally envious of Lissa's sultry Neapolitan olive-skinned beauty, her wonderfully sinuous dancer's body, her hypnotic eyes. Hers were mad, crazy eyes, but in this case madness was an aphrodisiac. The boys at Beverly Hills High shared a collective wet dream over Lissa. Lissa was runner-up for "Best Looking" in the senior-class yearbook. If the princess platoon hadn't voted in a bloc against her, she would have won hands down.

Lissa didn't care about accolades. She didn't even care that much about boys, although she enjoyed her effortless power over them. Lissa took a perverse sadistic pleasure in making them act like fools for her favors. "My body is a temple—the temple of doom," she would quip, and once she seriously considered getting a tattoo over her mons veneris of the Dante line about another Italian inferno: "All hope abandon, ye who enter here!"

What Lissa was convinced would bring her true happiness had nothing to do with love or sex. All she wanted was to be Jewish and rich, like the Beverly Hills High in-crowd. To that end, she successfully importuned her parents to let her have rhinoplasty to reduce her classic Roman nose. "It's roamin' all over my face," she insisted, and her parents gave in and gave her the graduation present of a pert and perfect retroussé nose just like the girls on North Rodeo and North Canon and North Palm. What Lissa's parents couldn't give her were the cars, the clothes, the coke, the comfort, and the confidence that came with never having to worry about money.

Money was *all* Lissa worried about, simply because she was in such blinding proximity to it. Although she had studied hard, made good grades, proceeded with her heiress friends to UCLA, and undoubtedly from there could have gone on to a successful white-collar career, Lissa was terminally impatient. She couldn't wait to be rich, Beverly Hills rich, and even a UCLA degree, summa cum laude, was no sure ticket to that special heaven. Besides, school was hell. Lissa thought her nose job would have made her a blood sister, but when sorority time came around the only rush Lissa got was the bum's rush. And when Robin and the rest of the JAP Pack discovered Alex, they refused to cut Lissa in on their fabulous new secret of "money for nothing." She just wasn't "one of us," they sniffed. But Lissa was smart and conniving and managed to find Alex through darker and more devious means, and quickly became one of Alex's stars. She dropped out of UCLA and spent all of her time fucking for the money that would finally enable her to become the princess she always wanted to be.

When Alex called her today about replacing Fifi, Lissa couldn't talk. She was in the middle of a session with the great New York dramatic actor Harris Fox, or rather Harris was in the middle of her, trying in vain to bring Lissa to orgasm.

"You're never going to come, are you?" Harris said, exasperated after having performed his very best cunnilingus on Lissa for the last half hour. Most of his millions of fans around the world would have died for this. Lissa was unmoved, bored.

"You want the truth?" Lissa asked him, knowing full well the answer. Harris Fox was famous for insisting on the "truth" of every part he played, and for driving writers, directors, and producers insane in a process that could send film projects years out of schedule and millions over budget. He came to Lissa not to get laid, but to get the truth, the hard truth about himself as a man.

"You're a little guy with a little cock," Lissa told him, flat out. "Little doesn't do it for me. I like big, hunky, laid-back guys who don't give a shit. Power and fame just don't ring my bell."

Harris, who had gone flaccid during his pussy eating, found himself getting hard again. He was getting angry. That was what he wanted. He studied Lissa's lithe, indifferent body, sprawled on her huge white bed. One of her hands stuffed Reese's Pieces into her mouth. The other stroked her clitoris. Harris Fox, for all his fame and power and Oscars and sex symbolism, might as well have not even been here. His cock was getting harder and harder.

"Napoleon complexes are a turnoff," Lissa said, staring at his erection and yawning. In real life, outside of session, Lissa, a child of Los Angeles, was as starstruck as any gawker on Hollywood Boulevard. But Lissa didn't worship stars because they were stars. She worshiped stars because stars were money. If she was acting blasé toward Harris Fox, it was because this was her job. This was a "corrective" session in which she was giving Harris the truth, which, in his case, was more like consequences.

Harris, fully aroused, spread Lissa's legs, moved her fingers aside, and began to enter her. He pumped away. She continued eating the Reese's Pieces. "Actually, Harris, it's better if you go down on me," Lissa said, pushing him off of her. "You're so small, this way I can't feel anything."

Harris Fox, who could make audiences cry, who could make Mike Ovitz cringe and Jeff Berg kowtow, got on his knees and did exactly what Lissa Trapp told him to do.

In the endless war between New York and Los Angeles, Harris Fox was one of the most frequently given reasons why New York was the better place. This short, ethnic, introspective celebrity, whose public persona was so anti-L.A. that he might not even turn right on a red light on general principle, had become a major consumer of Alex's California girls. He claimed he came to Alex out of sheer boredom when he was out doing a studio film. There were no streets to walk, no egg creams to drink, nowhere to go after eleven o'clock. Hookers were the only sign of life in this City of the Dead.

Until his breakthrough role as an alienated Ivy League sixties intellectual James Dean rebel with a cause in *Sit-In*, Harris Fox would have been considered a wimpy little bookworm nerd. But *Sit-In* made Harris and his type a new kind of anti-establishment sex symbol. Harris took his symbolism quite seriously. He thought he was beyond James Dean in his allure; he thought he was Clark Gable. Unfortunately for Harris, what played on the Upper West Side and in New Haven and Cambridge didn't necessarily play in Manhattan Beach. The California surf goddesses might have enjoyed Harris on the screen, but in real life they wanted California surf gods, rat-haired rock and rollers, sexy Latino low riders, Pendleton-shirted lumberjacks, bad gang-bangers. Whatever they wanted, Harris wasn't it.

Harris thus turned to Alex to buy the indifferent California goddess whom he simply couldn't seduce. And the Alex girl who got him off the most was Lissa, mainly because she seemed like the one California girl who *should* have gone for him, for nothing, a smart Jewish girl from Beverly Hills. (Lissa lied and told everyone she was Jewish.) This was Harris's constituency, but Lissa wasn't voting.

"Hey, Harris, cheer up," Lissa beamed, folding the ten hundred-dollar bills Harris had handed her into her Hermès money clip. "It's L.A. People are into looks. It's superficial. Who cares? The whole world loves you."

"You didn't come," Harris said dejectedly. "I tried so goddamn hard."

"For two thousand, I'll come." Lissa burst out laughing at her own joke. She slipped on her white silk panties. Harris stared at her, her bronze thighs and taut stomach offset by the shimmering white. He hated Lissa. He wanted to fuck her again.

"Bad boy." Lissa patted, then squeezed Harris's growing erection. He grimaced in pain.

"Let's do it again," he said, grabbing for her pointy breasts.

"Can't," Lissa denied him, slipping out of his clutches and into her Giorgio sweatshirt and Armani jeans. "Gotta go for my bikini wax." She grabbed another handful of Reese's Pieces and poured them into her wide-open mouth. Here was a star that kept the studio in a pathetic thrall. They would do anything for him, and Lissa Trapp was blowing him off for a bikini wax. It kept him honest.

Lissa called Alex from the car phone in her black BMW convertible.

"I drove Harris Fox crazy this morning," Lissa gloated.

"How crazy?" Alex asked.

"One," Lissa said, meaning a thousand dollars, which in turn meant a four-hundred-dollar cut to Alex. "I could've gotten one and a half, but I blew him off. I bet I can get two next time."

"He told me he found you obnoxious," Alex said. "A spoiled cunt."

"Then he'll *definitely* pay two next time."

Both women laughed. Lissa was one of Alex's pets. Alex loved Lissa's sense of humor, her flair for gossip, her greed. Unlike most girls, who might turn a trick every few days, Lissa would do two and three in a single day. Nothing was off limits for her. This afternoon she was scheduled to see the famous producer Carlos Wynburg, who would pay five hundred dollars to lie under a glass coffee table and watch Lissa defecate on top of it. To her that was easy money. Lissa adored making money as much as Donald Trump or Mike Milken did. As much as Alex did. That was their bond. Also, Alex was very maternal toward the young Lissa, who had just turned twenty and had turned her back on her own mother. Lissa had great potential, and Alex wanted to see her realize it. In return, Lissa was Alex's own truffle hound, Alex's eyes and ears. Because Alex, who was bedridden with heart problems and diabetes, rarely left her home, she relied on her girls to tell her *everything* that went on on their dates. No girl was a better, more vivid, reporter than Lissa. There was a true symbiosis between the two women. In some ways, Alex and Lissa were the same woman, Alex the brains, Lissa the body. Their adventures were one.

"Do you know any Arab girls?" Alex told Lissa of Fifi's stabbing and the high-and-dry OPEC minister.

"I'll go fuck him," Lissa volunteered.

"He wants an Arab."

"I'll be an Arab. I'll wear a veil. I'll put on an accent. Come wiz me to zee Casbah, babee. I fucka you gooood."

"I can't afford an international incident," Alex said, remembering how Lissa had misbehaved with the last Arab Alex had sent her to, arguing with him about Israel. Sex and politics were combustible. Alex opted for safety.

Lissa came up with someone, a Persian girl she knew from the nightclub scene. This girl worked as a receptionist in a Westwood real estate firm and always wanted more money for more clothes. She was Jewish, "but she looks like a Bedouin," Lissa insisted.

Alex was dubious, but agreed to have Lissa send her the Persian for an interview. Alex would have to call the minister and propitiate him with the vision of a thousand and one Arabian nights if he could wait one more day. And then there was Sir John to take care of. "What about WASPs? Have you met any classy WASPs who want to work?"

The minute Alex told Lissa about the New York assignment, Lissa sunk into the deepest trough of jealousy and depression. It wasn't over not being a country-club WASP. It was all about money. It was about hearing of OPEC ministers and British takeover lords and $10,000 weekends. In her first year with Alex, Lissa had earned nearly $150,000. She was one of the most highly paid twenty-year-old women in the world. This was amazing for someone who had dropped out of college, wasn't tall enough to be a model, and couldn't sing. Yet Lissa had nothing left, not after her three-thousand-a-month rent, the BMW, the clothes from the Beverly Center, Rodeo, and Melrose, and, of course, the drugs. There was nothing left, and nothing else to do but give blow jobs and shit on glass tables and dump on movie stars. What was it going to be like at thirty, when she developed *real* taste?

And how much more could she make as a call girl? Most tricks were $300 to $500. The $1,000 Harris Foxes were rare. And Alex had never sent her on a $2,000 overnight, much less a $10,000 weekend. On a great day, three tricks, Lissa would gross $1,500, and net $900, but she usually had no more than two great days a week. Some days all she could eke out was a $300 missionary. With $100 to Alex, the remaining $200 wouldn't even buy her the shoes she needed at Charles Jourdan. Yet at $150,000 in a year, Lissa was close to a call girl's peak. It wasn't going to get that much better, and it might get a lot worse. Lissa wasn't one for planning for the future, but as she saw it, ten years from now $150,000 wasn't going to get her much further than being a Beverly Hills bag lady. That the bags would be from Neiman-Marcus didn't make that future seem any more appealing to her.

Lissa gave the finger to a Beverly Hills High brat in a Testarossa who cut her off as Lissa made an illegal turn off Olympic and onto Century Park East and toward the Century City high-rise where she was going for her bikini wax. This wasn't Elizabeth Arden or Georgette Klinger but the apartment of the would-be producer Nicky Kroll. It wasn't often that Hollywood producers gave bikini waxes, but Nicky Kroll loved pussy so much that he would do anything to be close to it. If Alex was Lissa Trapp's mother figure, Nicky was her father, or godfather. In some ways, he played Erich von Stroheim to Lissa's Gloria Swanson, in their own version of *Sunset Boulevard,* grooming his star's pussy and scoring her coke. However, Nicky was far more the Svengali than the slave. Just as Alex had Lissa play out the active part of her life, Nicky had Lissa perform all the fantasies of his feminine side. Lissa was the woman Nicky had always wanted to be.

Nicky Kroll was a producer with the soul, if he could be said to have a soul, of a pimp. A Brooklyn College dropout, the satanically goateed, cocaine-skinny Nicky, who was now forty, had gone to Paris in 1969 to sell mutual funds of questionable provenance for Bernie Cornfeld's Investors Overseas Services. Adept at languages, Nicky quickly traded his Canarsie accent for a Parisian one and transformed himself into a suave *boulevardier.* He was less adept at selling his funds to unsuspecting buyers than selling himself to the young whores of the Rue St. Denis and the clip joints of Pigalle. Somehow he had the knack for getting *les girls* to bestow their favors *gratuit.*

Nicky realized he could get even more women by cloaking himself in the wolf's clothing of a film producer. Accordingly, he sweet-talked some gullible IOS investors into backing a couple of disastrous ersatz Sergio Leone spaghetti westerns and an even worse ersatz Dario Argento spaghetti horror film at the crumbling Cinecittà Studios in Rome. At most, fifty people ever saw the movies, but they gave Nicky a new identity as a film mogul, which he played to the hilt on the decaying Via Veneto, again proving as slippery in conning the Italian *putane* out of the price for their pleasure as he was with the French *putains.*

Like all great film moguls, Nicky, in the early eighties, found his way to Los Angeles, where the would-be impresario ended up doing plumbing contracting to support his big-producer charades. He was always ready with a million excuses why he had just missed being Sam Spiegel or the Salkinds. What Nicky hated most about Los Angeles was not so much the shortage of good work, for his producing was just a cover to get women, but rather the shortage of good whores. When he found out about Alex, he was dying to meet her, though he had no intention of ever giving her a cent.

Nicky got to Alex through a rich Beverly Hills strip mall developer for whom Nicky was installing bidets in his nine bathrooms on Sierra Alta Way. Using his charm, his multiple European dialects, and his some-times amusing war and whore stories, Nicky ingratiated himself into Alex's salon. What he gave Alex back, in addition to his tall tales of self-promotion, was that he found her amazing girls to stoke the unquench-able fires of her clients' endless demands for new, new, new. Nicky would find them everywhere. He'd park the old red Ferrari he'd won in a poker game in front of Beverly Hills High at lunchtime and pick up girls with that prop, one that invariably worked in a town that measured your cool by your wheels, and assumed you *were* what you *drove*. He'd don his most expensive European business suit and stalk the cafeterias of Century City, trolling for secretaries and administrative assistants who looked as if they wanted to supplement their salaries, and then he'd hit the win-dow shoppers on Rodeo and pick the longing ones who might make a Faustian deal to make their material dreams come true. He'd put on his tennis whites and visit the courts at UCLA, pretending he was on the French Davis Cup team. And then he'd put on his boots and leather jacket and his gold chains and do the town, the bars and clubs, from the Marina to Pasadena, in search of potential creatures. He positioned him-self like the emissary in the old TV series *The Millionaire*; he was offering these girls the chance of a lifetime. Of course, he had to sample them first to see if they were truly Alex material. By appealing to their greed, their unvarnished Southern California all-American greed to have all the "stuff" that Beverly Hills could offer, Nicky rarely got turned down. Cloaked in Alex's ungiven authority, Nicky was back to his old European tricks. He was fucking whores for free. The only difference was that these girls hadn't even become whores yet. But they would.

Nicky's greatest discovery was Lissa Trapp, whom he found at Squeeze Box, a hip, star-filled, weekends-only club. When he met Lissa while reaching over her for a Corona and lime at the bar, Lissa saw the nasty forbidden father figure her own father had never been, and was instantly entranced. Lissa had a divining rod for pain and trouble, and Nicky Kroll was that in spades.

Nicky took Lissa in his Ferrari back to his all-white Century City high-rise, which was an inconvenient color scheme in that his cocaine tended to get lost. The next day Nicky went to see Alex and boasted, like a high-schooler over his first conquest, that he had given her head until she was so out of control that she peed in his mouth. All Lissa cared about was sex and money, he said. She would make the perfect whore. The trick was to turn her out.

Nicky quickly learned that Lissa, who was eighteen at the time, was a compulsive shopper. So Nicky let her run up a several-month tab on Rodeo Drive and then called in the I.O.U., insisting he was desperate for the money. When Lissa couldn't pay him back, Nicky suddenly turned on her and became the very strict father. He gave her a week. When the week ran out without the paying of the debt, as Nicky knew it would— for every cent Lissa earned from her waitress job at Stratton's in West-wood after classes at UCLA went to the Beverly Center for clothes or to her dealer for coke—Nicky gave Lissa the option of repaying him by turning a trick for Madam Alex or never seeing him again.

Loving Nicky's brutal lovemaking (he specialized in bondage and anal sex), Lissa had no choice but to go with Alex. Lissa saw a visiting Arab at the Beverly Wilshire, and totally enjoyed it. Instead of losing what little innocence was left in her waning teenage years, Lissa found that she had gained true sophistication. She had hit the jackpot of easy money.

Although she was supposedly Nicky's mistress, she called Alex after her first date and immediately asked for more. And Alex sent her off to give a prostate massage to an aging ad exec in from Manhattan. Lissa would do anything for money. Anything. Golden showers. Excrement sandwiches. Nipple piercing. She'd give and she'd get, as long as the price was right. "Do you want to see more of me?" the executive, who was in town for the week, asked her, after she had made him come like he'd never come before.

"I'd like to see more of your money," she shot back, all sass and nasti-ness. Lissa's bitchy repartee made her the Don Rickles of hookers. A lot of Alex's clients enjoyed being roasted. Lissa would do everything in her repertoire to force the client to have a premature ejaculation, whining how long he was taking and what a rush she was in, and then she'd mock him for being so quick on the trigger and suggest he could use some counseling. Or she would deflate another by asking, poker-faced, if he had looked into all the new, safe methods of penis enlargement. Lissa knew precisely where it hurt, and the show-business guys in particular went for it, hooker, line, and sinker. Movies were the most vicious, ruthless business, and when one of these warriors wanted to bring the business, or its hostility, to bed with him, Lissa quickly became *the* wildcat to call.

Dressed in his artsy-look outfit of black jeans, black turtleneck, and black studded cowboy boots, Nicky was snorting some top-grade medicinal coke and watching *La Grande Illusion* when Lissa burst in, in the midst of her anxiety attack. Still viewing himself as an impresario manqué, Nicky, if he would ever come down off the coke to take a look at his own life, might have had an anxiety attack as well. Although he was continually boasting about his various projects that were in development at Fox and Paramount, his only meetings with studio executives were off the lot, to sell them drugs, which, in addition to the plumbing, was how he supported his luxuries. He would also traffic in stolen paintings and hot jewels, and even purloined cameras when times were hard.

"I can't stand it," Lissa whined. "I'm finished at twenty. I'm fucked. It's hopeless."

Nicky handed her a Valium and laid out some white lines on his glass table. Lissa plowed through them, and demanded some more. "Oh, God, I'm so hot," she wailed. "How can you dress like that? It's fucking hot." Lissa stripped off all her clothes. She lay on the couch naked, played with her breasts and her clitoris. Nicky didn't even look at her. He was immersed in Jean Gabin. Restless, she went into the two Theodore bags she had with her and tried on some Italian dresses, pouring herself some Stolichnaya into a large tumbler. "What do you think?" she asked Nicky.

"Great," he said without looking up.

"I fucked Harris Fox this morning," Lissa told him.

"Great," Nicky replied.

"Do you realize how much money Alex is making?" Lissa went into her lament, ticking off the open assignments with the OPEC minister and Sir John Ponsonby and the ten-thousand-dollar Carlyle weekend. "And I have to go shit on Carlos Wynburg. Shit. Fuck. I wish I could be like Alex."

Nicky was deeply annoyed at Lissa's obsession with Alex, mainly because Lissa had become more fascinated with Alex than she was with him. He could not stand not being the cynosure of any woman's attention. He wanted Lissa in his thrall, just as he wanted all women in his thrall. To that end, he broached a proposition that he had long been cogitating. "Why do you want to be *like* Alex? Why don't you just *be* Alex?"

"What do you mean? Me become a madam?"

"Not a madam. *The* madam," Nicky said. "With you running the show and me running the business. We could be global. We could be the Elite of hookers. London, Paris, Tokyo. Rome. I mean, try to get laid in Rome. Forget it. Some pathetic old whores on the Via Veneto and a lot of Brazilian transsexuals out on the Raccordo Annulare. A bunch of massage ads in *Il Messaggero*, but who reads Italian? Not the rich American tourist, not the Jap businessman. So what do they do for kicks? Jog in the Villa Borghese. Walk up the Spanish Steps. I can see it now. One call fucks all. Dial 1-800-PUSSY." Nicky was snorting line after line as he got himself worked up.

"But what about Alex?" Lissa tried to bring him back to earth. "I can't be Alex. *Alex* is Alex."

"Alex is old. Alex is rich. Alex doesn't give a shit," Nicky wailed. "She stays in bed with her fucking cats. She's a one-woman cottage industry. This should be a conglomerate, with computers and all that shit. Pussy's the biggest business in the world, but it's all piecework, small operators. Even Madame Claude wasn't that organized. All she really had was France. We could have memberships, credit cards, like American Express. Pussy Express."

"Hey, Nicky, it's not so easy. I tried setting up some girls. Most of them never showed for the dates. The ones who did never paid me." Lissa haunted the nightclub circuit, where most of the talk was about drugs or money to buy drugs. She thought it would be easy money to turn some of these MAWs on to her tricks who wanted variety. "All a hooker needs to be a madam is another chick and a telephone," Lissa said. But she quickly found out how flaky and unreliable the world of prostitution was, which made her respect Alex enormously for making it so businesslike. How Alex kept her sanity and good spirits in the face of her girls' insanity and her clients' fickleness was astonishing to Lissa, as was Alex's ability to avoid legal difficulties. Sure, Alex had a real money machine, but only she seemed to know how to operate the equipment. It was both an art and a science, and Lissa was overwhelmed by it. "It's so tough. Everyone is fucked up. What about the cops? It's worse than running a club. Forget it, Nicky. You're just high."

"*Buy* the fucking cops. Think of the money there is. Look at those sex charter flights to Bangkok and Manila. Why fly across the world to some sweaty hellhole when all you have to do is pick up the phone? And why fuck some little gook if you can have an Amazon goddess?"

"What goddesses? How many of them do you see out there?" Lissa asked.

"Eastern Europe, baby. They grow 'em big and beautiful. They're pouring out of there. They love to fuck and they're desperate for hard currency. Russia's one giant brothel waiting to happen. And *I* speak the language."

"So go do it."

"We will. But we have to start with a going concern."

"So tell Alex. She loves money," Lissa said.

"She doesn't think big. She doesn't want to grow. She wants to keep it in her head. She likes running a Girl Scout troop."

"Oh, Nicky," Lissa said with a yawn. She took off her Italian dress. "Fuck me and do my pussy. I've got to get to Carlos Wynburg's. Would you give me a pedicure, too?"

Nicky wasn't even listening to her. He was on a tear, captivated by his cocaine brainstorm. "If we could get her clients, we'd be set. They're the Who's Who. We build from that base. You know I'm an organizational genius."

"Now you're going to take over her business." Lissa shook her head in dismay. "Those johns are loyal to her."

"Not if she's out of business," Nicky averred. "They still have hard cocks. They still have to fuck. And we'll own her list. We'll be the Rolls-Royce of sex."

"What are you going to do, turn her in to the IRS? Have her killed?" Lissa was mocking him.

Nicky was serious. Dead serious. "She's all alone, got no family living with her. You think any john is going to stand up for her in public and demand an investigation? In six more months you can meet all her top clients. They'll know you. *Her* girl. Then we can do it. We can get the jewels, too, and the art. That stuff's worth millions."

Lissa reached over and unzipped Nicky's pants. She began stroking his penis. "You're such an asshole," she said. "Come on."

"She's got to go." Nicky *was* obsessed. "We can do this, baby, me and you. Think of all the shopping you can do. Saint-Honoré. Ginza. It's all yours, baby."

"Shut up and fuck me already," she said. But Nicky wasn't interested. "Besides, Alex is our friend."

Suddenly Nicky burst out laughing. In convulsions. At first, Lissa thought he was having a stroke or a seizure. "What's wrong?"

"Did you hear what you just said?"

"What? That Alex was our friend?"

"Your *friend*? Since when did *you* start making *friends*?"

Lissa thought about this for a second and started to laugh too. Maybe Nicky was on to something.

| The Sexaholic

Back on Doheny, palace coups were the furthest thing from Alex's mind. Rival madams had come and rival madams had gone, but Alex had rolled on, getting bigger and bigger. Alex never looked over her shoulder. She just took care of business, took care of her men, took care of her women. The main reason she wasn't worried was because she couldn't imagine anyone else loving her job as much as she did. One of the things she liked the most was the stories she heard. She came from a long tradition of oral history, the Filipino version of the general-store cracker barrel. No other business could have kept ears burning so.

Alex, like any major Hollywood agent, spent the greater part of her day on the telephone. The difference between Alex and, say, Mike Ovitz was that her callers never felt pressured to dish and dash. Alex relished long conversations, long tales. She always had time for a good yarn. She got one from Walter Burke, one of her favorite phone pals.

Walter was also one of Alex's most prolific customers. He didn't spend the most money by a long shot, but he did volume and was a great raconteur who always amused Alex with his Holy Grail quest for the perfect girl. A handsome thirty-something Yale grad writer-producer with several smart hits that had made him a studio darling, Walter was one of the most sought-after bachelors in show business. Women loved him for his courtly indifference. He never pushed, never pressured, was always the perfect gentleman—to the point where some women started to wonder if he was gay. That was precisely the point where Walter made his move and proved beyond the shadow of a doubt that gay was something he was not. Nevertheless, none of his relationships lasted that long. Women thought it was because of his dizzying array of options. None knew how dizzying the options really were. The main reason Walter could be so cool with all his inevitable conquests, the reason he could take his time and become friendly and get to know the "real them" before he segued into bed, the reason he was under no pressure to score, was that Walter was compulsively seeing as many as three or four different call girls a day.

Walter's mother had been a minor though beautiful movie actress in the forties. She had been a trophy for Walter's banker father and a millstone for Walter, who felt that unless he had a woman who could match her, he would be a failure, all his many other successes notwithstanding. Things weren't helped by the fact that Walter's mother dismissed all his girlfriends, from the first time he had girlfriends, as "sweet but homely." His mother had since died, though her ghost hovered over Walter's subconscious, telling him that whatever girl he was with, whether for love or money, wasn't good enough for him.

As a preamble to asking Alex for someone new, Walter gave her an update on his last twenty-four hours of sexual activity, which was more action than most men would get in a normal month, or a Hollywood week. Alex listened as she always listened, first because she was insatiable for gossip and loved to know what was going on in a town she rarely stepped out into, and, second, because a great part of her indispensability to her clients was as a mother confessor. The other madams were all business. They lacked her charm and empathy, and shortsightedly thought that their girls were enough.

"I was writing this sex script and it got me incredibly horny," Walter told Alex.

"All your scripts are sex scripts," Alex said, laughing.

Walter described how he had been stuck in the middle of a hot love scene when he got a call from Bobbi, a West L.A. madam, describing a new girl. Pushing their latest specials, madams would call like encyclopedia salesmen, especially to someone like Walter, who had a high propensity to consume. Bobbi's latest was a 5' 11" blonde whom she described as looking like one of the prize girls on *The Price Is Right*, that is, perfect and vapid. Walter was intrigued. "I would've been intrigued by anyone, just to avoid writing that scene. I rationalized it to myself that I was doing research." He called the girl, whose name was Heather. They were all called Heather, the most popular of all *noms de boudoir*. Because Bobbi had been so vague in her description, Walter was forced to get it out of Heather herself. Not wanting to be crass, Walter asked her first where she grew up, which was Washington, D.C., and about her college, which was the University of Miami, which meant nothing other than that she had a tan. He asked her what she did. She said that she had been a model in Europe, which sounded promising, and that she had recently been working in real estate, which did not, for she had been laid off and therefore had the time to be on the phone with him at that very minute.

Walter pursued the modeling angle. "Which agency were you with?" If she said Elite or Ford, he needn't ask another question. That would say it all.

"I wasn't with an agency. I was freelance."

Walter's heart sank. "Did you do the collections in Milan and Paris?"

"What kind of collections?" Heather asked.

Walter's heart sank further. "So what kind of modeling did you do?"

"Fashion stuff."

"Bobbi said you were five eleven and really beautiful."

"She did?"

"I really love tall girls. I have a thing for tall model types. I'm into natural . . ." What Walter was fumbling for was to find out if she had silicone breasts. He hated them. Yet they were as ubiquitous in Los Angeles as bleached blond hair, particularly on ectomorphic models whose body type was normally at odds with being voluptuous. After more fumbling, Walter decided to be direct. This wasn't a blind date; well, it was, but for the three hundred dollars (other madams' rates were half of Alex's, or less) he was going to pay for an hour work break, Walter felt he had a right to know what he was buying.

"I'm not into silicone breasts," he said, flat out.

"You don't have to worry here," Heather said.

"Do you have pretty breasts?"

"I haven't had any complaints."

"What are you, like a thirty-six-B?"

"About."

"I love beautiful breasts, like the girls at the Crazy Horse in Paris, you know what I mean?"

"Never heard of it"

Walter's heart sank again. "It's the most famous strip club in the world. All the girls are your height, with these gorgeous breasts. They look like those champagne goblets turned upside down. Are you like that?"

"I have nice nipples. They're really sensitive."

"What do you weigh?" Walter ventured, boldly now. "About one twenty?"

"Are you kidding?" Heather shot back, her voice alive for the first time in the conversation. "At my height? I'd be anorexic."

"So how much do you weigh?"

"About one fifty."

Walter kept the conversation going, but he had suddenly become ambivalent. He had been with so many women, maybe a thousand, that he knew exactly the type he wanted—a Crazy Horse girl. These girls usually were fine-boned, narrow-framed, 5' 10", and no more than 120 pounds. He knew feminists would despise him for liking that type. He remembered the book *Fat Is a Feminist Issue*. He acknowledged his sexist-pig tendencies. Yet what turned him on was what turned him on, and that's why he used call girls.

Walter told Heather he'd call her right back and got Bobbi on the line to try to ascertain how modelly Heather really was.

"I never saw her without clothes," Bobbi said. "She had on a nice pants suit."

Walter didn't care about her pants suit. He wanted what he wanted, and he was happy to pay for it. What he hated was to go over to a girl's apartment and find something completely different from what had been described. Bobbi had stung him before, promised him Madonna, gave him Mama Cass. He'd give the girl a hundred and be out the hour of driving and out of his mind with frustration. His mind raced. If Heather admitted to 150, she could weigh 160. And 5' 11" could be 5' 5". The only madam he could trust was Alex, but he had been through her list. He wanted new. Heather was new. But was she good? Walter called her again.

After chatting some more about a Europe he wasn't sure she had ever visited and about a Washington, D.C., that she said she couldn't remember, Walter got his first question from Heather. What did he do? He told her the truth. Heather had never heard of his movies. She did say that she knew a lot of writers in Santa Monica, where she had a typing service that she had advertised in the Writers Guild magazine. "If we get to know each other, maybe I can type your scripts," Heather volunteered sweetly.

"Why would you go back and earn twenty bucks an hour when you can get five hundred?" Walter asked.

" 'Cause I'm fast."

Then Walter asked Heather the most common of all Hollywood call-girl questions: "What movie star do you look like?"

"Mostly like Peggy Lipton," Heather said. "But a little bit like Susan Dey."

Suddenly Walter was smitten. *Mod Squad* and *Partridge Family*. Two of his all-time adolescent-crush dream girls. Now Heather was perfect. He didn't care that she didn't work for Elite and didn't know Europe and didn't know his movies and didn't know anything. He didn't care what she weighed. Peggy Lipton. Susan Dey. Magic words. "When can I see you?"

Heather had a "normal" job interview that afternoon, something in telemarketing. She told Walter she'd be back to her Brentwood apartment around five. Call then and come over. It was one of the longest afternoons of Walter's life. Sherry Lansing called from Paramount to talk about a project, but Walter was too distracted to call her back. All he could think about was Peggy and Susan, or, rather, Heather. His anticipation was heightened when he was talking to a writer friend and fellow call-girl habitué who lived out by the beach. Walter told his friend about this typist-turned-hooker Peggy Lipton look-alike whom he was going to see today and maybe forever. This was just like a regular blind date, and Walter was a true romantic. Anyone might be Miss Right.

"I think I used her," the other writer said.

"As a hooker?"

"No. As a typist. There was this girl. She looked just like Peggy Lipton. I had the biggest crush on her."

"What was her name?"

The writer paused. Walter paused. "What was it?" The writer groped. "I think it was . . . Heather. Yeah, Heather."

"I can't believe it," Walter said.

"You mean I could have paid to fuck her? Shit. I would have paid anything. She completely tuned me out."

"And she wasn't heavy?"

"Heavy? Man, she was perfect."

Walter called Heather's number every five minutes starting at four-thirty, thinking she might be back early. He lived in Laurel Canyon. The drive to paradise would be an eternity. He couldn't wait to take off. All he got was her machine. "Hi. I'm sorry to have missed your call . . ." At seven, Heather finally answered the phone.

"Where have you been all my life?" Walter asked, almost tasting the ecstasy that was ahead of him.

"Listen, I'm not going to do this," Heather said.

"What?!"

"All these questions about my tits, about my weight. It's so degrading."

"I didn't mean anything. I'm dying to meet you."

"No, I'm too fat." Heather slammed down the phone.

Walter dialed again. Frantically. "Hey, I'm really sorry. You know Bobbi's really flaky, and she's burned me before, and the only way you can really know . . ." Walter was at a loss for words. All he could do was grovel. "Come on. It'll be great."

"I am *not* interested. Forget it. You're an asshole." *Click.*

Walter called again and got the machine. Then he called Bobbi, who promised to intercede, and failed. Walter had never wanted anyone more. "Give her a few weeks," Bobbi suggested. For Walter, whose entire existence was predicated on instant gratification, that was cold comfort.

"Curiosity killed the cat," Alex chided Walter. "It's not like you're buying a VCR at Adrays and you have to ask about every feature."

"No," Walter said. "It's more like buying a stolen one in Tijuana. Bobbi lies to you. She'll sell you anything."

"You've got to stop treating women as objects," Alex said.

"If I did, you'd be out of business," Walter parried.

"You were very rude. You should be spanked."

"If only by Heather. What'd I do wrong?"

"You asked too many demeaning questions. Just go see her."

"It takes so much time. All the driving."

"Stop whining," Alex said. "Talk on the car phone in your Porsche."

"And I hate to walk out. It's so embarrassing. I never know what to say. 'You turn me off'? 'You're ugly'? Come on."

"You say, 'I'm sorry but you remind me of my sister.' "

"That's pretty good."

"But your problem is you're thinking negative. If you had just gone, you'd have had your Peggy Lipton. But of course you'd be sick of her after one more time and you'd find some new way to torture yourself. And you know you love it."

"You think so?" Walter replied. "Talk about torture. Listen to what I did next. I was going crazy." Because he had already gone through Alex's "new" list, Walter had called a dozen other madams and other call girls he knew, looking for Peggy Lipton and/or Susan Dey. Alex wasn't jealous that Walter had looked elsewhere. Madams could be proprietary about their girls, but not about their clients. The customer was always right. By the same token, the customer was never faithful. For customers like Walter, the mandate was identical to that of the studios, to constantly reinvent the wheel.

By eight o'clock, Walter had struck out. There *was* no one new under the L.A. moon. If they were new, they weren't available. Refusing to extinguish hope, Walter decided to explore a new venue. A womanizing member of the Beauty Bunch had tipped Walter off to a place his nutritionist had tipped *him* off to. None of the tippers had actually visited the place, but it sounded intriguing: a "Seven Sisters" massage parlor in Beverly Glen. Run by a graduate of Bennington and Yale, the establishment was supposed to employ only classy, preppy, eastern-educated young thespians-in-waiting. Walter had a number. The girl who answered was incredibly charming and accommodating. "There're two of us here tonight. I'm five eight. She's five nine. We both weigh one twenty. I'm a B, she's a C, we're all real. I have killer legs. We both look like Kelly Emberg. It's sixty dollars for a half hour, a hundred for an hour, full body massage completely nude. We happily accept tips. Come and see us." No feminist indignation here. Walter jumped into his Porsche in a Le Mans start.

Every L.A. canyon has its own personality. Laurel was a rock-and-roll hideaway, Coldwater was for big stars, Benedict was for tasteful money. Beverly Glen was for hippies, with the wooden shacks of the pot smokers and pot dealers still holding their precarious ground against the encroaching postmodern Santa Fe blockhouses of the agents and television producers of the New Age. Sliding his Porsche through the canyon where Steve McQueen used to race motorcycles, Walter arrived at the most vertiginous of these crash pads, so high up a hill that he couldn't see it. Two Mercedeses and a new BMW were parked on the street below, a sign inspiring the confidence the habitation above did not. Walter pressed the buzzer next to a large metal door and announced himself. The door released, and Walter was confronted with a daunting ascent of maybe a hundred flimsy wooden steps, with a rickety wooden railing on one side and a muddy slide to oblivion on the other. Some stairway to heaven, he thought, and began his climb.

At the top, Walter was breathless from the trek and with anticipation. There was an etched-glass mandala set into the front door of what was no more than a cabin. Walter went in. The first thing he noticed was the *Exorcist*-green hideous shag carpeting and several frayed sofas. Then he noticed that on the coffee table, next to the *Vogues* and the *Elles*, were Samuelson's *Economics*, Janson's *History of Art*, and the Oriental Humanities anthology text he had used in graduate school at Columbia. He rounded a corner and he stopped short. Talk about truth in advertising. Standing at what Californians call a "wet bar," which was topped with a bank of six Plexiglas telephones, were indeed two Kelly Embergs. They were barefoot in bright leotards, and they flashed Walter the most welcoming of smiles. One was Toby, the other Kim. Both were amazing.

Why these knockouts were giving walk-ins sixty-dollar rubdowns in a hippie crash pad when they could have been catering to stars and senators for Alex was one of Los Angeles's great inequities. But it was the same reason Bruce Willis can get ten million a picture while thousands of other cool Jersey types are out of work: luck and access. Getting to Alex or another top madam was extremely difficult, both for the putative call girl and the prospective client. It was like getting Mike Ovitz to represent you. Toby and Kim were not in the loop. Like most lovely women in a city glutted with them, they were undervalued assets. In terms of the commerce they were in, they were an incredible bargain.

"I'd love to take a session," Walter said to both, confused by this dual embarrassment of pulchritude and already in agony as to which one to choose.

"Well, I've got a booking coming in," Kim said.

"So that leaves me," Toby said.

Which made Walter automatically want Kim. Nevertheless, Toby, who was the B-cup with the great legs, was so alluring that Walter was able to distract himself from this Groucho club syndrome of not wanting any woman who would have him. Anyhow, he had the perfect solution. He would see Toby, and later on, when Kim was free, he would see her. That would be having his cake and eating his caviar.

Toby led Walter up a ladder to a loft bedroom area, which she sealed off from the rest of the house by closing a trapdoor. She asked him for the sixty dollars and asked him to sign a release:

"I declare under penalties of perjury that I am not an agent or employee of any law-enforcement agency. I am only interested in a presentation of WonderRub Miracle Lotion and a massage and do not anticipate any sexual encounter. I agree to pay $60.00 for the presentation and product."

Walter scribbled his initials and gave Toby three twenties. How much more the "tip" would be was an unknown. Whatever, it would surely be a bargain compared to Alex's rates. Toby asked Walter to "get comfortable," which was a euphemism for undressing. She took the release and the money and disappeared through the trapdoor.

Walter took off his clothes and listened to a Doors album on the CD player. It was perfect mood music for this house. He lay on a foam-rubber mattress on the floor covered with fresh beach towels. It wasn't San Simeon, he thought, but it was all in the game, part of the thrill of the chase. Then the real thrill returned. Toby was carrying a plastic box of hot water to warm the four bottles of WonderRub she was carrying. Then, nonchalantly, she stripped off the leotard. She was wearing a black satin demi-bra and matching bikini panties. These came off, too. Walter was in ecstasy. Better yet, he was in the Crazy Horse Saloon.

As Toby rubbed Walter's back with the hot oils and lotions, she told him a little about herself. The child of French parents, hence the Crazy Horse body, she grew up in Manhattan, then moved with her family to Des Moines, where her father worked for a pork processor and she had been a professional dancer. She had gone to Iowa State. It wasn't Wellesley, but at this point Walter didn't care about anything other than turning over and making insane love to her.

Walter turned over and Toby sat astride him, rubbing hot oil on her breasts, letting Walter help her until her nipples stood hard and firm. Then she rubbed her glistening body all over his. She turned around and sat on his chest and stretched forward to massage his feet and to give him a disquieting view of the perfect crescent of her derriere, all sleek with the hot oil. Walter was breathless.

When it was almost too much for Walter, Toby rolled back over and continued her ministrations, working all around Walter's erection and pretending not to notice it. All the while she talked about her acting classes and how eager she was to get into the movies. Walter, of course, told her about his films and how he was a real producer who could help her. He felt like a cliché, but right now he would have hired her over Greta Scacchi or Kim Basinger or anyone. He thought about offering to introduce her to Alex, but that would have spoiled the bargain. Walter couldn't stop fondling Toby's breasts, though when he reached between her legs to stroke her, she pulled away and giggled. "I'm so sensitive there," she said.

So am I, Walter sighed to himself. "I'm dying to give you a tip," Walter said.

"I see," Toby said, looking between his legs. "You know how it works here."

"How?"

"We can't have sex."

"What?"

"We can't make love."

"What do you call this?" Walter asked petulantly.

"A massage."

"I can't stand it. I've gotta . . ."

"I see," Toby giggled. "These are house rules."

"What about the tip?"

"Well . . . ," she said. "For forty dollars I can give you a manual release and you can give me a manual release."

Is that sex talk in Iowa?, Walter thought. "What if I give you more money?"

"You're more than welcome to do that, but that's all we can do here."

"Could you give me your number? I'd love to take you out."

"If I get to know you better," Toby evaded.

"I think you're stunning. I'd love to put you in something. I've got two major features about to start." Walter felt incredibly sleazy. An erect penis has no conscience, no shame.

"Let's get to know each other better."

So he agreed to the tip and they got into a sixty-nine position with Walter staring at the bikini-waxed mons veneris he wanted to dive into more than any other he'd ever seen, and Toby's hot-oiled fingers stroked him and she guided his finger into her and she groaned and spasmed and got incredibly hot, and if this was an act Toby deserved an Oscar, and Walter lasted at most a minute. He never realized that safe sex could be so exciting.

After a minor anxiety attack about contracting athlete's foot or some more major fungus from the shower floor, Walter scrubbed as much of the greasy WonderRub off his body as plain soap and water could remove. Now, twenty minutes after his trip to the Crazy Horse, Walter was horny all over again. It was the erotic equivalent of the Chinese-restaurant syndrome. Walter knew he was a sexaholic, but he loved the addiction. He was a foodaholic, a travelaholic, a dealaholic. He saw himself not as a terminal neurotic but rather as a pure-gusto, bon-vivant sensualist who was willing to endure immense inconvenience, even pain, to get to the finer pleasures life afforded. And the finer pleasure of this moment was Kim. He zipped up his New Man jeans, straightened his Armani jacket, and emerged from the bathroom for round two of eros, Beverly Glen–style. But Kim wasn't there. Nor was Toby. In their place were two short, squat girls in overstretched black Danskins. Maybe they were Radcliffe girls. Wherever they were from, Walter felt like Michael Redgrave in *The Lady Vanishes*, thinking he has found the sweet and saintly Miss Froy, only for her to turn her head and be the fright face of all time.

"Where're . . . the other girls? Kim . . ."

"They're gone. We're the night shift. I'm Tabby. This is Lulu."

Walter forced himself to be polite. "Does Kim work tomorrow?"

Tabby checked the chart. "Kim's off for Tahiti. Lucky her."

Jake, the manager, arrived from the back. Six feet tall, curly hair, lush in an Italianate Sophia Loren way, she took Walter's agony away. Wearing skintight jeans with peace-symbol patches and an Indian tie-dyed blouse open in the front to reveal a heroic cleavage, her attire matched the aura of the house. She had a throaty, knowing voice. She inspired confidence. She inspired lust. This was the Bennington and Yale girl. She grew up in Europe, her father a diplomat. She knew about the collections and the Crazy Horse and had modeled for Wilhelmina. The more Walter chatted with her, the more he wanted to date her, not just fuck her. But he would take what he could get. First things first.

"I'd love to take a session with you," Walter said.

"Only if you want to be whipped," Jake said with an apologetic smile. "I'm gay and I only do domination."

"It was the end of a perfect evening," Walter concluded with Alex.

"You should have taken the whipping," Alex said. "You're such a masochist."

"I'm a hedonist. It's just tough being one. Alex, I've never been so insanely horny. You've gotta give me someone new today. I'm going out with this incredible girl tonight."

"So wait for her," Alex told him.

"It's a first date. I'm a gentleman."

Alex just cackled, her trademark all-knowing cackle.

"She's a neurosurgeon. She's not from here. She's from Philadelphia. She could be the one."

"Yeah, but how tall is she and how much does she weigh?" Alex mocked Walter, and he loved it. She finally hung up, promising to find him someone that afternoon. She had her feelers out. Someone, someone great, would materialize. That was Alex's magic.

| The Lunch Bunch

Now it was time for lunch. Lunch at Alex's was always an event. It was invariably casual—Alex would never change her muumuu—and usually ad hoc—whoever was in the neighborhood was welcome to drop by. She would usually serve salad, and lots of vegetables, and beef—yes, beef. Alex was oblivious to Los Angeles dietary phobias about cholesterol and saturated fat. Beef, in Alex's mind, was the food of kings. Real men didn't eat quiche, and real men, the kings of the land, were whom Alex had for her lunches.

Today's special guest was Brent Wexler, a famous show-business lawyer and legendary roué, counsel of stars, courter of starlets. In his late seventies, he showed no sign of slowing down. He regretted nothing, except that all his friends were dying off. He used to love to sit at what was known as the comic's table at the Hillcrest Country Club in Beverly Hills, the club with its own oil well on the golf course. He would sit at the round table with the great Jewish entertainers—Groucho Marx, Jack Benny, George Jessel, Eddie Cantor, George Burns, Sammy Davis, Jr. Now only Burns was still around. The shadow of death had driven Brent away from Hillcrest. Ma Maison, his other favorite, was gone, and he hated all the agents at Le Dôme, which had become lunch central. No, Brent liked to stop by Alex's. She made him feel young.

Alex's other guest was Cyrus Firuzhi, one of the richest Persians in a Beverly Hills whose economy was dominated by them. Cyrus, at sixty, was a tiny, sleek silver fox of a man who dressed in Lanvin suits and always seemed as if he had just stepped in from his office on the Place de la Concorde. He even drove a Citroën, in contrast to the Rolls-Royce that was standard issue for his fellow countrymen. A major real estate developer, Cyrus was one of the leaders of the community of Persians who had descended on Los Angeles after the fall of the Shah, and whose gates had been stoned by enemies of that imperial regime. Many would-be home buyers in Los Angeles felt the same way, for the Persians were the single most influential force in driving local real estate prices through the heavens. Long-term residents were more ambivalent. In one fell swoop, the Persians made net-worth millionaires out of almost everyone north of Wilshire in Beverly Hills, Bel Air, Westwood, and Brentwood, people who had bought their houses in the fifties for well under a hundred thousand dollars.

Yet this was an area where envy was the first deadly sin. Because the Persians were richer than anyone else, save the Sultan of Brunei and the odd oil sheikh, everyone tended to hate them, a resentment compounded by their darkness, their clannishness, and their guttural language that no one else could understand. In response to this hostility, many Persians were forced to "pass," often ludicrously so, opening "Dutch" ice cream shops, and "Greek" restaurants, and even "Scandinavian" furniture shops. The most popular cloak was "French," as many of the Persians had spent time and money in France, and now they were in Beverly Hills, the sister city of Cannes, where fake transformations and façades were the order of the day, where a Persian could become a Parisian (with a tan) in the blink of an eye.

Cyrus Firuzhi hated such persons. They made him look bad. A true cosmopolitan, educated at Le Rosey, Charterhouse, and the Sorbonne, Cyrus had built architecturally distinguished skyscrapers everywhere from Brasília to Tokyo. He kept a triplex in Paris overlooking the Esplanade des Invalides. Because he had superb taste, he was one of Alex's prime "tasters," just as he had been for Madame Claude in Paris. He would meet the new girls first. This was part of Alex's unfailing politeness to her applicants. Although she might be scrutinizing them with X-ray eyes, she would never demean them by asking them to undress or, worse, by demanding sexual favors, as several of her rival madams insisted on before sending any new girl on a date. Bobbi, for one, would always require that a new girl strip and go down on her as a measure of fealty, as well as flexibility. Alex was too much of a lady for that. Cyrus, and several other select connoisseurs, took care of all that, reporting to Alex things about the girl that only men could tell her.

What made Alex's lunches so special was that lunchtime was also interview time. The way for a girl to meet Alex was to be introduced by one of Alex's current girls or, alternatively, by one of Alex's clients who had met the new girl either through another madam or as a "straight" girl who wanted to change her life.

The day was warm and radiant, so they ate amid orchids around the pool. Otherwise, they might have lunched on trays in Alex's bedroom, where she preferred to hold court. Although Brent, who breathed show business, and Cyrus, who was appalled by it, had zero in common, Alex kept the dialogue neutral, on current events and earthquakes and Brent's old apartment on the Ile Saint-Louis, until the girls arrived.

First in was Paola, a Brazilian bombshell who worked part-time as a receptionist for a prominent plastic surgeon. Herself the handiwork of Dr. Ivo Pitanguy, Paola was a great advertisement for the field, and her employer paid her disproportionately for her time, and overtime. It was he who had introduced Paola to Alex, and now she in turn was introducing Eve, a platinum-tressed Swiss ice goddess, all dressed up in an icy-white linen pants suit. Eve said she was an aspiring composer who had come to Hollywood to work on film scores. Next to arrive was Daisy, a big blond Colorado cowgirl turned stand-up comic, wearing a blue-jean jacket, a miniskirt, and Tony Lama boots. Daisy was all ebullience, in contrast to her friend Ann, a downtrodden Denver divorcee who was thinking of moving to Los Angeles and starting a new life. With her excess Pan-Cake makeup and eye shadow, and her JCPenney clothes, Ann looked completely out of place.

Most of the lunch talk was sexual gossip. Paola recounted a story about one of the most celebrated of all actresses, who had hired as a lesbian call girl the crack-addicted but outwardly together daughter of one of the city's premier record moguls. The S & M scene the actress had requested got out of hand; she beat up the record heiress so badly that she had to call an ambulance. However, remembering the recent scandal at the Cedars-Sinai emergency room, the actress didn't dare call a Cedars ambulance. Instead, she called the most discreet of all local hospitals, St. John's in Santa Monica, where the priests and the sisters knew how to keep secrets. But somehow the police picked up the dispatch and sent two squad cars up to the actress's mansion. She had to lie and say that her "friend" had fallen while helping her hang a painting. She turned on the charm, gave the cops autographed pictures, and the entire matter stayed under wraps.

"I just saw this super-famous actor who thought I was so stupid that I didn't know who he was," Daisy said.

"Nobody I sent you to, was it?" Alex said.

"No. Marlene," Daisy answered, referring to the Woodland Hills madam she also worked for. Most girls weren't exclusive these days, just as most actors weren't under contract to one studio as in the good old days. On the other hand, because Alex's rates were the highest in the business, most girls would have preferred to work only for her if she had enough assignments for them.

"Who was the star?" Paola asked.

"Can't say." Daisy put her finger to her lips.

"Come on."

"Uh-uh," Daisy persisted, mostly for Alex's benefit, to demonstrate her discretion.

"Client privilege," Brent the lawyer said, as much a warning as an explanation.

"Tell us what happened," Alex prodded her.

"I meet him at Marlene's and he tells me his name is Mr. Verdoux."

"Mr. *what?*" Paola asked.

"See, he coulda fooled you," Daisy said, spelling the name.

"The Charlie Chaplin character," Alex identified him. "The one who murdered his wives. Were you scared?"

"No way. He comes up to my chest. So, listen, I get naked, and he gets down to his boxer shorts, and he starts directing me in this love scene. He's a big director, too."

"Who?" Paola repeated.

"No names."

"Boring."

"What was the love scene like? What did he want you to do with him?" Alex asked.

"It wasn't with him. It was with his wife," Daisy said.

"You didn't say he brought his wife," Cyrus said.

"He didn't. She was imaginary. He wanted me to act out a sex scene with this imaginary woman named, let's say, Mary, but when he said her real name, I knew that was his wife's name because she's famous, too, but he thought I was too dumb to know. Really, didn't he think I watched *Entertainment Tonight?*"

"Was she an actress? I bet I know," Paola intruded again.

"Shut up," Alex silenced her.

"It wasn't, so there," Daisy said. "So he says, 'Make love to her, eat her pussy, go around the world,' and I'm there licking the sheets and humping the pillows. 'Oh, Mary, you're so beautiful, ooh, aah, Mary, Mary, Mary.' And this guy thinks he's like Fellini in 8½. All he needed was the whip."

"That's all he did, direct you? Was he whacking off?" Alex queried.

"No, just directing. He was into it. But then when he had me on my knees, munching the down comforter, he jumps out of the chair and onto the bed and starts doing it to me from behind, doggy-style. Just for a few seconds, because he then pulled out and started screwing Mary. 'I'm coming inside you, baby,' he kept saying to her, and then he shot it all over the sheets. God knows what he did to the real Mary when he got home."

"He gave her the Oscar," Alex said, cackling away.

The normally sedate Cyrus then told about an assignation Madame Claude once made for his friend the Shah. The girl sounded great, a brainy Catherine Deneuve type who was a law student at Nanterre. In dark glasses and black mink, the beauty was dispatched first-class on Iran Air to the palace in Tehran. What Claude, and the Shah, didn't know was that the star pupil had once been the girlfriend of Daniel Cohn-Bendit, aka "Danny the Red," the ardent French radical. She still remained a devout Communist. At the moment of truth, instead of performing for the Shah, she attacked him as the ultimate fascist pig, her ideological scruples triumphing over her economic necessities. Deeply embarrassed, Claude sent the Shah a ménage of three cover girls, gratis, as consolation. Cyrus also described how a government factotum had arranged for Claude's girls to dote on a leading diplomat when he was in Paris for the Vietnam peace talks, to keep him in a positive state of mind so that he would be negotiating from—if not a position—a mind-set of strength. The diplomat may have presumed, as Henry Kissinger always did, that power was the great aphrodisiac. He never knew that his own idolators had been on retainer.

As the lunch wound down to ambrosia and fresh mangoes, Brent retired with Daisy to one of the four bedrooms. There he gave her head for an hour before going back to the office to pretend he was still a force in the business. Daisy knew not to give anything back, for it would remind Brent that the days when he was known as "the Battering Ram" were behind him. Accepting his favors was easy for Daisy, especially with the five hundred dollars he always left behind as a party favor.

Alex sat on the terrace with the others, stroking the cat Georgie in her lap, making conversation between the endless phone calls. One was from

a new client, Hy, a television producer whose show's star had introduced
him to Alex as a reward for the star's winning his first Emmy. Alex's clientele was like that. Being rich wasn't enough; you had to have "arrived"
in some way. It wasn't written that that was the way in, though it worked
out that way. Alex herself wasn't a snob, far from it. Her *clients* were
snobs. They didn't like the idea of mere mortals, even mere millionaire
mortals, having access to the same women they did.

"I have the same taste as Woody Allen," he said, trying to describe the
shiksa goddess he was looking for.

"Why does every small New York Jew in Hollywood want to be Woody
Allen?" Alex teased him.

" 'Cause we can't be Robert Redford," Hy said.

Alex knew that some clients, like Hy, got off more on who else might
have seen her girls than on the girls themselves. In that sense, she preferred the legends rather than the successful wanna-bes like Hy. Yet she
wasn't about to turn down a good, easy client like Hy, whose main obsession was to have "star pussy." Alex would feed that obsession, never denying the widely held assumptions that certain stars were clients, even if
these assumptions were incorrect. She knew a lot of stars, though by no
means all of them.

"I don't even know Woody Allen," Alex said, knowing full well that
the mere mention of the name got Hy going.

"Come on, Alex, just find me a young Diane Keaton. Please. Okay?"

"I think I'm gonna find you a young Louise Lasser," Alex cackled, and
hung up.

When Eve, the Swiss girl, asked Alex whether it was true that a certain
blond superstar had gotten her start working for her, Alex flashed a
Mona Lisa smile. "Don't you love my little Georgie Porgie?" she
beamed, picking up the cat and making it dance on its hind legs in her
lap.

Eve, like every other outsider, was dying to pierce the veil that Hollywood's establishment had placed over itself. The insiders were sanc-
timonious. Alex? Who's Alex? Pay for sex? Please. Maybe some de-
bauched Arab, but one of *us*? Really! Their Hollywood was a pure meri-

tocracy, where actresses never slept with producers to get ahead, where anyone could walk into Spago whenever he wanted, unannounced, and sit next to any stars he desired. Their catchphrase was "Be positive," and their Beverly Hills was still an Ozzie and Harriet place, notwithstanding the death of poor Ricky, smoking the crack cocaine that set his plane on fire. In the words of the twelve-step programs that half the town seemed to be enrolled in, this establishment was "in denial." More than anyone else in this town, Alex knew what they were denying. Grinning like the Cheshire Cat that had swallowed a whole cage of canaries, she wasn't about to serve her secrets like petits fours after lunch. She was saving them for special occasions.

When Eve had first arrived, Alex thought the girl had something. The more Eve talked, however, the less Alex liked her. Eve claimed she had given all her money to her black boyfriend, who had promised to "manage" her musical career. Of course the boyfriend not only stole the money, but also absconded with all Eve's recording equipment and beat her up to boot. Alex had heard it all a thousand times. She knew that the shorthand here was cocaine. While Eve was trying to come off as a pathetic victim, the anger in her voice marked her as a victimizer. Alex wasn't at all surprised, then, when Cyrus decided to leave without seeing anyone.

Alex walked him to the door. Aside from Eve's personality deficiencies, Cyrus noted her bitten nails, her pretentiously "cultivated" accent, and the coffee stains on her linen suit. Alex had toyed with sending Eve to Walter Burke for the quickie he wanted before his *real* date. He'd never see her again, anyhow. Cyrus's dismissal scotched Alex's notion. She didn't want to get involved with Eve. Despite her friends at City Hall, Alex was always vigilant about getting busted. You couldn't be in this business without having enemies—other madams, angry call girls. Never customers, because Alex's customers were never dissatisfied, but ambitious police and self-righteous politicians and reporters looking for a scoop. Eve was potential trouble. Alex would avoid her. "What about Ann?" Alex asked Cyrus about the Denver divorcee.

Cyrus simply cocked his eyebrows in his most understated "Don't be absurd" glance, kissed Alex on both cheeks, and was off in his Citroën.

Ten minutes later, Serge Gilbert arrived in a battered Mercedes, which was odd, in that Serge owned one of the toniest car dealerships in the city. But he wanted to be low-profile here. Serge was late for lunch. He was late for everything. He had only twenty minutes, which would work out to fifty dollars a minute, yet that would be worth it to him for some stolen kisses from Paola. He had spotted her at the office of her plastic surgeon boss, who had done Serge's wife's eyes. Serge went straight to a bedroom. He didn't have time for introductions, though Alex insisted he stroke Georgie hello. Alex called Paola away from the pool and sent her in to Serge. She ordered a maid to bring them some flutes of champagne. And some caviar, from which Serge would make a quick lunch by nibbling it off the huge Dr. Ivo Pitanguy breasts Serge had been fantasizing about. Yes, he sighed as Paola undressed. Alex could arrange anything.

Back at the pool, Eve had stripped off her clothes and decided to go skinny-dipping. Alex admired her body, and wished her character had been better so that Alex could have used her. Eve was showing off. She knew her body was good. She was pushing it hard, auditioning. It didn't matter. Of course, Alex wouldn't reject her on the spot. That wasn't how she operated. She just wouldn't call her. If Eve called *her*, Alex would tell her there wasn't anybody right now, and she would continue to tell her that until Eve got the message.

As Eve swam and floated on her back, flaunting assets that Alex had already fully depreciated, Alex took a harder look at Ann. Cyrus's disinterest, even contempt for her, aside, Alex spotted something in her she couldn't ignore. Beneath all the Pan-Cake were high, fine cheekbones. Alex looked at Ann's legs. The ankles, the feature that psychological studies Alex had read said men noticed first, were slim and tapered. She had a certain languor that Alex thought was sexy. Probing Ann about her past, Alex learned that she had been her high school's homecoming queen runner-up, as well as one of the finalists in the Miss Colorado beauty pageant. She had just missed making the cheerleading squad at college, and her husband had just missed making a fortune in the real estate market, which, like their marriage, had collapsed before he could cash out. He had left Ann for the Oriental girl who worked at the dry cleaners they used. Jilted for a Chinese laundress. Alex was instantly sympathetic. All her life, Ann had been an also-ran, an underdog. Now it was time for her to be top dog. Alex was going to give her the chance, for which she sensed Ann would be extremely grateful. Gratitude was not normally a quality one found in this profession, which was even more opportunistic than acting. Alex had been wrong here before. For all the kicks in the teeth she had received from her girls who had married millionaires or become millionaires, Alex remained a bit of a Pollyanna. She loved discovering new faces, brightening sad faces, playing Pygmalion. Ann was the perfect candidate for an Alex makeover.

"Do you have a bikini wax?" Alex asked Ann.

"No," Ann replied, taken a bit aback by the question. "Why?"

"My men hate hairy twats," Alex cackled, amused by Ann's surprise. "I guess we're going to have to do a head-to-toe on you." Alex called her friend Nance Mitchell on Burton Way and scheduled a facial, an eyelash tinting, and a waxing. She called her friend René at Cristophe on Beverly Drive to redo Ann's hair, "to take Denver out of the girl." She called her friend Linda at Linda's Nail Care One on Wilshire to do Ann's hands and feet, and she called her friend Cathy, who used to model for Chanel in Paris and now fucked arms dealers for ten thousand a weekend, to take Ann shopping and make her chic. If anyone could make a silk purse out of a sow's ear, Alex could.

CHAPTER FOUR

THE LIFE IN A DAY, PART II

| **Big Spender**

*W*ith Ann dispatched for her makeover, Alex decided to call Jock
Palfrey, her very biggest client, to entice him with the new discovery that
Ann was going to be by the end of next week. Jock, forty-five, a Pennsylvania blue blood, was a freebasing modern version of Cary Grant in *The
Philadelphia Story*. Although Alex's reputation was made as madam to
the stars and madam to the sheikhs, she made an important part of her
fortune as madam to the high-leverage, low-visibility super-rich. In the
last year, Jock Palfrey had spent an incredible $1.4 million on prostitutes.
By comparison, Alex's next top spenders, a playboy producer and a studio lord, had tied for second place in the high-roller-in-the-hay depart-

ment at barely $250,000 each. Small wonder then that Jock got first dibs on all the new talent.

It had been a busy day for Jock, who had been luxuriating in the living room of his Lexington Drive mansion, located behind the Beverly Hills Hotel. The house had been featured, under its former owner, in *Architectural Digest*. Now the grand room was littered with coke paraphernalia as well as *Playboy* and *Hustler* centerfolds, Norma Kamali swimsuit ads and Lily of France lingerie ads, and enough head shots to cast a dozen Prince rock videos. Jock had had them all, having bought them the way a normal person would buy something from a catalog. The world was Jock's catalog. He would see someone, he would want her, he would challenge Alex to get her. Most of the time Alex was able to rise to the challenge, though not *every* woman in Hollywood was for sale.

Jock had said good-bye to Rona, a young Valley madam who had brought her friend Chris over to meet Jock. Like old-fashioned rug merchants, the madams of Los Angeles would come by with their wares to present to this major buyer, the john to end all johns. Three others had already dropped by today, each with a big blonde for Jock's delectation. Unfailingly polite, he had given each of them wine and some coke, taken the girls' head shots and modeling composites, and sent them on their way. It was an endless casting call.

Rona couldn't understand why Jock wouldn't see Chris, who in her white minidress seemed precisely like Jock's type: blond, 5' 10", endless legs, huge tits. "And she's all real," Rona assured him, hoping he would take a thousand-dollar session with her on the spot. "No silicone, nothing phony."

"That's too bad," Jock said. "I like phony. I *prefer* phony. So why stop with their tits? Why not go all the way?"

Jock's type—the plastic Vegas bleached blonde, the big-titted Barbie show girl—was the epitome of the cliché Hollywood starlet, from Marilyn Monroe in her grave to Angelyne on her billboard above Sunset. This type was the total antithesis of Jock's ex-wife, Merrie, a willowy, understated, no-makeup, freckled, Katharine Hepburn tomboy. That was the

WASPy type Jock's friends all wanted to fix him up with when Merrie left him, but that was a road he vowed never again to travel.

"Jock, why don't you try her?" Rona urged him, hating to leave empty-handed. "Try her for five."

"She doesn't do it for me," Jock demurred. Rona's bargain gambit was a foolish one to use on a man who always overpaid. Ten thousand dollars for a hand job was not unheard-of, although the same girl might come again, fuck for a week, and get nothing. Jock liked to torture the girls. It was the only control he had. Invariably, he would make it worth everyone's while. He was, after all, a Philadelphia gent.

Soon after Rona and Chris left, Lissa Trapp stopped by. Her coffee-table session with Carlos Wynburg had been canceled at the last moment, when Carlos was called to a meeting with Jane Fonda about a prospective Edith Wharton project. Lissa was at loose ends. She was furious at missing out on the money. She needed some good coke, and Jock's door was always open. Even though the dark, thin Lissa was anything but Jock's type, for some reason he often threw her three hundred for a quick, empty fuck, which he did today. The reason was that he liked to *be* tortured as much, if not more, than he liked to torture. Jock reveled in pain. "I wish I could make you come," he said wistfully when he finished his two-minute quickie in his bedroom overlooking the clay tennis court he had turned into a kennel for his menagerie of snarling pit bulls, Rottweilers, and other attack dogs.

"You did make me come last time I was here," Lissa told him. "I came twice."

Jock's sad countenance lit up. That was his fondest wish: to bring a hooker to orgasm. "You did? Really?" He beamed with amazement.

"You bet," Lissa said, hitching up her panties and her miniskirt without even a post-coital washing. "I came, all right. Once when you paid me, and again when I spent it." Ha! Ha!

Jock knew what a fool he seemed. "There isn't enough blood in the human body to let you *think* and have a *hard-on* at the same time," he said in his own defense.

Lissa thought about Nicky Kroll's idea to take over Alex's business. Jock alone was good for half a million in commissions. At three hundred, Lissa felt like an exploited illegal-immigrant scullery maid. She felt angry, ripped off. Why should Alex get half a mil while Lissa got a pathetic three bills? Because Alex owned Jock; because he needed her desperately. Could anyone else get him to spend so insanely?, Lissa wondered. It was certainly worth thinking about.

There was a price to pay for dealing with Jock. Lissa had to sit with him and his foaming Rottweilers while he showed off his new pearl-handled gold-and-silver Colt .45.

"And look at this one," Jock said, whipping out a tiny gun, no larger than a cellular phone, from an ankle holster. "I can hide it in my cowboy boots and beat airport security. Those metal detectors only go down to the knees." He made Lissa accompany him to his basement firing range, and he forced her to shoot an Uzi. "If *that* doesn't get you off, nothing will," he said. It got Lissa off, all right, off the premises. It was hard to take Jock for more than an hour. Alex *earned* her money, Lissa reflected, having to baby-sit this wacko, who was rich, educated, handsome, cultured, and completely bonkers, especially since he had started freebasing. Jock had gotten more and more paranoid, and his gun collection and dog collection had grown accordingly. The two guards at the gate of his three-acre estate, as well as his English chauffeur and his black-belt Korean houseboy, were all armed and dangerous.

Dawn, a very slim twenty-year-old aspiring porno star, was in the television room catatonically slurping on a straw stuck into a giant, empty 7-Eleven cup that she grasped like a security blanket. Dawn wasn't at Jock's for sex, just to keep him company while he did drugs. Jock sat down beside her and used his little acetylene torch to heat the Pyrex globe of crack cocaine. He took a deep hit, then offered some to Dawn, who shook her head. Wearing very short shorts with an American-flag patch across the seat, Dawn seemed miserable.

"What's the matter, honey?" Jock inquired.

"The shot." A diabetic, Dawn had just given herself an insulin shot.

"How's your chest?"

"It's okay. A little sore." Dawn's breasts hurt from the silicone implants Jock had just bought for her. They were a must for her X-rated career, though way out of scale for her tiny body. Jock was nothing if not generous.

"What else, baby?"

"Nothing."

"Tell me."

"Nothing."

"Tell me, or I'll put you out," Jock warned her, in a martinet/paternal tone.

"Last night I had a date in Bel Air."

"What kind of date? A date date? Or an Alex date?"

"A Bobbi date."

"With?"

"Some agent. He lived in Bel Air."

"What agency?"

"ICM."

"I can call Jeff Berg right now. Did he hurt you?"

"No, no. Nothing like that. He was a young guy, sweet. I gave him my portfolio."

"Did you fuck him?"

"No, just head. But what happened was, when I left, this cop stopped me on Roscomare Road."

"For what?"

"He said he would bust me. He said he had seen me come up there before. He said he knew I was a prostitute, and that he could send me to jail."

"He can't do shit. He didn't see you with the agent. He saw you driving in the car, right? That's all, right?"

Dawn nodded. "But he scared me. He seemed to know. He took me down a side road. And he made me give him a blow job. And then he also made me give him all my money, the two hundred dollars the agent gave me." Dawn started crying.

"Did you get his name?"

"No. He was Bel Air Patrol."

"Oh my God, how stupid can you get!" Jock blurted out, aware too late that he had further injured Dawn's fragile feelings. "The Bel Air Patrol's *private*. They're not *cops*. They can't do anything to you."

"But he had a badge," Dawn said, embarrassed at her own naïveté. "He had a gun."

"*I've* got a gun. That son of a bitch. You think you'd recognize him?"

Dawn nodded. "I think so. He had a mustache."

"Okay. Let's get the cocksucker." Jock tightened his ankle holster, pocketed his new Colt .45, and went into his gun chest and pulled out a Clint Eastwood .44 Magnum. He sheathed it inside his shoulder holster, threw on his navy Brooks Brothers blazer, and dragged Dawn, 7-Eleven cup still in hand, into his supercharged, bulletproof Land-Rover. They were off to war. The one thing Jock liked better than sex was playing vigilante.

A combination of luck and strategically distributed hundred-dollar bills enabled Jock to find his prey, one Dante "Danny" Spinaro, having a burrito at La Salsa at Pico and Sepulveda before beginning his shift. Trailing Spinaro's patrol car into the hills of Bel Air at the Bellagio gate, Jock beeped to get Spinaro's attention. He waved for him to pull over. When a blond WASP in a Brooks Brothers blazer driving a spotless Land Rover beeps, the Bel Air patrol listens. This was probably someone who paid his salary, Spinaro thought, a rich banker who was locked out of his house or who had car trouble.

"What can I do for you, sir?" asked Spinaro, who had pulled off on a deserted stretch of Chalon Road.

"You can get out of your car and suck my cock," Jock said, jamming the .44 Magnum square between Spinaro's eyes. "Now, I was decorated in 'Nam, I've killed for my country, and I'm rich enough to ruin your life and I'm mad enough to cut your balls off and ram them down your throat, so don't even think about talking back."

Trembling, Spinaro got out of the car. Holding the gun to Spinaro's head, Jock pushed the patrolman into a eucalyptus grove. He motioned

Dawn out of the Land Rover. "Time for *The People's Court*," Jock said. "Is this the guy?" he asked Dawn.

"Yes."

"Reach into his pocket and take his wallet," Jock ordered her. Dawn obliged. There was almost three hundred dollars in cash. "The extra's your interest. Take it." Then Jock unzipped his fly. "This is *my* interest. Suck it, asshole. On your knees!"

"I'm sorry. I'm really sorry," Spinaro begged. "I was drunk. I was crazy . . ."

"You're gonna get a lot crazier. Suck me!"

"No way!" Spinaro grimaced.

"It's all right, Jock," Dawn said. "You showed him."

Jock released the safety and set the trigger.

"I don't suck cock."

"You do now." Jock pushed the cold gun to Spinaro's burning forehead. Faced with death or dishonor, the terrified patrolman chose the lesser evil. For once in his life, Jock was a man, a real man, in total control, even though it took an act of homosexual vigilantism to give him this freebase rush of masculinity. Dawn watched the showdown in a trance. Spinaro gagged but kept at it, and Jock thought about Perri, the whore who had transformed him from a wholesome preppy into a freaked-out, paranoid gun, drug, and sex addict. Magnum to his head, Spinaro got the rhythm. Perri on his brain, Jock got hard.

Three years ago, Jock Palfrey had never used a call girl, had never dreamed of using one. Nor had he ever tried cocaine, or dreamed of that either. Jock had always done the right thing, matriculating from Penn Charter to the Hill School, then on to Princeton, where he spent a little too much time at the Ivy Club and required an extra year to graduate with his gentleman's C-minus. Jock didn't need the grades. He was going into the family real estate firm. From the days of Benjamin Franklin, the Palfreys owned some of the best land in Philadelphia and across the Delaware River in Camden, and ultimately created an empire that included high-rises in Tokyo, industrial parks in Milan, and shopping centers in California, which was what had brought Jock west.

Jock had married Merrie Wetherill, a Daughter of the American Revolution, whom he had met at the Merion Cricket Club. They had two sons and lived in San Marino, across from the Huntington Library, in a WASPy, clubby existence that approximated their Main Line lifestyle, except with better weather. Although Jock had gone to prep school with Oliver Stone, he would have never dreamed of calling him. Psychologically and socially, Hollywood was as far from San Marino as it was from Bryn Mawr.

Then Hollywood intruded. Jock's oldest son was expelled from the Thacher School in Ojai for dealing drugs with the son of a flashy woman film producer. Jock blamed it on Thacher's admitting this "new element" into its once Old Guard midst. Then Jock caught Merrie *in flagrante* with their insurance agent, who was a failed soap actor, and Merrie insisted everything would work out if Jock would just start attending A.A. meetings. Jock couldn't believe it. His wife and son had been Hollywood body-snatched. Merrie got ten million in the divorce and married the insurance agent. Jock got increasingly drunk and miserable. He was going to move straight back to Philadelphia, where such things would have never happened.

Then he met Alex. One of Jock's Princeton friends, who was now a Barbarian at the Gate investment banker on Wall Street, was in L.A. on a deal and wanted to cheer Jock up. He called Alex and arranged a double date with two gorgeous creatures, not revealing to Jock the provenance of his prospective good fortune. Jock was, after all, a puritan and a Philadelphia prig. He wouldn't understand. Perri was a twenty-something Hawaiian Tropic bikini-contest finalist from New Orleans, a blond Creole goddess with voodoo eyes. Jock had been married, faithfully, for sixteen years, sexlessly for the last seven. He had forgotten what lust was.

Perri was quite a homecoming for him. Jock took his friend, Perri, and Perri's girlfriend Cass to the funereal California Club in downtown L.A. for dinner. Perri and Cass, both in skintight Alaias, were probably the hottest women ever to grace those hallowed precincts. Back in San

Marino, at Jock's estate, Jock's booze led to the banker's coke, which led to a strip-croquet game, and then to sex with Perri in his son's elaborate tree house, followed by the pool house, and then the main house. The next morning Jock was in love, both with Perri and with California, which Perri and the cocaine enabled him to see in a more positive light.

No sooner had Jock's barbarian banker friend departed than Perri also disappeared. The number she gave him was disconnected. Her alleged agency, Elite, had no idea whom Jock was talking about. When his friend told him the truth, Jock was crushed. The double date had been a double cross. But instead of blaming Perri, Jock blamed Hollywood. And he blamed this Madam Alex, whoever she was, for taking this innocent flower of the South and leading her down the primrose path to hell. Jock had taken two bullets in Vietnam. He had killed there. Now he wanted to kill again. He wanted to kill Alex.

The alcohol, the drugs, and Perri's own charms had come together into a speedball of emotional deception that convinced Jock that Perri had been, for at least one shining moment, smitten with Jock. Given all the pain he had been through, Jock needed that moment again. Despite his atavistic urges, Jock was a civilized man. He suppressed his rage against Madam Alex, the serpent of this bogus Eden that had somehow ensnared him. He still vowed to kill her. With kindness. He would use Alex to free Perri, to save her, to make her his. He had no idea how much this knighthood fantasy was going to cost him.

The serpent Jock wanted to kill soon became the mother he never had. Then again, who had a mother who would get him laid by the most incredible women in the world? Introduced by the banker, Alex gave Jock the red-carpet treatment and disarmed him completely. Nothing would make her happier, she assured him, than to see Jock ride off into the sunset with Perri. But that sunset, she warned him, could cost more than a studio western. Perri, the illegitimate daughter of a Mafia kingpin from the wrong side of the bayou, was one of the most mercenary women Alex had ever met. And that was saying something.

"I've got the money," Jock said, almost proudly, as if the matter were settled.

"She wants it her way," Alex countered. "She's a free spirit."

A very expensive free spirit. Jock began seeing Perri for two thousand dollars a night. Even though he would have seen her seven nights a week, she would never give him more than one. Eventually, Jock tried to buy Perri off the market, paying Alex her full commission *not* to send Perri on any more dates. Because Perri was one of Alex's racehorses, this was a major sacrifice. There was a big demand for Perri, and Alex had to disappoint a lot of important customers. Nevertheless, she was growing fond of the needy, lonesome Jock, and she was growing even richer off him. Trying to cure him of Perri, she sent him other girls, groups of girls. Price was no object. His shopping centers gave him a personal income of over ten million dollars annually.

For a while, Perri seemed to relent. She went with Jock on trips to Italy and to Bali that were the most romantic of his life, notwithstanding her charging him two thousand dollars not just every day, but every time he wanted to have sex with her, which was frequent. He wanted her to come, and she was being honest with him. Her G-spot was a cash register. Paying her was the only way she could get off.

But money wasn't enough. Perri simply didn't, couldn't, love Jock. He was too needy. Perri wasn't even looking for Mr. Right. She was looking for a City of Rights. She begged Alex to send her out again. Alex kept her word with Jock and refused. Other madams had no such compunctions. So Jock got to them and tried to buy them off as well. It didn't work. They were too greedy. They thought they could get away with lying to Jock, taking his money, and sending Perri out anyway. In the end, it was hopeless. There were too many madams, too many clients, too much demand. Jock did get something of a last laugh, though it gave him cold comfort. Furious with Perri, he sent her a 1099 for $500,000 in "miscellaneous income." The IRS swooped down on Perri and began an audit. The tax man thus accomplished what no one else could. He drove Perri out of Hollywood and out of the call-girl business, though rumor had it she had resurfaced in Tokyo as the mistress of one, if not several, of the electronics barons there.

The Perri quest transformed Jock from a buttoned-up socialite into a decadent sex addict. He stopped going to his downtown high-rise, and worked at home. Then he sold the San Marino mansion and bought a new one in once despised Beverly Hills, so he could be closer to Alex and closer to the action. More remarkably, he began investing in low-budget sex-and-action films to showcase the starlet/harlots he happened to fancy at the moment. Power may be an aphrodisiac in Washington; in Hollywood the aphrodisiac is celluloid. Jock thus became what he most despised: Mr. Hollywood. Yet his main motivation was romance. He was literally looking for love in all the wrong places, but he had been so square, so married, for so long, that he didn't have a clue how else to do it. His life had been so perfectly ordered that once it came apart, he couldn't put it together again.

Back from his triumph over evil in Bel Air, Jock heated up another vial of crack. He breathed in the vapors and felt good and strong and positive. It wasn't the blow job that he had forced the patrolman to give him that contributed to his euphoria; it was the chivalry. Jock was an old-fashioned guy who, despite his bad habits, saw himself as a shining knight of virtue in a sordid world of vice, a Lancelot, a John Wayne, an Alan Ladd in *Shane*. To him, Dawn wasn't a hooker–porno slave; she was a damsel in distress. He wasn't really looking to get laid; he wanted to love and be loved. But the pain of his wife leaving him had turned him into a pain addict, a super-masochist, with his endless casting calls for the hooker Cinderella of his dreams who would only charge him, hurt him, and leave him.

"This one is different," Alex told Jock over the phone. "Not only are *you* going to fall for *her*, I think *she's* going to go for *you*."

"How much will that cost me?" Jock shot back.

"Don't be cynical," Alex said. "If you'd only listen to me, you'd get the girls. For nothing."

"Ha!"

"You're a very brilliant man. This one can appreciate you. You've got to stop going for the bitches."

"They're all bitches," Jock roared. The Rottweilers snarled.

Alex felt sorry for him. She refused to accept any responsibility for his sexual addiction. But she genuinely cared for him and wanted him to be happy. "Ann is vulnerable. She's wounded, just like you."

"How does she compare to Perri?" was the most important question in Jock's mind.

"Perri was a killer. She was a narcissistic sexual vampire," Alex told him. "All she wanted was your blood. Ann is sweet, like a doe in the forest. You're very lucky you're getting her first. Because once I finish with her, all she'll have to do is look in the mirror, and her stock in herself will go straight up."

"And then she'll be just another whore cunt bitch," Jock said.

"Not if you behave yourself. She's sweet. You're sweet. Just be yourself."

Alex could only hope that, once transformed, Ann would like Jock. Despite his fortune, it was by no means a sure thing. Not one of Alex's girls had been able to put up with Jock. He was too much of a mess, and far too scary. He had several thugs in his employ, and he was constantly threatening to have them "take out" or at least disfigure Rob Lowe or Charlie Sheen or Sean Penn or whomever in the Brat Pack the call girls seemed to have crushes on. They were usually in that hip under-thirty young-actor group, not the rock stars that most of the hookers gave it away for. The girls that Jock liked were more practical than that, practical enough to have at least considered Jock for his money and then dismissed him, practical enough to calculate that they might have a better chance, however slight, with Judd Nelson than with Bono. Starved for even spurious affection, Jock made the most of whatever attention these call girls gave him. He bought elaborate electronic eavesdropping equipment and Space Age magnifying cameras to spy on them, and when he witnessed the girls "cheating" on him, he would buy them Mercedes convertibles and Cartier jewels to lure them back.

When he failed, Jock would rant and rave about hiring a hit man to take the Brat Packer out. On coke, Jock sometimes thought he was John Gotti. He blustered and raged and issued death warrants. "I'm going to bring her to heel," he would say about the infidel of the moment.

"Just give her a dog biscuit," Alex would say, making a joke of it. "You bring dogs to heel, not people. Go play in the kennel." The Brat Pack should have been thankful for Alex's levity. Without her and with enough coke, Jock was crazy enough to go through with it.

In trying to find a Miss Right for Jock, Alex had a slightly ulterior motive. Alex had other things on her agenda than just Ann. More important was establishing a rapprochement between Jock and his father, from whom Jock had become completely estranged. The problem for the elder Mr. Palfrey was that Jock had a Midas touch for making money that transcended his ability to squander it. Even if the Palfrey patriarch disowned him, Jock still had his own properties, which he had expanded into strip malls and a storage chain that had made him fortunes of his own. Not that Jock didn't have his cash-flow problems. He drove his accountants mad, and would run two- and three-hundred-thousand-dollar sex tabs with Alex for months on end, until even *she* would despair of ever collecting. Then a seven-figure check would arrive from selling a mall or a warehouse, and the debts would all be settled and the party would begin again.

In the course of one of these massive overextensions, Jock's harried creditors had descended on his exasperated father, whose private eyes traced one of the money trails to Alex. A dialogue began, and in light of Alex's empathy, Palfrey *père* concluded that perhaps she could be the key to bringing Jock back into the real world, or at least the real world of the Main Line. The objective was to get Jock into the Betty Ford Center, but since the Palfreys were in Pennsylvania and Merrie and the children had moved to Hawaii with the insurance agent, there was no blood relative in California to pursue a legal commitment procedure, which was next to impossible anyway. Besides, Jock had so many lawyers on his payroll that no one would be able to stop his gravy train. Thinking that an outlaw might accomplish what the law could not, Jock's father offered Alex half a million dollars if she could get his son clean and sober.

Even though putting Jock away would have been cutting off her own nose to spite her face, Alex's humanitarian side (as a mother, she more than had one) was certain that if Jock didn't stop freebasing, he might not be alive to call hookers—hers or anyone else's—for much longer. On the other hand, she was realistic enough to accept that only one trick in her book could persuade Jock to go cold turkey and that would be the ultimate trick—another Perri, hopefully one with human emotions, whom Jock would fall madly in love with for more than three sessions and would change himself for. This, too, would not be simple. If Alex ever got her reward from Jock's father, she would have earned it.

"I'll see her when her tits heal," Jock said.

"She doesn't need new tits," Alex said.

"She does for me," Jock insisted, very ornery.

"You haven't seen her."

"She's not a whore if she doesn't have fake tits."

Alex dismissed the comment, which, like most of Jock's comments, was a mask, a cocaine viciousness to cover up the stabbing emptiness of his billionaire-playboy existence.

While Jock talked, Dawn came back into the room and began paging through the centerfolds and lingerie ads of his "conquests." She wondered if maybe she should have had her breasts made just a little larger. If she decided to redo them, she knew Jock would pay. He was that kind of guy. The hounds howled outside. Jock fingered his new gun and let his mind open to the possibility of a new romance, as Alex, the Dolly Levi of lost souls, stoked the fires of his pathetic quest for Miss Right.

| Hollywood Princess

Alex got off the phone with Jock when Brooke Kuhn arrived. Brooke, in her mid-thirties, was one of Beverly Hills's premier socialites and party givers. Her estate, Alhambra, near Alex's place off Doheny, was considered one of the most tasteful and charming of all local homes, and the food she served was indisputably the best in the city. Everyone swooned over her grilled partridges, her white asparagus, her super-sweet mangoes flown in from Cochin. But it wasn't the mangoes that made Brooke's parties such a draw. It wasn't even Brooke, who was either so high on coke or so low on pills or so depressed about always being on a diet and never getting to eat this great food that the only people she really bothered with was whoever had the top-grossing film in *Variety* that week. It was Brooke's father, Caesar Kuhn, the great studio lord, the quintessence of moguldom, who wielded more power from his retirement wheelchair than Jeff Katzenberg did from the car phone in his Mustang. Not only did Caesar know where the bodies were buried; he was often the one who had manned the shovel.

Why Brooke, with her unlimited access to glittering celebrity, chose to hang around at Madam Alex's was something of a mystery. That her father had hung around there for years, though not anymore, may have had something to do with it. What was more likely was that, just as she was for Jock Palfrey, Alex was a mother figure for Brooke Kuhn. Brooke's real mother, Felicity, was dead; Felicity had been the ethereal daughter of one of Hollywood's founding families, and she had transformed Caesar Kuhn, a onetime traveling dress salesman, then a two-bit Broadway talent scout, into one of show business's most ruthless arbiters of the movies America would see.

The young Felicity had fled her family's privilege to move east and try to make it as a theater actress under an assumed name. Alas, she had less talent for the stage than even Lee Radziwill, whose name couldn't do the job for her. Felicity's actual name, as far as show business was concerned, was even bigger, but it remained a secret to everyone except Caesar Kuhn, who "discovered" her and loved her as if she were the poorest, most wonderful girl in the world. When Felicity returned west, she presented Caesar to her family as a fait accompli. They had lost an actress, she conceded, but they had gained a son. Grateful that Felicity had outgrown the actress phase, the family embraced Caesar with open arms and gave him their empire to rule so that their daughter could reign.

While Brooke had inherited her parents' mantle as toast and host of Hollywood, she wore it much more uneasily. She turned to Alex, whom she could never invite to her parties, for ideas on menus and floral arrangements. She never bought a painting without consulting Alex, or an antique, or, especially, a jewel. Alex's own collection was surpassed in Hollywood only perhaps by Doris Stein's or Elizabeth Taylor's. She had the keenest eye, the same eye she used on her girls, and Brooke, who was a jewelry junkie, depended on Alex to keep from getting ripped off. That was the worst thing that could ever happen to a daughter of Old Hollywood who was supposedly born to be above such errors of judgment.

Brooke, through the injustice of the genetic lottery, had inherited her father's simian looks and her mother's less-than-rocket-scientist brains. Had it been the other way around, she would have been a force of nature. Alex had met Brooke at an antiques fair five years ago. They bonded when Alex rescued Brooke from a dealer who was trying to get a small fortune for a chair he said was a real Hepplewhite but which was actually a fake Chippendale. Brooke thanked Alex by giving her a small music stand that Ira Gershwin had given Felicity. Alex thanked Brooke by baking her cookies and sending them to her in an eighteenth-century cookie tin. A friendship was born. They talked about astrology, about which Alex knew a lot, and about movies, about which Alex could care less, and about art and diamonds and high-ticket consumer items that Brooke loved, but they never talked about Alex's business. To Brooke, Alex was the sweet lady next door, a den mother to the beauties who came in and out all day with their fat white envelopes. Naturally, Brooke couldn't help but be a bit titillated when a big star called and asked for something, or someone. But Brooke was her father's little girl; she had grown up among starlets and mistresses, she had seen call girls become stars and stars become call girls, so nothing much could shock her. For Brooke, Alex's was an escape, a place she could be herself, if she could ever figure out who that was.

Today, Alex decided to enlist Brooke's help in finding someone to send to Sir John in New York, a WASPy deb who could play field hockey in the afternoon and then change into Trashy Lingerie for the evening and give Sir John a hand job under the table at "21" while she was talking to his friends' wives about the Pre-Raphaelite show at the Met.

"I've got just the girl," Brooke exulted, happy to be of help to Alex, whom she had almost never seen at a loss for girls. The girl's name was Courtney Van Ness. She had gone to the Marlborough School with Brooke, who had been one of a handful of token Jews in this blue-chip finishing school. Courtney, who lived near Marlborough in Hancock Park, was Old California, Gold Rush California, on both sides of her family. Her mother was a McAllister, one of San Francisco's pioneer families. Her father was the vice president of a downtown brokerage firm, a leader of the Jonathan Club, and a major golfer at the Los Angeles Country Club, which had even fewer Jews than Marlborough did. Although Courtney looked the part, and *was* the part, her heart definitely was not in fulfilling her birthright. Discovering drugs and rock and roll in her early teens, she fulfilled the sex aspect of the unholy trinity by surrendering her virginity to Jim Morrison in a cheap La Cienega motel when she was fifteen and topping that off with a ménage à trois with two of the Family Stone, though not Sly, on a backstage pass at the Greek Theatre. Blessed with high S.A.T.s, Courtney majored in philosophy and psilocybin at Reed College in Portland, then moved to Berkeley and supported her psycho-bohemian lifestyle working in the kitchen of Chez Panisse. The moment the eighties arrived, though, at a Russian Hill New Year's Day party she was catering, Courtney met another forty-niner scion, a druggie turned yuppie venture capitalist. She married him within three months, moved to Pacific Heights, joined the Junior League, and started wearing pearls. This year, however, the yuppie had gone bust, as had the marriage. Courtney was back in Los Angeles, Brooke said. She needed money.

"For starters, she's too old," Alex said. For Alex, anybody over twenty-five was too old. Thirty-five was for the Smithsonian.

"She still looks great," Brooke said, slightly offended. "Gorgeous blond hair, not a wrinkle, amazing body. She always rode, until she had to sell the horse. I saw her naked when I took her swimming at Hillcrest. Not an ounce of cellulite."

"Children?" Alex asked.

"None. Her body's perfect. I'd die to have a body like that. And listen to this. I took her to a party for Barbara Grant, Cary's wife, and Kirk Kerkorian was really checking her out, and Courtney said, 'I wish he wasn't taken.' "

"What's that supposed to mean?" Alex asked.

"It means she likes older men. That this wouldn't turn her off."

"It doesn't mean she'd sleep with him for money. Americans are very touchy about that," Alex said. "They love money and they'll do just about anything for it, but they're hung up about sex. That's where they draw the line. The last thing a woman here wants to be thought of is a whore."

"Since when did you get so shy?" Brooke wondered.

"She's your friend. I don't think you should get mixed up in this."

"You asked."

"I was looking for a whore, not a Junior Leaguer. And you know I need young."

Brooke pointed out to Alex that she had girls on her rolls in their thirties, and even in their forties.

"I never started someone at thirty-five," Alex said. "And anyway, what makes you think she'd ever do it?"

"She needs the money," Brooke explained. "She used to screw everything. She was a hippie, she lived in communes, she went to India to that sex ashram."

"Rajneesh?" Alex mentioned.

"Yeah."

"I had a lot of friends who knew him," Alex said. "Two of my creatures went there once to meet rich men."

"See," Brooke said. "Courtney could do it. I know Sir John. I met him at Alice Mason's. He'd love her."

"But she's not a working girl," Alex said, exasperated with Brooke's gung ho enthusiasm. "Working girls aren't made in a day."

"She's been preparing for this part all her life," Brooke insisted. "She just doesn't know it yet."

"You really want to turn your friend into a hooker?"

"Absolutely," Brooke declared gleefully. "It's a big fantasy. A lot of women are thinking about it. How much could she make?"

"Maybe ten thousand. Maybe more," Alex said. "Depends on what Sir John thinks. He is a little lonely."

"I want to do this for her. It's a perfect match. Give her a chance.

Please," Brooke pleaded, as if working for Alex would be the greatest honor in Courtney Van Ness's life.

"Get her out here," Alex said, giving in. "Fast. This is a rush job."

| Secret Agent Madam

With Brooke off to track down her friend, Alex began having second, paranoid thoughts. What if Courtney was a cop? What if Courtney was so offended by the proposition that she would turn Alex in to the cops for pandering? Legally, being a call girl was scary. Being a madam was high-risk. Prostitution, at the worst, might bring a night in jail, a suspended sentence for a misdemeanor, and a scarlet letter of embarrassment. Pandering, on the other hand, was a felony that could be, and often was, punished with years in prison. The eyes of the law took an equally dim view of the maternal madam as they did the brutal pimp. The madam often fared worse because the wages of her sin tended to be much higher.

The law, then, always hovered in the wings of Alex's consciousness, like death and taxes. Over the last two decades, Alex had been visited only a few times by the law, and the charges had always been dropped. Alex's girls never ratted on her. She was too good to them, or, as others suggested, they were too scared of what the reprisal might be. More important, Alex had friends in high places, including in the L.A.P.D. To the police, Alex was a valuable resource, a clearinghouse of gossip, rumor, and, often, real leads. It wasn't that the cops wanted to spy on movie stars, or shake down philandering politicians. They were after crime, real crime—drugs, counterfeiting, S & L master scams, that sort of thing. Big-time criminals were just as interested in using Alex's girls as big-time stars or big-time producers were. Alex was an integral part of the top-dollar, high-roller, deluxe L.A. consumer package. What better way to celebrate closing that multimillion-dollar cocaine deal than buying a Testarossa, leasing an estate in Trousdale, buying a silk jacket at Bijan, eating foie gras at L'Orangerie, and partying with one of Alex's divine creatures? Closing Alex would be as inconceivable, as sacrilegious, as closing Chasen's or Mortons. Alex in business was worth infinitely more to local, state, and federal authorities than the smug self-satisfaction that would be enjoyed by the Beverly Hills bluestocking moralists from shutting her down.

Forever mindful of her quid pro quo social contract with the authorities, Alex called Captain Tom Freihof at L.A.P.D. headquarters downtown to give him a report on an out-of-town client Freihof had under surveillance. Identifying herself as "Mrs. Morgan," Alex quickly got Freihof on the line.

Although they had been talking for five years, the two had never met in person. Alex had many such phone-pal relationships. She considered Freihof a friend, and wanted to be of help. She might have sent him cookies, or a painting, or even a girl if he were anyone else, but she knew precisely where to draw the line. Their friendship was strictly business, *his* business.

"His name's Dickie Roberts," Freihof told Alex matter-of-factly.

"Never heard of him," Alex said.

"Didn't expect you to," Freihof replied. "British. Fortyish. Retired career soldier. In the last ten years, he's lived in Tripoli, Djakarta, Tehran, Entebbe, and Belfast."

"He likes the quiet resorts," Alex deadpanned.

"Lists his profession as an electrical contractor. M.I.5 thinks he may do more for Qaddafi than install light switches."

"What can I do with a guy like that?"

"Entertain him. He's staying at the Century Plaza. We have a bartender over there. Informant. Gotten chummy. Said he could find him a call girl. Can we give him your number?"

"What do you want to find out?"

"We don't know. Anything suspicious. He listed the purpose of his visit as tourism, but M.I.5 doesn't believe it. They're real curious. Will you help us?"

"Have I ever said no?"

"Thanks, Alex."

"Have the bartender have him call me. Dickie Roberts?"

"That's right."

"*Dickie?*" Alex played with the name.

"I know, I know," Freihof said. "British."

Alex set Roberts up with an Australian blonde named Emma, who, like Roberts, had had an internationally checkered career. Emma had worked as a model in Mexico City for a South African–born jeans manufacturer. Now she was in L.A., living in a Polynesian apartment complex in Marina Del Rey and trying to sell real estate in a nonexistent market out of the Jon Douglas office in Westwood. That one-two punch was usually a dead giveaway to cognoscenti who would meet Emma at the bar of the West Beach Café, where she often hung out alone. A beautiful blonde in tight black Lycra, a Chanel belt, and high heels who had been a model in some off market and was now in real estate was a safe bet to be a working girl. More than a few of these cognoscenti, upon picking up on this, would steer the conversation around to how bad the property market was and how unfair it was that such a beauty should be stressed for cash. After a few expensive vintage cognacs, they would find themselves with Emma on Bora Bora Way, for a cheap $150, which was less than what she could get from Alex, but given the time and not having to pay 40 percent commission, Emma was happy to do the deal.

Normally, the least Alex would charge even her oldest and most favorite customers who were on tight budgets was $300 for what was basically a one-hour quickie. Alex would waive her cut. This was known as a "courtesy fuck," as opposed to a "freebie," for which Alex paid the girl herself. Freebies were quite rare. Since Dickie Roberts was a self-proclaimed tourist, Alex didn't want to scare him off with her normal rate, which was $500 for a two- to three-hour session in which the client was entitled to come twice, if he was up to it. Even the charity rate was too expensive for most Century Plaza guests. So she called on Emma, who was one of Alex's $300 "utility girls," who would get more if the traffic would bear it but who would "fuck for scale" if times were hard. Some of Alex's racehorses were very strict and would never turn less than a $1,000 trick, like actors who had struggled to establish their price and had a point of honor about ever cutting it. Most, however, had a more flexible, realpolitik approach to what their pussies were worth.

Alex did not tell Emma about Captain Freihof. She never told any of her girls that Big Brother might be watching. The girls were nervous enough without that, and neither Alex nor the powers that be wanted to risk the girls' safety, which could be jeopardized if they knew they had beans to spill. All Alex told Emma was that Dickie came via a London connection, and was a businessman. She didn't even tell her to keep her eyes open. Emma knew to do that, for Alex always loved to interrogate the girls about every gory detail when they arrived with their white envelopes. Aside from what she had heard from Captain Freihof, Alex had nothing much to tell Emma about her client. Alex's phone conversation with Dickie had been generic, polite. All he wanted, he said, was a "nice girl." He didn't ask for blond, or big breasts, or long legs, or domination, or anything else kinky or even specific. "I'll leave it to you" was all he said.

Emma's first encounter with Dickie was completely unremarkable. A wiry, tan man in a khaki safari suit, a colonial type, he knew the exact neighborhood in Melbourne where Emma had grown up. The sex was pro forma: a vodka from the mini-bar, a flattering comment on Emma's sleek bronze legs, then a hand on them, which led to Dickie's taking off her panties and going down on her on the couch. Emma rated him "quite nice—for an Englishman" in the cunnilingus department, and later told Alex that he had an average-size uncircumcised cock and had come in her mouth in about ten minutes. To Emma, he just seemed like a lonely middle-aged man who wanted some company. What he seemed most interested in, above all else, was going to Spago. He asked to see Emma again, and to take her to dinner at the celebrity pizza house, offering her another two hundred dollars for her extended company. Calling for a table, she was told there was nothing at eight o'clock for the next month, six or ten only, and surely in the Siberia in the back of the restaurant. Emma had to enlist Alex's aid.

The next night they had an "A" table in Star Country in the front room overlooking the bright lights of Tower Records and a Clint Eastwood billboard. They had had sex, so Dickie was in an expansive mood, talking monotonously about electrification problems in the Third World and the annoyances of laying cable during the monsoon season in Indonesia. Dickie had no idea who Joan Rivers was, or Veronica Hamel. They were unknown in Entebbe. He paid no attention to countrywoman Jackie Collins. But he was obsessed with wanting to see television actor Bruce Boxleitner, so much so that, after dinner, he insisted on buying a map of the stars' homes, which turned out not to have been updated since Sammy Davis, Jr., lived in Holmby Hills, and which didn't include Boxleitner at all. Captain Freihof made a thorough check on Boxleitner to see if there were any possible terrorist links, family roots in Northern Ireland, Richard Gere–like Buddhist sympathies or antipathies to Sikh separatists or something like that. But there was nothing.

This was Alex's final report on the matter to Captain Freihof, who had been off fishing at Catalina yesterday when Emma saw Dickie once more. Again, an easy blow job and nothing more. "A boring engineer" was how Emma summed him up. Alex knew that Emma was no Mata Hari, and like most of the L.A.P.D.'s other surveillance requests of Alex, the final result here was nothing to declare. The main thing was that Alex had tried, and her accommodation earned her Brownie points so that the force would be with her when the shoe of the law fell again, as it inevitably would.

| Valley Girls

Roddy Winston, boy-wonder studio executive, had left Burbank in his Porsche convertible to try to sell Jessica Lange on playing Emma Bovary. He thought he could get Adrian Lyne to direct, and if he couldn't get Jessica he knew Debra Winger would jump at it, but he *really* wanted Jessica, wanted her so much that he picked up the car phone.

"Do you want the greatest fuck of your life in fifteen minutes?"

"Roddy?"

"Who else?"

"I'm already getting wet. You won't believe this but I had this dream about you last night. You had this *football* between your legs."

"Fifteen minutes. I'm going to eat your pussy and drive you crazy and then fuck you up the ass without a rubber."

"I want you to fuck my pussy, Roddy. You're the only one who can make me come that way. I need an hour."

"I don't have an hour. I've gotta meet Jessica Lange. Fifteen minutes."

"Jessica Lange?"

"I'm gonna put her in *Madame Bovary*. Know what that is?"

"Madame who?"

"*Madame Bovary*."

"Is she in Beverly Hills? She works with Alex, right?"

"It's a French *classic*. Doesn't anybody read out here?" Roddy yelled into the phone through the Cahuenga Pass. "Fifteen minutes."

"Roddy, I need to take a bath, get myself all nice for you. I want to wear this new black bra and these lace panties you're gonna want to eat right through. Give me an hour, please."

"Fifteen minutes."

"I'm getting really jealous."

"Why?"

" 'Cause you're gonna fuck Jessica Lange."

"It's business."

"Where are you meeting?"

"Her hotel," Roddy said.

"You're fucking her."

"Who said?"

"Don't expect to come over here and fuck me if you're fucking Jessica. Forget it. You're a pig."

The line went dead. Roddy called again.

"Why are you such a cunt?"

"You're cheating on me. Star-fucking. I wanna be the one, the only one. I need you."

"Fifteen minutes," Roddy promised.

Marti Gold hung up and laughed to herself. She figured Roddy Winston had the highest car-phone bills in the city. Every time he went to a meeting, he had to call her, or whatever call girl was home at that moment, and pump himself up to think he was the coolest, sexiest Lothario-Adonis ever to hit Hollywood. Despite an industry consensus that Roddy was likely to be running a studio well before he was thirty-five (he was only twenty-six), despite his marriage to a lovely young nursery-school teacher, despite his Porsches and Armanis and Colony house, Roddy Winston inside was still fat little Ronny Weinstein.

As one of the emblems of his rise, Roddy had become a call-girl addict. He had married his wife soon after his first big script sale. She was the first woman he had slept with, and at the time he saw her as way out of his league. Now he was out of hers, but Roddy was still socially maladroit and had no idea what to do with the starlets who were willing to throw themselves at him. He had no moves with women other than to the telephone and to his wallet.

Marti Gold, even more than Jessica Lange, was the type of girl Roddy had most fantasized about in his long nights of obscurity. A blond, bubbly head cheerleader from Reseda, in the Valley, she had been a state gymnastics champion; she was a Nadia Comaneci with long legs, an archetypal shiksa goddess who had the added benefit of happening to be Jewish. She reminded Roddy of Cybill Shepherd in *The Heartbreak Kid*, the blond icon who wrecked Charles Grodin's honeymoon. Marti was precisely the sort of girl who could wreck Roddy's marriage, if only she weren't a whore. He couldn't leave his wife for a prostitute, not even a Jewish prostitute.

The story of Marti's becoming a call girl was as unlikely as she was; Marti was turned out by her boyfriend's mother. While Marti was going to UCLA, Buck, a hunky guy on whom she had an unrequited crush, helped her get a cheap off-campus apartment in Culver City in a building his mother was managing. Marti hoped the little studio would come to be her and Buck's love nest. Buck paid no romantic attention to her, however, taking her on mountain hikes and bicycle trips but never making a move. Trying to get to him, or at least understand him, by getting to know his mother, Marti found out that Buck had been sexually traumatized by his mother's "other" profession, as a fifty-year-old hundred-dollar hooker who saw older traveling salesmen and waiters between shifts in the afternoon.

Marti's frustration and fascination with Buck finally brought her so close to his mom that Marti began doing threesomes with her to defray her rent and pick up spending money. It seemed easy; it was also a way of trying to provoke the reluctant Buck. When Buck finally began to suspect the unholy alliance between Marti and his mother, he beat Marti up, and then he finally had sex with her. To her it was divine retribution, what she had been longing for for months. An extremely violent relationship ensued, after which Marti was so battered and embittered that she dropped out of gymnastics as well as UCLA and linked up with a Marina madam, selling herself for what she could get and recovering her self-esteem in the process of losing her innocence.

Marti had a Valley girl's adoration of money and "things." Alex, to whom she had graduated, called her "my worker bee." Despite a clothes habit, a furniture habit, a BMW habit, and a coke habit, Marti, at twenty-three, had nearly $300,000 at Merrill Lynch and a spiffy duplex in Westwood. She was even going back to UCLA at nights to get her degree, though she had no idea what she was going to do with it. Marti also had a plastic-surgery habit. Most men would have rated her gymnast's body a perfect 10, but she had gotten hooked on breasts, and had had hers enlarged by two successive plastic surgeons, both of whom did their work for barter and ended up spending far more money on Marti than she could have ever spent on them. Months later, she decided that she looked better without the implants, and she found a third plastic surgeon to seduce into removing them. Now her breasts were tight, pert, and perfect, except for the scars, which she had been promised would heal.

When Roddy called, Marti had just come back from fucking her plastic surgeon, who had removed the bandages afterward, and from fucking her lawyer, just two buildings away in Century City, in return for his suing her upstairs neighbor for a flood that had ruined her new sofa and

Aubusson carpet, both of which Alex had helped her pick out. In fact, she was late in getting over to Alex's to give her her four-hundred-dollar cut of the easy thousand Marti had received for giving an hour's head in a night of coke to an English drummer at the Sunset Marquis.

Marti met Roddy at the door in a black bra that concealed the scars of her breast reduction. She held a whirring vibrator in her hand. "I was getting so horny waiting for you that I had to do myself." She gave him a big, wet kiss on the lips. "You look fabulous in that Versace."

"Armani," Roddy corrected her. "Did I tell you I think we're getting Gere?" What he didn't tell her was that he had seen another call girl this morning just to get himself psyched up for that meeting. "Am I cool or what?"

Marti stroked the front of Roddy's trousers. "I'd say you were hot. I want you to give it to me up the ass, right now."

"Don't you want to hear what Stanley Jaffe said?"

"Later. Feel how wet I am." Marti took Roddy's right hand and guided it inside her black G-string panties. "Feel this."

"Jesus," Roddy gasped. "You're ready."

"I want you to shoot your hot sperm straight up my ass," Marti murmured, kissing him again, unzipping his pants, taking off his jacket. She led him into her bedroom, where a single foil-wrapped Trojan sat on her nightstand.

"I can't believe how wet you are," Roddy marveled.

Marti controlled her amusement. Roddy couldn't tell passion from K-Y jelly. "Fuck me, Roddy. Fuck me for hours. Fuck me all over. Fuck me now." Roddy was still wearing his shirt and tie. He lay back on the bed. Marti tore the Trojan packet open and slipped on the rubber. She started to mount him, but before she could get him inside her, he had already come. "Oh, yes. It feels so good, so hot, so good. Yes. Oh, oh, oh." So much for the incredibly hot unprotected anal sex. Nevertheless, Roddy was completely satisfied. This was as hot as he could handle. He got off on the bullshit, on the hype, the same way the stars and the agents got off on *his* bullshit and *his* hype. He was so self-absorbed he hadn't even noticed Marti's new, streamlined breasts.

"From behind next time. I promise," Marti said, washing Roddy's genitals with a hot towel, like a geisha.

"Definitely," Roddy said. "When I have more time, I'm going to really fuck you great. This Jessica Lange deal . . ."

"Hey, I understand," Marti said. "This is the big time."

She helped Roddy into his Armani, adjusted his pocket square, and sent him off to work his magic on Jessica. The whole encounter had lasted under a quarter of an hour.

When Marti arrived at Alex's, the maids were serving tea to Alex and Lori Schwartz, a raven-tressed eighteen-year-old freshman at UCLA.

"You two have got a lot in common," Alex said. "You're both from the Valley, you both went to UCLA, and you're both bad girls." Alex cackled. "Show us your new tits."

"They're my *old* tits," Marti said, and unbuttoned her blouse. Women in Los Angeles liked to show off their redone breasts as casually, and as proudly, as their engagement rings.

"I love your bra," Lori Schwartz said. "Where'd you get it?"

"Victoria's Secret at the Bev Center. They're having a sale. Do you really want to see them? The scars are kind of icky," Marti said.

"Show us. I was thinking of getting mine done," Lori said.

Marti unsnapped the bra. "Voilà!"

"Nice," Lori said. "Perfect."

"I prefer the small boobs on you," Alex said. "They're much more elegant."

"They're not too small, are they?" Marti asked.

"They're great." Lori admired them, coming closer to inspect. "Perfect B's."

"She wanted B-52's," Alex joked.

"Who did them?" Lori asked.

"Gottlieb in Century City. The best."

"How much?"

"Four fucks and two blow jobs," Marti answered.

"He's one of mine," Alex said to Lori. "If you ever need anything, he'll take care of you. He loves eating pussy."

"He's good at it, too," Marti said. "Where are you from?"

"Encino," Lori said.

"Where else?" Alex added. "I'm introducing her to Ari Gratsos."

"Mr. Baby Pussy." Marti knew him well.

"How gross?" Lori wondered.

"Gross but not disgusting. I hope you're a Laker fan." Ari was a big Hollywood producer who was an integral part of the club because he was a superb poker player, and he was a fixture in the Beverly Hills high-stakes league. He had owned a chain of coffee shops, which had given him the grubstake to get into the picture game by buying the rights to a KGB espionage novel called *Molehill* as a Stallone vehicle. The movie never got made, but Ari was a high roller, and the big studio people found him simpatico. Every year they'd throw him a cinematic bone or two. He could fuck a few starlets, rake off his million-dollar executive-producer fee, and show up for the premiere of the invariably no-brain action flicks. The rest of the time he spent gambling and chasing "baby pussy," i.e., the teenage girls who had been one of the prime staples of Hollywood desire from Chaplin to Polanski to now.

"What's it like?" Lori asked Marti.

"Easy. You watch the Laker game on this humongous TV, and you pretend you're really into it. Go Magic. Go Worthy. Go Kareem. Rah. Rah. Strong to the hoop. Amazing reverse layup. Just say things like that. And he'll play with your tits and . . . Oh, wear some really ridiculous lingerie, something really tight and complicated. It turns him on if you look uncomfortable."

"What else?"

"Well, every time you think you'll have to fuck him, Magic'll save you with a layup, and Ari'll call his bookie and bet some more. Basically, it's head at halftime and then you'll get on top of him at the end, cause he's too fat and lazy to do anything else."

"You forgot the best part," Alex reminded Marti.

"Oh, yeah. If the Lakers lose, he'll be too depressed to fuck you."

"Go Celtics," Lori said. "Juwan's being scouted by them."

"Juwan who?" Marti asked.

"Juwan Jefferson," Lori said, proprietarily.

"I don't mean to be dumb, but who's that?"

"The center for UCLA," Lori said.

"And her boyfriend," Alex chimed in.

"Now I get it," Marti said. "No wonder you're here."

Lori Schwartz was a major find. The Demi Moore look-alike was from a rich family that owned a car dealership and lived down the top-dollar block in Encino from Michael Jackson. Lori and Marti may have both been from the Valley, but the gap in their level of privilege showed just how big the Valley was. Yet here they both were.

The Schwartzes expected their daughter to go out with nice Jewish boys. When she brought home the 6' 10" Juwan, whom UCLA had re-cruited from the playgrounds of Bedford-Stuyvesant, the Schwartzes weren't impressed that a lot of coaches thought Juwan was going to be the next Kareem Abdul-Jabbar. Adding insult to this *Guess Who's Coming to Dinner* injury, Lori refused to take any more money from her parents (though she did keep her Corvette and her platinum AmEx).

To support herself, she responded to an ad in the *Daily Bruin* to work as a masseuse at Beach Ball, a no-fucking hand-job parlor next to the Chicken Natural take-out on Little Santa Monica and Sepulveda, similar to the one Walter Burke had visited in Beverly Glen. While that one had a Seven Sisters hook, Beach Ball's pitch was its UCLA coeds. Lori had been there less than two weeks when another of Alex's sexaholics, a madam-and-massage-hopping CAA hotshot, "discovered" her after lunch one day at the Grill when he had a half hour to kill on his way to TriStar. He introduced her to Alex in return for a free hand job. Out of technical "loyalty" to Juwan, Lori didn't want to fuck the guy, but once she started with Alex, that technicality had to go. Juwan had shown re-markable understanding, though it should be noted that most of the money Lori was making went to buy him new clothes at Maxfield and take him on weekends to Cabo San Lucas.

So here she was, baby pussy personified. It was only fitting that the moguls who were slaves to the youth market in their films would, in their private lives, be a market for youth. Alex courted this market as aggressively as Warner Bros. did. The cutoff for Alex, if not for the moguls, was eighteen. What happened to Polanski would be a garden party compared to what Alex might expect. Most girls usually didn't get to Alex before they were twenty-one. The kind of special beauties she required took at least that long to get disillusioned enough to come to her. Even the dreamy teen coke whores needed a few years before they started thinking like businesswomen. Hence legal, high-quality baby pussy was in short supply. It commanded double the normal rate.

| The Player

Marti went off to her condo, Lori to her dorm. It was getting dark. The lights of the L.A. basin began to twinkle as the sun set over Century City, then Santa Monica. Sir John called again from New York. "Any luck?" he pressed Alex, who bought two more days of grace with the promise that Courtney Van Ness was everything that Brooke Kuhn said she would be. Alex was going on more faith than Brooke deserved. Alex called Brooke, but only got her machine. Brooke was prone to make cocaine promises and never deliver. Had she even tried to get Courtney? Would she ever? Brooke could disappear for days, even weeks, at her horse ranch in the Santa Ynez Valley.

Alex began dialing for hookers. It was six-thirty. The other madams should be wide-awake now, planning the evening's assignations. Carole wasn't there. Brenda was in Las Vegas. Dixie was at Gelson's. Nobody had what Alex needed. It was like the main branch of The Gap calling the satellite stores looking for an out-of-stock-color in a T-shirt.

Alex set up a date with an even bigger producer than Ari Gratsos, albeit one who never gambled and never lost. Dixon Blake was so fastidious that many people thought he was gay, notwithstanding his role as mentor to several of the women in key positions in the Men's Club of Hollywood. Never married, Dixon seemed too controlled, too mannered, too discreet, to have taken advantage of these situations. Dixon lived in a landmark Richard Neutra house, he had a museum-level modern-art collection, he had been photographed for *Vanity Fair* and *Vogue Uomo*. And his best friends were the Hollywood gay power elite who had quite a Men's Club of their own, as powerful, if not more so in some ways, than its hetero counterpart.

Dixon Blake was anything but gay, and no one knew this better than Alex. Not only had he bedded all of his mentees, as a condition of his mentorship and their advancement, but he had also slept with every actress who had a part of any consequence in any of his films. Like Arturo Toscanini, who liked to sleep with all of his divas prior to their performances, to loosen them up, Dixon liked to get his leading ladies "ready" for their parts. Additionally, Dixon basically distrusted women. Even if he had no particular lust for them, he had to have them before he could work with them, if only as a matter of proving their good faith. When it came to sex for sex's sake, he preferred Alex's girls. He had had at least a hundred of them. Dixon Blake may have slept with more women in Hollywood than Wilt Chamberlain had, but he had done it so discreetly that most local gossips would have laid heavy odds that he was a homosexual.

Dixon was planning a late dinner at Mortons, and he asked Alex to send him something for the cocktail hour, as it were. Dixon had never met Alex in person. So many of her clients had not. Yet he trusted Alex's taste completely. She knew what Dixon aspired to. She only sent him the "refined" type, the Audrey Hepburns, the Catherine Deneuves—the "unfuckables," as Alex called them. Tonight's selection was Arianna de Montrachet. Arianna, born Alicia Muñoz in the border town of Matamoros, had turned her first trick at twelve in a sailor's bar called the Don Quixote. A rich Midland, Texas, oilman discovered her at fifteen and set her up in his pied-à-terre in Dallas. By eighteen, Arianna had been to Europe with her sugar daddy a dozen times and had begun to put on airs. By twenty-one, she had her new name, spoke French, wore Saint Laurent, stayed at the Plaza Athenée, and sat at the Paris collections in the same row as Lynn Wyatt and Nan Kempner. Two years later she was out in the street.

The oilman died of a heart attack eating foie gras at Robuchon while Arianna was shopping at Christian Lacroix. There was no legacy, no palimony, only an outraged widow who threw Arianna out of the Dallas flat and ripped much of Arianna's couture wardrobe to shreds. Like so many courtesans, then, Arianna came to Los Angeles to reinvent herself once more, this time as an interior designer. She attended Otis/Parsons downtown, got her certificate, and met Alex through another Dallas hooker-socialite gone south. Alex liked Arianna, and helped her modify what was considered good taste in Dallas to something a little less Reign of Terror that could pass for good taste in Los Angeles, if not New York.

Arianna wanted nothing less than to be the Mark Hampton or Mario Buatta of L.A. She had the looks; she had the bullshit style and phony accent that L.A. took for real class. All she needed was a couple of "A" clients, and no one in town could be a better reference than Dixon Blake. Arianna was dying to get to him. She never bothered to consider why someone with genuine good taste like Dixon Blake would want to hire her, with her ersatz good taste. As Arianna told Alex, "Just let me fuck him, and I guarantee he'll recommend me." Alex wasn't sure it would be so easy where the decor was concerned, but as for the sex, she knew that Dixon would enjoy the lanky gamine with her Jerry Hall French and her Avenue Montaigne finery.

The Filipino houseboy led Arianna through the silent white-and-gray house of granite Buddha heads, pre-Columbian gods, and Hellenistic busts. The walls were hung with Schnabels and Salles, and the effect was very powerful and very cold. Dixon could use some chintz, Arianna thought. The houseboy pointed her toward a long corridor and disappeared. At the end of the hallway Arianna found the master bedroom, with its wall of glass looking east toward the floodlit Griffith Park Observatory.

A single filled flute of champagne stood on a silver tray atop a black marble pillar. Arianna drank it. Alex had told her the routine. She would strip down to her lingerie and high heels, then wait for Dixon to arrive in his gray silk robe. Without a word, he would take off his robe and seduce her, making love to her on this football field of a spotlit bed flanked by statues of the Hindu husband-and-wife gods of destruction and rebirth, Siva and Kali.

"When do we talk?" Arianna had asked Alex, eager to introduce herself and her interior-design skills to this pillar of Hollywood style.

"After you've come, you have a little chat, but not too much. Don't try to drop names. He knows them all."

"What do you mean, come?" Arianna was nervous that a sophisticated man like Dixon would be able to tell that she was faking an orgasm. She wasn't sure what a real one felt like. The traumas of her adolescent prostitution had left her oblivious to sex, impermeable to feeling.

"He wants you to come."

"I never really come. Not really. I mean, I'll give him a show."

"Dixon hates shows," Alex warned her. "Let him do it. He'll make you come."

"Come on. No way. What do I do?"

"You'll come," Alex assured her.

Yes, she would come, somehow, Arianna willed herself. But when would Dixon? Lounging on the bed in her elaborate black French bra and panties and garter belt and silk stockings, after a half hour Arianna was unable to cool her Manolo Blahnik super fuck-me black silk backless high heels another minute. She wandered down the corridor, looking for someone, anyone. She called out for the houseboy. There was no answer. Her voice echoed off the marble and the statues. Had she been stood up? She looked for a phone to call Alex, but she couldn't find one.

Arianna went back into the bedroom. She didn't want to walk out on this thousand-dollar gig and, more important, the contact of a career that might one day free her from these five-hundred-dollar gigs. But this mausoleum of a house was freaking her out. She had to find a phone. She saw some switches by the bed. She pushed one, and the lights went out, which terrified her further. She pushed another, and a large screen came down from the ceiling. But no phone. On another wall, which was completely mirrored, Arianna noticed a panel. She pressed it, and the mirror opened to reveal a huge closet full of a hundred suits and even more mirrors. She pressed another panel, and another closet opened up. And then Arianna screamed louder than anyone has ever screamed.

Hanging in this closet amid all the Turnbull shirts and Charvet ties and Battistoni pajamas was Dixon Blake, impeccably dressed in his bespoke Kilgour suit, his eyes bulging out, a trail of blood trickling from his mouth, a rope around his neck fastened to a clothes rack. Arianna didn't even put her clothes on. She didn't dare call the police, even if she could have found a phone. She grabbed her Escada dress and dashed out the door in her garter belt and silk stockings and Blahnik fuck-mes, through the box hedges, down the hill, past a startled coyote, into her car, and down to Sunset, where the sight of this distraught pretty woman behind the wheel of her Golf Cabriolet, top down, wearing nothing but an expensive French bra, made everyone who saw it glad they lived in Hollywood, after all.

One person who didn't see her was a man in a smoked-window Bentley who had just been stood up by Prince, whom he had wanted to talk to about playing the Cary Grant role in a remake of *Notorious*, with Madonna in the Ingrid Bergman part. Dixon Blake was late, but he wasn't the *late* Dixon Blake, as the hysterical Arianna truly believed. For all his fastidiousness, Dixon was a great practical joker. He had had the Paramount prop department prepare the lifelike effigy of himself, which he loved to show his guests as a party favor. He had no idea that Arianna would find her way into his closet, and was sorely disappointed when he finally arrived and found that she had fled. He wanted her back; the ones that got away unseen were always the most intriguing. But Arianna refused, career goals notwithstanding. She was too rattled by that haunted museum of a house. Alex told her on the phone to take a Valium, then go back and meet Dixon after Mortons. She refused. Dixon, intrigued by her resistance, offered to come to her. She still refused. Another night, Alex promised him. She would bring Arianna around. To be sure, Dixon sent Arianna an anonymous bouquet of roses and a rare Egyptian ankh, the symbol of life, to remind her he was still kicking. "I've already *died* to see you," the note said. "Let's live a little."

Alex lost that two-hundred cut. She still had nothing for Sir John, and she had waived Lynn Armstrong's fee. It seemed as if she were running a charity today. But then she added up the credits: the senator, Brent and

Daisy, Serge and Paoloa, Roddy Winston, Ari and Lori, and, of course, Rex Fried's bachelor party, which was coming up tonight. All in all, on this charitable day, Madam Alex had earned almost three thousand dollars. Not a bad haul, not for a slow day like this. Maybe Mike Ovitz had made more on the phone today than she had, Alex reflected, but not by much.

The phone was silent. Los Angeles, Alex's Los Angeles, was taken care of. Somehow, however, she couldn't take her hands off the phone. She called Jock Palfrey again, to invite him over for the sukiyaki her maids did so well. Jock was freebasing with Dawn. He dropped the phone, and Diablo and Judas, his two pit bulls, barked into it. Alex hung up. She called Lissa, but Lissa wasn't answering. Lissa was making the move of her life. Being twenty and adrift had given her the fear. Nicky Kroll and the coke had given her the courage. She was over Kansas on a United 757, winging her way to New York City to meet Sir John. Sir John? Was she mad? Lissa was almost as different from Candice Bergen as Grace Jones was from Princess Grace. She hadn't called him. She was just coming. She didn't want him to be able to call Alex and ask about her. That, she knew, would have been fatal, maybe even literally, so Lissa had a plan. She believed she could "get" Sir John, and if she could get Sir John, she could get the world. With no cut to Alex, except to cut her *out*. It was a brazen gambit, a big risk. But Lissa didn't have time to waste. She was already twenty, and on the Hollywood time by which she paced her life, the clock was ticking.

Poor Alex. She ate her sukiyaki on a tray in bed by herself, feeding slivers of the prime beef to her true loves Georgie, and Georgie, Jr., and the others. She read the new *People* and *Hello!* and the *Globe* and the *Star* and the *Tatler*, and smirked about how wrong they all were about all of her "friends," none of whom was around to talk to her tonight. She watched more of these friends on *Entertainment Tonight*, and then she watched *Carousel* on cable. And didn't cry, not even once.

CHAPTER FIVE

THE BACHELOR PARTY

*I*n a Hollywood whose bottom line is often to prove "who has the biggest dick," it was rather curious that at Rex Fried's bachelor party, which was shaping up to be one of the sexiest events of the year, the last thing any of the studio macho types wanted to do was to show his dick to anyone else.

It had been a he-man day. The boys, all twenty of them, had played a ruthless game of touch football on the flat and WASPy lawn of Ross Chandler's socialite aunt's estate in Hancock Park. Ross was the one pure WASP in the group, their "Bel-Aryan," as they called him. Behind his back they had laughed at him for trying to be an agent; he was too tall and blond and preppy to be an agent, not to mention too polite and too rich and without anything to kill for. Now that Ross was succeeding because his Anglophile boss was living out his Social Register fantasies through him, the guys hated him for it. They did, however, love his playing field. For a few hours they all imagined they were Kennedys.

Now they were imagining they were wiseguys, tearing into charred twenty-ounce New York strips at Dan Tana's. The venue had been shifted at the last moment from the Steak Pit when that speakeasy's mercurial proprietor decided, as he was wont to do, that he didn't feel like opening that night. So he'd lose a few thousand from the party. He may have been the one person in this town who couldn't have cared less about money. Tana's was the perfect fallback for a bachelor party. The guys had taken over half the restaurant, the half that Magic Johnson and James Worthy and the other Lakers would usually claim as their own on Sunday nights. Tana's was L.A.'s version of a New Jersey roadhouse. There were red-checkered tablecloths, and red leatherette banquettes, and Chianti bottles hanging from the ceiling, and sports on the giant bar TV, and thick-haired old waiters in black tuxes. But instead of button men at the tables, there were "cool" stars like Bruce Springsteen and Sam Shepard, or Peter Falk and Ben Gazzara, and "cool" producers like Sidney Beckerman of *Marathon Man* and *Kelly's Heroes.* Beckerman was a former Golden Gloves boxer who once punched out an effete British agent at Ma Maison for casting aspersions upon Beckerman's daughter. These were earthy he-men, just like Rex Fried's buddies were trying to be tonight, talking deals, thinking hookers, worrying and machinating how to actually fuck one of Alex's legendary creatures without getting blackmailed to their wives by the dear buddies they were breaking sourdough bread with.

No group of friends could have wished each other more ill. These young men, the pride of the system, feasted on their colleagues' failures, and choked on their comrades' successes. This round table of purported bonhomie was in truth a circle of deceit. Barry "Bookie" Feinstein, the one writer in the group, who wore a diamond stud in his ear to proclaim his creativity, hated Jake Gewirtz, the tiny, even for an agent, ICM powerhouse with the natty tie collection that made the low-key ICM head,

Jeff Berg, slightly nervous. The cause of the hatred was that Jake had turned Barry down as a client, which was the most crushing rejection Barry had had since Harvard's no had forced him into Penn. Jake, in turn, hated William Morris agent Bobby "Bluto" Miller, not just for his piggish slovenly dress habits—his shirttails always hanging out of his Armani suits—but because Bluto had sold Bookie's script to Universal, which had made it into a huge success. It was one of the rare times Jake looked like a fool for having passed on something.

Bluto Miller *should* have liked Avram Gund, the Universal executive who had championed Bookie's script. Instead, he hated him because Bluto coveted Avram's beautiful rich wife, Trina, whose father owned a huge chunk of MCA stock and had gotten Avram, who had previously sold bogus gems in a mail-order telephone boiler room, his high-level job without Avram's having paid any dues at all.

Avram, for his part, reserved all his hatred for the handsome Jeff Simon. Normally, Avram would have pitied Jeff, for being trapped in his boring business-affairs job at Fox, and for his inability to leverage himself into one of the glamorous creative-exec posts like Avram had, where all you needed was an opinion. But Avram despised Jeff because Jeff was reputed to be the Milton Berle of his generation, with the biggest cock in young Tinseltown, with which Jeff had rogered Trina for several years before Avram came along. Avram was completely paranoid that Trina still longed for Jeff and, worse, might even have acted on her yen while Avram was away on one of his location trips, visiting Jack or Warren or Meryl.

Jeff hated Avram for making the commitment to Trina that her narcissism and selfishness had always deterred him from, his career goals notwithstanding. Jeff would gladly have fucked Trina again, but Trina wouldn't have him, especially since he had married her friend and fellow Jewish debutante Roxie, whose theater-chain-owner father's unexpected distaste for the studios further anchored poor Jeff into his hopeless corporate tedium, writing contracts that Oliver Stone said were never enough. Jeff also hated public relations whiz Ernie Le Vine, for his obsessive Francophilia, his obnoxious sycophancy, and the fact that it all worked to make him the dark horse who actually *was* having the affair with Princess Trina.

Ernie hated everyone, not least himself for having to kiss the collective studio derriere, which was the biggest butt in the universe, and for having to sing the praises of movies that stank and stars who spit on him. His worst enemy was his best friend, Jake, his onetime debating partner at U. S. Grant High in Van Nuys, the best man at his wedding, who had promised, as Ernie had, that whoever made it first would help the other. When Jake became the star of the mail room at William Morris and was thrown a life preserver from that then sinking ship by ICM, he became the Mustafa Kemal of ICM's Young Turks. Diller and Eisner both tried to recruit him as an executive, but he decided he would wait and run ICM and then take on Disney and be the next Katzenberg. Jake left poor Ernie drowning in a third-rate flackery, despite Ernie's entreaties to help him be a *real* agent, not a *press* agent. Ernie's anger had fueled his rise, up through Rogers & Cowan and PMK and now into his own very hot shop, yet he was still a flack and not what he wanted to be, which was Mike Ovitz.

They *all* wanted to be Mike Ovitz, except for Peter Greene, the brilliant lawyer everyone assumed *would* be Mike Ovitz. Peter Greene wanted to be Bookie Feinstein. He wanted to sell million-dollar scripts, not negotiate the deals for them. Peter was the star of Rex Fried's class at Harvard. He had married a Harvard girl, the daughter of a rich Boston Brahmin, and he had come back to Sinclair & Roth, L.A.'s best firm, and then into Field and Schwartz, the hottest entertainment firm. And still he wrote scripts all night. Each time he thought he had the formula, and would send it out to some big agent, though never under his own name. "A friend wrote this. Could you give him some input?" And the superagents would always call back and say, "Tell your friend to keep his day job."

Peter never could figure it out. He blamed it on the stupid readers that the big shots passed on everything that wasn't written by Robert Towne or Joe Eszterhas. Or he blamed it on his friends' own stupidity. The studio executives were either like Avram, a know-nothing nepotistic plant, or like David Bleeker. Bleeker wanted to grow up to be Ray Stark. His highest goal was to make Spielberg movies like *The Color Purple*. Raised on television, he had never even seen any movies made before *Jaws*. He wouldn't know Eisenstein from Einstein. He barely knew Hitchcock, and that only from the TV reruns.

All these friends were busy toasting Rex Fried—whom they really detested because he was a legacy, and political, and would surely be running a studio one day—when Jeff Rosenberg, the Century City lawyer who had made the Alex connection and who hated Peter Greene for being a brighter, smoother, and more successful lawyer than he himself could ever be, spotted a girl at the Tana's bar whom he knew from his days working on Wall Street.

Her name was Judy Breitling. She was 5'4", slightly mousy, and wore her brown hair tied back in a bun. Her glasses made her look secretarial, and the guys were surprised to learn that she had an MBA from Michigan and a financial-analyst job at Merrill Lynch. She had met Jeff on a case where he was doing some first-year-associate drudge work. She was still at Merrill Lynch, out in L.A. for a seminar on some obscure aspect of the aerospace industry, and meeting a girlfriend from her hometown, Pontiac, who worked at TRW, for a Hollywood evening. Alone at the bar in the crush of molls—big bleached blond hair, big silicone tits, acres of thighs—Judy seemed lost.

To be gallant, Jeff insisted Judy join his table until her girlfriend arrived. A few of the guys seemed a bit taken aback by Judy, Jake and Avram and Peter in particular. This was a *guy* night out, not the Welcome Wagon. They were fantasizing about the Alex girls to come, visions of Sean Young and Daryl Hannah, not poor Minnie Mouse. Rex whispered to his friends that they should be sports, show a little hospitality to a stranger, and, he added snidely, "remember the neediest," referring not only to Judy but to Jeff, who was unmarried, unstudly, and lucky in his friends' eyes to get *anyone* into bed. The goddesses that were soon to be arrayed before him weren't even on his radar. However, when Judy's friend never showed and Judy called her down in Torrance and found out that her Celica had broken down, Jeff's suggestion that they invite Judy back to the Beverly Hills Hotel bungalow was met with incredulity and derision.

"Are you fucked up or what?" Rex snapped at Jeff. "What's she gonna do at a bachelor party?"

"She's totally cool," Jeff said. "She knows what's going on."

"Yeah, with the world's most expensive hookers. Give me a break."

"She can't come," Peter Greene said, looking at Judy, who was waiting for the phone across the bar. "This isn't for her."

"What if she's some kinda feminist?" Avram added. "Look at her. She'll hate these hookers. Feminists hate hookers worse than they hate rapists. It's like seriously threatening."

"She's a fun girl," Jeff insisted. "She just looks uptight."

"Forget it," Jake Gewirtz shot out, in the same peremptory way he would pass on a script. "This is Rex's party."

"But I have a chance to score," Jeff said. "She likes me."

"So that's it," Ernie Le Vine said. "Jeffrey smells *le parfum d'une femme.*"

"Speak English, asshole," David Bleeker said.

"He smells pussy," Ross Chandler said.

"From *that?*" Jeff Simon, the "other" Jeff, laughed.

"Listen, guys," Jeff Rosenberg pleaded, "I may have a chance to score with her tonight. She's all alone. We had something going back in New York. Come on."

"So take her home and score, but don't bum out our party," Avram said.

"I only *organized* your fucking party," Jeff retorted. "And I'm not planning to lay out a grand for twenty seconds to pork a Sean Young lookalike. I'm not drawing a studio salary."

"Hey, keep your cork on, Jeff," Bluto Miller said.

"The girl just isn't appropriate." Peter Greene issued his verdict in his mellifluous, Solomonic lawyer's tones. "And this isn't appropriate for her."

"Let Rex decide," Bookie Feinstein said. "It's his party, and he can blackball her if he wants to."

The burden was on Rex. He looked around at his friends, who didn't seem to want this outsider in their ordered, privileged, and snobbish midst. Then he looked at Jeff Rosenberg, who had worked so hard to put the evening together, and Rex could see how much Jeff wanted this girl, though he couldn't see why. She wasn't beautiful. She wasn't powerful. She wasn't rich. She couldn't advance his career. Rex pitied Jeff for wanting her. Rex *liked* pitying Jeff. It made him feel superior.

"Fuck it," Rex decreed. "Let her come."

Drunk from scotch, Barolo, and grappa, they swaggered like an Armani army into the Polo Lounge to commune with the spirits of Zanuck and Warner, Hawks and Hayward. They ordered tureens of the house's famous guacamole, and drank margaritas. They sprawled in the green leather banquettes, calling their wives on the house phones, telling them what clean, good-guy, all-guy fun they were having, and not to wait up for them. As long as the debauch was confined to food and drink, as their wives assumed, no questions would be asked.

The one modern touch of this phase of the evening was chemical. Jake and Ernie had had a high school classmate at U. S. Grant—who, in fact, had been named "Best Dancer" in their senior yearbook—who had become a major drug dealer in Calabasas. They thus took charge of the narcotic aspect of Rex's night and brought with them a cache of cocaine, Ecstasy, and bootleg Mandrax that would add several thousand dollars to the rapidly mounting tab. They passed the Mandraxes around under the Polo Lounge tables. About half the guys took them, washing them down with tequila sunrises. The hookers were coming. They couldn't wait. They wanted to be primed.

Jeff offered Judy a Mandrax as well. She hesitated for a while. Then she smiled, a little nervously, and popped it. Jeff looked at Rex with a big grin. See, his eyes said, she's one of the guys after all. Rex was surprised the mousy MBA did such a thing. He started to pay more attention to her.

Reeling through the tropical gardens of royal palms and banana trees and night-blooming jasmine, the group arrived at their bungalow. Liz and Mike had stayed there, and Liz and Eddie, and possibly even Liz and Dick. There were at least four iced champagne buckets filled with bottles of Dom Pérignon. A VCR had been installed. Bluto Miller had brought some porno tapes, *Slippery When Wet* and *Rear Admiral* among them. There were slabs of foie gras and tins of beluga caviar and beautiful flowers none of the guys even noticed. By now they had forgotten everything, the history, the tradition, their contempt and jealousy for each other, everything except one thing.

"The chicks, man. Where are the chicks?" Bookie Feinstein wailed.

Alex's girls were supposed to have arrived at ten-thirty. It was after eleven. Nor were the strippers in evidence. All eyes focused on Jeff.

"*Cherchez les femmes*, counselor," Ernie Le Vine challenged him, and Jeff called Alex.

"This isn't exactly the fire department." Alex made light of the girls' tardiness, though she knew full well that a girl's reliability was usually inversely proportional to her pulchritude. By that measure, there was a distinct possibility that either Sarah or Liz, or both, might not show up at all. Despite the money they stood to make, there was always someone who might give them more. Or there might be a star, or a pretty boy at the car wash, or tickets to Aerosmith, or Aerosmith themselves. Their options were endless. If Alex punished them by striking them from her rolls, which was her only form of reprisal, another madam would gladly grab them. Nevertheless, these were the best boys, who said they wanted the best girls, and Sarah and Liz were ideal for this under-thirty billionaire boys' club. Rather than lose face to these prospective lifetime clients by ordering up two other girls, Alex elected to play poker. "They're on their way. The best things are worth waiting for."

The guys drank champagne, ate caviar, smoked Havana cigars, bragged about deals, and snorted coke to fill the time. Soon the first stripper arrived, to a collective hurrah. She was a 5'10" brunette named Kim, and she was wearing a black vinyl raincoat. She looked part-Mexican, but when her two impassive Korean "managers," or bodyguards, came in behind her, nobody was quite sure what she was. The two Koreans were wearing black leather jackets. The handle of a gun protruded from the waistband of one of them.

"They're fucking Yakuza," Bluto Miller whispered to Jeff. "They're gonna take us out. Where'd you get her from?"

"I told you, *L.A. Weekly*."

"It looks like *Soldier of Fortune*."

"They're just here to keep us from raping her. It's okay," Jeff reassured them. Frankly, Jeff was quite disappointed, not just by the presence of the hit men, but by Kim herself. He expected someone classier, more refined, more "appropriate." Someone like the amazing dancers he had seen at Star Strip—L.A.'s premier temple of ecdysis, just a block down La Cienega from the Beverly Center.

Star Strippers tended to be Alex-level blondes who not only didn't fuck, they didn't even speak. They were Stepford strippers, perfect and perfectly impenetrable. They'd do their routine to three rock songs. In the first, they'd doff their robe, getting down to their bra and G-string. By the end of the second, breasts would be on display, vaginas would be flashed. The third number would feature the naked dancer writhing on a towel on the stage so that each Oriental, and occasional Occidental, gentleman could have a gynecologist's-eye view of the action. Tips, usually fives and tens, would follow each round, and, finally, applause, after which the strippers would don Trashy Lingerie and serve Coke and Perrier for $7.50 a glass.

Jeff had scouted Star Strip numerous times, but had never gotten one of the girls to so much as communicate with him. Apparently, the commonest pickup line was a proposition to work a big-bucks bachelor party. No one would believe Jeff that he had a real one. Consequently, when he read the ad for "Star Strippers," and when the Etonian English voice on the phone promised him the same girls he'd seen at the club and was totally empathetic about how hard it was to recruit the girls on the premises, Jeff instantly whipped out his MasterCard and made a phone guarantee. Now he felt like a sucker.

Kim was no Star Strip girl. She was, at best, a Bare Elegance girl or a

Jet Strip girl, from those tough clubs down by the airport, or, more likely, an Oddball girl, from that even tougher joint deep in the Valley. Jeff was losing face. His peers would all be running the town soon, he thought, panicking, and he would still be their lackey lawyer, all because he had screwed up Rex's bachelor party.

Kim barely spoke to anyone. She barely smiled. Instead, she went into a bathroom to prepare her act, as her handlers set up a ghetto blaster in the living room. She came out in a black spangled evening gown, reeking of perfume like the entire ground floor of I. Magnin, and caked in makeup. The Beatles' "Baby's in Black" came on the blaster. The Koreans retreated to the kitchenette and ate caviar, as the guys settled into the couches.

"Who's the bachelor?" Kim asked, and Rex was reluctant to step forward until Ross Chandler gave him a shove.

Kim had him take off his double-breasted jacket and seated him in a chair in the middle of the living room. Rex felt like a dunce who was about to be given a lashing by his teacher. Instead, he was given a rather mechanical treat. Kim wrapped her long scarf around his head and drew him to her heaving bosom, which was so hard from its encapsulated silicone implants that for a moment Rex thought he had broken his nose. The guys—drunk, stoned, and generally fucked up—cheered, every one delighted that Rex and not he was on this firing line. Kim had Rex remove her gloves and unzip her dress, from which she wriggled to a new tune, the Stones' "You Can't Always Get What You Want."

Now Kim was down to what looked like a metallic black-and-white drum-majorette costume, if the drum majorette happened to be a dominatrix. Oblivious to the other men in the room, Kim continued her number solely for Rex's discomfited benefit. The Stones yielded to Jackie Wilson's version of "Higher and Higher," and the majorette gear gave way to a studded leather bikini. Kim was remarkably muscular, almost like a weight lifter. Her size, her enormous fake breasts, her rippling biceps and calves, gave Rex pause that she might be a female impersonator, a pause that ended when she swung one leg around Rex's head and pushed what turned out to be the cutout crotch of her bikini square in his face.

Soon Rex was dragged out of his chair and pinned to the floor between Kim's vise-like power thighs. She slammed his head to the floor time and again in what was supposed to be simulated cunnilingus but which was more like simulated Hulk Hogan. As a finale of safe yet profitable sex, she had Rex pull out a twenty-dollar bill and pass it from his mouth into the lips of her waiting, grasping vagina. Again the boys cheered, though when Kim canvassed the room for other adventurous tippers, there were none.

Even though another stripper was due to arrive shortly, the entire group might have packed it in in despair had the phone not rung at the crucial second of Young Hollywood's lowest ebb. It was Sarah calling on her car phone from Newport Beach. She gave some convoluted apology about a volleyball tournament, then promised that she was en route to pick up Liz in Venice and would be "all theirs" within the hour. "You've gotta wait," she said. "We've heard all about you. You guys sound like a trip." There was division in the ranks, but as several of the guys got on the phone to chat with Sarah, the double entendres started flying ("I'm coming as fast as I can," Sarah promised; "so will you"), and the heat began to rise again. What turned the tide, and the guys on, the most was that Sarah had a car phone. "A cellular hooker," Bookie Feinstein observed. "She must be hot."

In the end, only five of the golden boys went home to their wives, three of whom were pregnant and impatient. This left the hard core, which crowded around the giant-screen Sony to watch the hard-core *Rear Admiral* and shout at the assorted couplings on the screen as if this were a Laker game. They were all relieved to see the last of Kim and the Yakuza, none so much as poor Rex, who sprawled in a chair in the far corner of the room receiving consolation from Judy, who he was amazed hadn't left in disgust.

"Your poor head," she said, casually stroking his slightly balding pate. "She could have killed you."

"You must think we're a bunch of pigs," Rex said.

"Naw. You're just guys. I've got brothers."

"You're a good sport. I'm sorry your friend got messed up. You could've been out on the town with Rob Lowe and Charlie Sheen or someone instead of here with all these perverts."

"This is an experience," Judy said.

Rex looked over at Jeff, in the crowd by the television. Why wasn't he paying more attention to his "date"? He was being a good guy, a hail-fellow-well-met. But how was he expecting to score with Judy later after letting her see him watching *Rear Admiral*? Maybe he didn't even want to score. Rex looked at Judy again. She was little and mousy and you'd never call her sexy, but after Kim she was starting to look better. Maybe it was the hour, maybe the drugs. Rex leaned over and took off her glasses.

"What do you wear those for?" Rex asked, almost amazed at the transformation. She had big blue eyes with thick lashes.

"To see. I lost one of my contact lenses today, and I didn't bring a spare."

"Do you ever wear your hair down?"

"Sometimes."

"Could I see it?"

"Sure." Judy undid the bun and shook her hair out. It was rich and thick and auburn.

"God, you're hot," Rex said, and meant it.

"Hot? Me?"

"Well, all-American. Like Grace Kelly."

"That's the opposite of hot."

"If you're Jewish, it's the hottest thing you can be," Rex said. He recalled the old English Leather ads where the schoolmarm with thick glasses let her hair down and took her specs off and turned into a bombshell. He told Judy about them, but she was too young to remember. Still, she was completely flattered. "How come you're in hiding?" he asked.

"I'm a banker. I have to look responsible."

" 'Call me irresponsible,' " Rex crooned off-key. "Kill the glasses, go with the hair, you'll be running the place."

Judy giggled. "You think I'm too straight, don't you?"

And all of a sudden, Rex was overcome with a desire for her. He was awash with "curiosity" that was mutating into lust.

Rex got Judy to talk about her wholesome midwestern *Annie Hall* upbringing, her father who was in product safety at General Motors, her housewife mother, her jock brothers, one a Chicago commodities broker, the other, the wild one, a Milwaukee disc jockey. She talked about being "average" in high school and going to Ann Arbor and being in a sorority and now being a Columbus Avenue yuppie in the Big Apple. He asked her if she was in love, and she said she wasn't. Then she asked him if *he* was in love, and he was floored by the question.

"What do you mean? I'm getting married next week."

"I almost got married once, after college, back in Michigan, when I was working in Detroit. But I lost my nerve at the last minute."

"How come?" Rex asked.

Judy paused. "We were on different wavelengths. He was a radiologist . . ." She paused again. "You really want to know the truth?"

"Yeah. Sure."

She waited. She blushed again. "Bad sex," she said.

"Oh" was all Rex could say. The comment made him extremely uncomfortable, because he had never really reflected on the kind of sex he and Sindee had. It was . . . all right, he supposed. What it was was Hollywood sex. What turned him on about Sindee Cohen was not her looks or what she was like in bed. What turned him on was her drive to power and that she had been the mistress, as part of this drive, of two powerful older moguls. When Rex Fried was in bed with Sindee, he wasn't fucking her. He was fucking the moguls. That got him off. He wasn't sure *what* good sex was. And he stared at Judy, this low-key embodiment of family values, and wanted to find out.

Rex looked over at Jeff, who was still engrossed in *Rear Admiral*. "I'm going to go into the bedroom to go to the bathroom. Would you go into the kitchen first and then meet me in there?"

"Why?"

"I want to tell you something, but I'm a little self-conscious."

"You can tell me here. Nobody's paying any attention."

"Do me this favor. Okay?"

In the bedroom, with the door locked, Rex told Judy that he really wanted to make love to her. Judy seemed totally shocked and surprised, though by no means insulted. "But you've got two call girls on the way," Judy said.

"I don't care. I want you," Rex said, and began kissing her; she kissed him back. He felt guilty. For a second. He fumblingly, nervously undressed her. He was amazed by her sexy black garter belt. He was more amazed by her body.

Judy, the little nothing, had one of the most wonderful bodies Rex had ever dreamed of, much less seen. It was an androgynous body, with tiny upturned breasts and a narrow, boyish frame. It was a teen's body, pubescent. It was also an Olympian's body, with every muscle beautifully defined, ready for action, built for speed. It was definitely not the body of a financial analyst. "Incredible" was all Rex could say.

They kept kissing. Judy undressed Rex, without a word, no reference to Jeff, no reference to Rex's marriage. Rex saw it as a pure animal thing. Why hadn't he always been lucky like this? If he had, maybe he wouldn't even be getting married. Judy was a tigress in bed. She sucked Rex's nipples in a way that sent electric jolts straight to his penis, and just as he was about to come—he had no control whatsoever at this point—she writhed down his chest and put his cock in her mouth and let him erupt inside it. When he was hard again, for the grand finale, she took him and plunged him inside her, again without a rubber. Even with Sindee, Rex used a rubber. He was a terrible hypochondriac with a special phobia about venereal diseases. Ever since the advent of AIDS, he had always used rubbers; by now, he had forgotten what it was like without one. Here he felt the real thing again: It was magical, voluptuous, overwhelming. He didn't give a second's thought to risk. Judy was the cleanest, healthiest girl he'd ever seen. Worth dying for, but the only thing that was killing him was that he was getting married and he'd never be able to do this again, and all he really wanted to do was take this creature of infinite surprise and run away with her to some lost tropical isle. Judy moved rhythmically around Rex, squeezing him with her vaginal muscles, arching her back, letting him see her go up and down on him. It was a juggernaut, it was a carnival ride, and in a few seconds, it was all over.

Rex believed that he and Judy could ease back into the party without being noticed. If anybody asked, hey, they were just talking, having a quiet conversation. With her glasses and her bun and her business suit, nobody would ever suspect, just as Rex had not, that Judy was erotic dynamite. Rex grinned to himself. He had pulled a fast one. His only concern was what he was going to do with Alex's girls, if they bothered to show up. Whatever, he was sure he could rise to the occasion. Given the roll he was on, they would probably beg him for it, have multiple orgasms, and waive their fee. He could get anyone. He was hot. He was a sexual superman.

Expecting to find the guys sweatily glued to the television and the roiling seas of *Rear Admiral*, Rex opened the bedroom door to a wall of leering faces, a bottle of champagne, and a chorus of bravos. Not only were they all on to him, they had also been out in the bushes watching his Casanova display through the bedroom window, whose curtains, he noticed as he glanced behind him, had not been fully closed. At this point, however, Rex was so full of himself that he wasn't even embarrassed. He was proud of his performance, seducing the seemingly unseducible. He graciously accepted his buddies' accolades about his prowess. Rex loved the way the guys stared awestruck at Judy. He was gloating. They wanted her, but only he had had her. He was truly Bachelor Number One.

And then he linked eyes with Jeff Rosenberg. Poor Jeff Rosenberg. The poor cuckold. The poor lawyer. The poor schlepper whose date Rex had just stolen out from under him. Rex wasn't exactly known for his conscience—he loved screwing lawyers, and writers, and directors, but never stars, because he respected stars. Yet he did feel bad for Jeff. Maybe he'd help him get out of his sweatshop, into a studio. Jeff would never be a threat to Rex's plans to run the town. Rex could help him without hurting himself. Rex called Jeff aside.

"Hey, pal, I hope you're not too pissed off."

"Well," Jeff said.

"Jeff, face it," Rex said, swigging Dom from the bottle. "It's a chemical thing. She saw me, she wanted me, she fucked me. You don't pick women. Women pick you. I don't mean to say I'm *better* than you. You're just maybe not her type. I was her type. She was just into me. Totally into me. What the fuck can I say?"

"Say thank you."

"Huh?"

"Well, old sport," Jeff said, "she was incredible and she was into you because I paid her five hundred dollars to be incredibly into you. Congratulations, guy." Jeff shook Rex's hand. His face broke into the biggest smile. He had pulled it off.

"What are you talking about?" Rex sputtered.

Jeff knew it was Rex's party, but he still couldn't resist the sadism that underlay the matrix of these Hollywood friendships. "Judy's a hooker. We paid her."

Rex cast his eyes across the room. Judy, sedate little Judy, was surrounded by the guys. "Bullshit. She's an analyst. Fuck you, Jeff."

"She's an analyst, yeah. But not at Merrill Lynch. She lives out here, right on Curson and Franklin. And she moonlights as a call girl. I got her through Danny Latigan at Turner. He has her come out to the Colony and do him and his wife every other weekend."

"No. . . . No. I thought you were getting the girls from Alex."

"I am. They're coming. But we wanted to surprise you. You asshole."

"You're not kidding," Rex said. His ego became a pricked balloon. "I fucked a hooker." And then it dawned on him. "Fuck! Shit! I fucked her without a rubber. I fucked a hooker without a rubber. I'm fucking dead. I've got fucking AIDS." Rex went into a hypochondriacal frenzy. He wanted to kill Jeff. He wanted to kill Judy. He wanted to kill them all. Because here it was: His dearest friends had conspired to give him AIDS.

He was a dead man. He knew it. But instead of killing anyone, Rex ran into the bathroom and took a scalding, soapy shower, and used the bathroom phone to call a twenty-four-hour health-information hot line in Atlanta.

Unbeknownst to him, Rex wasn't the only one there who was upset by Judy's presence. The reason Jake Gewirtz, Avram Gund, and Peter Greene were all so reluctant to have Judy at the party was that each of them was her client, and each of them thought that Judy was his own private reserve and that he was the only man in elite Young Hollywood who had access to her special favors. Each of them felt betrayed by Judy. At the same time, watching her fuck their friend Rex made them want to possess her even more. Judy was all surprises. There was so much about her they didn't know. What was it about her that Jake, who dated starlets, and Avram, who had wed an heiress, and Peter, who had a perfect aristocrat wife, would risk the order and symmetry of their dreamy universes to steal away for an hour or two with Judy, like clockwork, every week? What was the addiction? And who else had it?

This most unlikely of call girls had stumbled into the oldest profession because she felt trapped in the most boring one—accounting. Her upbringing was pure apple-pie Americana in suburban St. Paul, where her father worked as a midlevel executive for Land O Lakes butter. Judy was an amazing athlete, a high-school champion swimmer, a compulsive runner. She got her MBA and then went to work for Price Waterhouse. When they offered her a transfer to Los Angeles, she jumped at the chance.

It took the high relief of Hollywood to show Judy how dull her existence was. She was earning fifty thousand dollars a year, which seemed like the big time until she tried to buy a new car, live in a nice Brentwood apartment, buy clothes, and go out at night. Judy was working to live, not living to work, but the life her work provided wasn't worth the bleary-eyed numbness it induced.

By the time Judy had reached Los Angeles, at age twenty-five, she had slept with a grand total of two men. One was her high-school sweetheart, who had broken her heart when he left her after college to go to Harvard

Business School and other points east. The other man was her father. She didn't like to think about that. It happened one summer at their lakeside vacation home, when Judy was sixteen and still a virgin, and her elementary-schoolteacher mother had gone to New York City to take a course at Columbia University Teachers College. It started out as a birds-and-bees discussion, and it became more show-and-tell, and her father was gentle, and, and, and . . . Judy wrote it all off, and at least she lost her virginity to someone who didn't dump her, and she had wanted to get it out of the way.

In any event, Judy was no easy mark. A lot of guys hit on her at Façade and Tramp, where she went with girls from the office, and she always said no, especially since most of these guys were either Persian or Israeli pretending to be French, and were clichés of sleaziness. One of these guys, a Tel Aviv–born electronics chain owner, was persistent. Night after night, week after week, he sent Judy champagne, until she finally started talking to him. When she wouldn't go for him because of his looks and charm, he offered to take her to L'Orangerie and L'Ermitage, the two most expensive French restaurants in the city. When that wouldn't get her into bed, he offered her drugs. And when that didn't work, he offered her money. He offered to give her three hundred dollars, which he told her was what he paid top call girls. That he bragged about using call girls was not exactly an aphrodisiac to an all-American girl from St. Paul, but the three hundred dollars, on top of the lobster and champagne, was not without a certain allure. Because she had gotten to know him, the Israeli didn't seem at all menacing or sinister, just an infantile playboy wanna-be, a Tel Aviv version of the Wild and Crazy Guys Steve Martin and Bill Murray played on *Saturday Night Live*. Furthermore, Judy lived in the very real world of numbers; she could see exactly how that three hundred added up—and what it could do for her at the Beverly Center. Plus, and this was a very big plus to her, it was tax free.

The Israeli was the beginning. It was quick and clean and easy, and when he offered to introduce Judy to his Beverly Hills lawyer, for the same deal, Judy wasn't insulted at all, because she was anything but in love with the Israeli. And so the network began. The Beverly Hills lawyer was a Harvard man who introduced her to Peter Greene. Avram Gund found her through another Israeli. And Jake Gewirtz met Judy through his Israeli personal trainer. And soon, Judy was seeing the toast of Young Hollywood. And loving it. She was amazed that all these happily married, exemplary-lived young men were paying for extramarital sex. Israeli sleaze bags, maybe. But *these* guys?

Judy was getting off on the money, getting off on the glamour, and getting off on the sex. That amazed her the most. She loved the sex. The Hollywood golden boys were genuinely thrilled to see her, and they came to see her again and again. Because she never used a madam—never even met one—Judy was insulated from the hard commerce of prostitution. Her business, and she didn't see it as one, was all word of mouth. Each "client" was a lover, each hour a mini-affair. Judy, who had never gone to a psychiatrist, somehow protected herself emotionally by not getting hung up on these clients, though each of them was invariably getting hung up on her.

Where Judy wasn't protecting herself was physically. With her Hollywood princes, as with Rex Fried tonight, she would give them that ultimate thrill of not wearing a rubber. Judy wanted to please them, just as she had wanted to please her father. This cautious woman of numbers was throwing caution to the winds. That these boys were straight and clean and innocent was her logic, if she took the time to rationalize. They were as safe as a man could be. She made the Israelis suit up for each encounter, but not her princes, which got them addicted to her all the more. She wasn't their whore; she was their mini-mistress. His *crise de santé* notwithstanding, Rex Fried would join her list, right after his honeymoon. Where princes led, kings would follow: the bosses, the moguls, the stars. She was making two thousand dollars a week, tax free. And she had been doing it for money barely one year. Her word of mouth was so strong that the sky was the limit. But as with any small business that succeeded, there was always the threat of a hostile takeover. Right now Judy was a private pleasure; she had no interest in being a public vice. Yet as the word got out—as it inevitably would after this bachelor party—the madams would find out about her. The call-girl business, as disorganized as it was, had certain union aspects. The others would want Judy to join them, and if she refused, as she surely would, her enjoyable life was going to get extremely complicated.

CHAPTER SIX

CREATURE

I took what should have been a reform school and turned it into a finishing school. In many ways I was a headmistress (no pun intended), though not as saintly as Mr. Chips or Robin Williams in *Dead Poets Society*, crossed with a drill sergeant, though not *quite* as tough as Lou Gossett, Jr., in *An Officer and a Gentleman*. Face it, the kind of girl who wants to become a hooker is a bad girl. She isn't Pollyanna. These girls were lazy and greedy and, above all, wanted something for nothing. They had all the selfish entitlement of homecoming queens and head cheerleaders, which most of them had been: I'm gorgeous, I don't have to do anything else, everyone wants to fuck me, and if you want me, you've *really* got to perform or pay up. Big-time. Being here in L.A., the world capital of self-absorption and narcissism, made them even worse than if they had stayed home in Sioux City. At least there, their parents would have made them go to church.

Speaking of parents, way over three quarters of these girls had been molested as kids by their fathers, or uncles, or someone. And when they hit their teens, they were molested again, and hit on by everyone else. I guess when you're beautiful, that's one of the prices you pay. No wonder so many of the girls hated men and were lesbians. Their big fantasy was to bite off a guy's penis while they were giving him a blow job. Sweet. And the drugs. Did they fuck for coke, or did they coke to fuck? What a vicious circle. Most of them said they needed the drugs to anesthetize themselves so they could do sex for money, yet the main reason a lot of them became hookers was because they wanted money for drugs. How they loved that coke. Because when they were on coke, they really believed that they were going to be stars, huge stars, or rich wives, or whatever they wanted to be.

What I tried to do was make them see that they could be what they wanted to be *without* the coke. A beautiful woman has every option in the world. *If* she's smart. Looks aren't the only thing. They're *everything*. I don't like it, either, but that's a fact of life, especially in Hollywood. Madame Claude always said she had three criteria: looks, brains, and skill in bed. Two out of three were good enough for her to justify taking on a girl. I had only one criterion. Brains in Hollywood? Give me a break. This was the Fertile Crescent of dumb blondes. How many guys whack off thinking about Meryl Streep? My men *loved* dumb. If they wanted Phi Beta Kappas, they'd go to Harvard Square. Even my geniuses had to play dumb. Jayne Mansfield supposedly had a 160 I.Q., and look at her breathless idiocy. As for good in bed, my men always preferred a "looker" to a "worker." Even if the girls were frigid bitches who gave more reluctant head than their wives, my men didn't care, as long as the girls were stunning. They'd get off on their looks. In Southern California, everyone judges solely on appearances. That's why everyone goes bankrupt having the flashiest house, and the flashiest car, and the flashiest call girls. I didn't create the place. I just played by the rules out here. Paris it is not.

I had the most gorgeous girls you could find anywhere. The best. With the worst characters. That's why I called them creatures. They were absolute monsters, but they were beautiful monsters. Even after I cleaned them up, taught them how to dress and talk, made ladies out of them, and not just ladies of the evening, most of them betrayed me, dumped me, tried to cheat me. Gratitude is not a call girl's long suit.

I'd like to say the nice girls were the ones who made it, and the bad ones got what they deserved, but I can't. Often the bad ones got what the nice ones deserved. The ones who ended up stars or Hollywood wives or Fifth Avenue socialites were usually more vicious and deceitful than the rest. What made the difference is probably that they used less coke and kept their eyes on the prize and used their pussy very strategically. The keys were maintenance and withholding. Maintenance, maintenance, maintenance, I'd scream at the girls. Being beautiful was a full-time job, and if you wanted to make a future just on your looks you had to work like a dog to keep them up. And then I had to teach them how to keep a guy longing for them, to never give him enough, to keep him wanting. It sounds like a big game, and it is, but it was certainly worth winning. In my Hooker Academy, I should have awarded an MM degree, Master of Manipulation.

Speaking of manipulation, one of the greatest creatures I ever created turned out to be my biggest nightmare, my own Lady Frankenstein. My favorite little Beverly Hills non-Jewish Jewish Princess, Lissa Trapp, paid me the ultimate compliment: She wanted to be me. A lot of my creatures thought being a madam was easy. All these girls thought they needed was a few pretty friends and a telephone. They were quickly disabused of that notion. Being a madam is a twenty-four-hour-a-day job. It's one part p.r. firm, another part modeling agency, and the biggest part psycho ward. Very few people can take it for very long.

With Lissa Trapp, it was a matter of greed conquers all. I never met a girl who worshiped money the way she did. She was so greedy that being a call girl, even one who would see five clients a day, wasn't enough. She wanted to be a hundred call girls; that's why she thought being a madam was the dream job for her. Now, Lissa wanting to be me might have been flattering. The problem was, *she* wanted to be me so much she didn't want *me* to be me anymore. And that was where the problem began.

Lissa Trapp had been in New York only once, a few years back, with her parents. All she remembered was that they had stayed at the Warwick, which was famous because the Beatles had stayed there on their first American visit, but which had seen better days. That had been a let-down, as had the steak at Christ Cella her father had raved about; it was of little interest to the bulimic teenager, who threw up the lobster they gave her. She didn't like *Cats* much better. The only thing she liked was the subways, which seemed dangerous and exciting.

This trip was different. She had ordered a Mercedes stretch limo to take her to the Carlyle, where she had reserved her own suite, so there would be no problem of getting past suspicious hall porters and desk men. As soon as she arrived, Lissa, who read *Vogue* religiously, went to Bergdorf's to get her hair done, and then on a shopping spree up Madison: a dress at Valentino, Montenapoleone for lingerie, and Boyd's for makeup. All the bills, well into the thousands within hours, were courtesy of Nicky Kroll, or, rather, the hot AmEx and Visa cards he gave Lissa and which he promised her would not be caught on to until she was safely back in Los Angeles.

The first night she was there, Sir John didn't come back to his room until three o'clock in the morning. Even with her stash of coke, Lissa was too jet-lagged and exhausted from shopping to make her move. She knew she would have one more day before Alex could find anyone to beat her to it.

The next evening, Sir John went to dinner at Le Cirque with real estate tycoon Mort Zuckerman and Lazard's Felix Rohatyn. He was back at the Carlyle before midnight. Lissa got the information from a horny junior concierge who believed Lissa when she said she had something to give Sir John.

"Room service."

Sir John, wearing his Frette robe, hadn't ordered anything, but the sexy, throaty promise in the female voice on the other side of the door made him curious to find out. Lissa, a sophisticated vision in black, was there with a large, elaborately wrapped gift box.

"Greetings from Alex," Lissa said, using the password to get in the door. Sir John was completely confused.

"She didn't tell me—"

"Surprise," Lissa cut him off.

"She sent you all the way from Los Angeles?" the towering Englishman sputtered.

"Where do I look like I came from?"

"No, no, quite right. Do have a seat. Drink?" He led her into his living room.

"Champagne," Lissa said. "But only if you are."

"I've got my brandy," Sir John said, and opened a bottle of Cristal from the mini-bar. "I'm a bit loath to say this, but I'm afraid Alex has gotten her signals crossed. Poor thing."

"Tell me," Lissa said, prepared for this eventuality.

"You're exactly what I *don't* want." Sir John was known as the rudest man in the City. "I ask for Eaton Square and she sent me Golders Green," he said under his breath.

"What's that?" Lissa heard him, but didn't get the references.

"I wanted a California girl. You're very New York."

Lissa was crushed. She had worked so hard to look glamorous, sophisticated, Fifth Avenue. And here was Sir John telling her, in effect, that she was straight out of Brooklyn. Lissa tried to defend herself: "I'm totally California. Native."

"Darling, it just won't do." Sir John went into his bedroom and got his wallet. He took out ten hundreds and offered them to Lissa. "I assume Alex got the airfare. I'll settle with her on that."

"It's really true what they say about you," Lissa said, turning away the money.

"What's that?"

"That you're an anti-Semite."

Sir John laughed. "Just ask Henry Kissinger. Are you Jewish? I would've guessed Italian."

Lissa was doubly insulted. "Have you ever fucked a Jewish girl?"

Sir John cogitated. "As a matter of fact, I can't recall. So that's worse, isn't it, a sexist anti-Semite? Oh well, when you're rich you can be as dreadful as you wish." He offered her the thousand again. "I've got a long day tomorrow."

"I can't believe you'd walk away from the hottest fuck of your life."

"That's precisely the point, my poor young lady. I don't want a hot fuck, I want a *cold* one. That's why I asked for what I did."

"Just try me." Lissa reached for Sir John's robe. He held her at bay, and began pushing her toward the door.

Lissa played her trump. "Wait till I tell Gwaine."

Sir John stopped short. "You know Gwaine?"

"I see Gwaine. He adores me. He sucks my toes. He licks out my ass. And you won't even touch me. Betsy said you were gay, but I don't want to believe that."

"You don't know Gwaine."

"Call him. I do him *and* Betsy. But I guess they're open-minded. They *like* me." Lissa was doing a high-wire act. She had never met Sir Gwaine Byrne, or his new wife, Betsy Martin. But she remembered every word Alex said and knew that Sir Gwaine was Sir John's archrival and that Sir John coveted Betsy. Jealousy, Lissa hoped, was the most powerful aphrodisiac of all.

"At this early stage, I can't imagine Gwaine needing marital aids."

"Believe what you want," Lissa said with a shrug. "At least open your gift before I go." She handed him the big red box.

Sir John looked more closely at her. The invocation of his adversary had indeed piqued his curiosity. Lissa sat on the couch and stretched out her long legs. Sir John stared at her. "Open it," she said.

Sir John cut his eyes from her and undid the ribbon. He removed the top. His eyes widened. He smiled, maybe not as big a smile as Howard Carter's when he opened King Tut's tomb, but big. He pulled out one by one a beautiful white garter belt, white silk stockings, a huge white bra, a peignoir—all delicate frilly things, but in a giant size. Again, Lissa had hung on Alex's every word. She knew Sir John's fetish, and she had told

Nicky, who had acquired Sir John's trousseau from a star back for the L.A. Raiders.

Sir John turned to Lissa with a huge grin and an even bigger erection that had snaked its way between the folds of his robe. Lissa let her Valentino dress ride up her thighs, so high that Sir John could see that she was wearing no panties under her expensive garter belt. She licked her index finger, slowly and deliberately, then she began to masturbate with it. Sir John walked over to her, his arms filled with his mammoth lingerie. He sat down next to her on the couch. Lissa offered him her wet index finger. Sir John sucked on it, then let go.

"Do forgive me," he said softly.

Lissa took the Frette robe off Sir John's bearish shoulders and held the super-bra up to his powerful chest. "Now let's get creative."

Lissa spent a week at the Carlyle, "getting creative" not only with Sir John but with several of his close friends, wizards of Wall Street. She came back to Los Angeles twenty thousand dollars richer, thinking she could pull a fast one on Alex by giving her the four thousand for her cut on Sir John and never disclosing the other men she had seen through him.

Alex, on whom Brooke Kuhn had completely flaked out, never making good on Courtney Van Ness, was relieved that Lissa had saved the day with Sir John. On the other hand, she was furious that Lissa had gone behind her back to do it.

"You would never have sent me," Lissa defended herself.

"You're absolutely right," Alex agreed. "You're too uncouth."

"It worked. He came from nowhere. I came from nowhere. He could relate."

Lissa, given her rousing triumph with Sir John, was drunk with her own possibilities. She wanted to be Madam 90210. To do so, however, would require getting Alex's customers. To get Alex's customers, Lissa could compete on price, or quality, or service. The problem was that

Alex's customers weren't particularly price-sensitive. It was hard to top Alex's quality. And no one gave better, more caring, and personalized service than Alex. Lissa's other route was to get new girls of Alex quality, which in Los Angeles, with its constant turnover of cinema hopefuls, was always a possibility, or to steal Alex's girls. In this latter area, price cutting held a distinct allure. If Lissa could offer these girls Alex-level clients at, say, a 20 percent madam's cut, she might get them to switch to her. Still, it was a vicious circle: You had to have the clients to get the girls, and you had to have the girls to get the clients.

In any coup, there was the threat of reprisal. As sweet and motherly as Alex seemed, Lissa had heard rumors that Alex could be as ruthless as any Mafia don whose turf was being invaded. How else had she ruled the most competitive sex market in the world for decades? Lissa put aside thoughts of winding up in pieces in a Dumpster or washing up onshore in Malibu with a broken neck and her tongue ripped out as a warning to any other potential madam to the stars. No, Lissa had Nicky, the ultimate protector. She also sincerely believed that Alex loved her so much that Lissa could always play the wayward-child act and be forgiven. Convinced she could get away with anything, Lissa set out to see how far she could go.

Even as Lissa was weaving her web, Alex continued to send her out. Lissa had a way with insecure Jewish superstars; she seemed like the perfect princess who had rejected them in high school. Theirs was the sexual revenge of success. To this end, Alex sent Lissa to Jonah Belasco, an intense diminutive superstar who was a West Coast version of Harris Fox. Jonah had grown up comfortably in Brentwood and gone to Uni High. As hyper as Harris, his only real angst concerned being second choice for all the roles Harris Fox turned down. Otherwise, Jonah Belasco was thrilled to be a movie idol and enough of a native West Angeleno to appreciate his access to Madam Alex as a token of his success, a Bar Mitzvah of stardom. Jonah scheduled Alex's girls as nonchalantly as he would a workout or a massage or a chart reading.

He would fuck them in his office in the famous Writers and Artists Building on Rodeo and Little Santa Monica, down the hall from Billy

Wilder's. To the outside world, Jonah's office in this 1940s building, without a secretary, showed what an artist he was. He was there to work on scripts, prepare his directing debut. What it really was was an escape from his wife and family and, most important, a place to see call girls.

"You know, I think you're better than Harris Fox," Lissa told him as they were dressing after a quick in-and-out on an ancient leather couch that had belonged to Nathanael West when he wrote *The Day of the Locust.*

"Then how come he has two Oscars and I've got zip?" Jonah asked.

"Not as an actor." Lissa stopped herself. "Actually, I loved you in *Day of Atonement.* You should have gotten something for that. I meant as a fuck." Lissa was breaking Alex's cardinal rule: Never reveal one client to another. Then again, she wasn't playing by Alex's rules anymore. She was in revolt, and there was a method to her indiscretion. She had lied to Sir John about Sir Gwaine. Now she was telling the truth, all to the same end.

"Harris Fox? You see Harris Fox?" Jonah's fascination—no, obsession—with Harris Fox transcended any anxiety of Jonah's that Lissa might tell Harris Fox that Jonah was a john. "Harris Fox uses hookers?"

"Lots," Lissa said.

"God, he's sick," Jonah said. There was a total, myopic double standard here. Jonah could see all the whores he wanted; his idol could not. "All that bullshit with his professor wife. He really goes to call girls?"

"Endlessly. He's a terrible fuck. I try to teach him, but . . . Well, forget it. You get the Oscar in my book. He gets the King Oscar." Lissa made a gesture with her thumb and forefinger to indicate how large—that is, small—Harris's equipment was. "He's like a baby sardine."

"I love it," Jonah said. "That is so pathetic. Mr. New York highbrow intellectual."

"Just another horny guy," Lissa said.

"Who else do you see?" Jonah went to his wallet to be sure he had another three hundred. He wanted Lissa to stay longer. He needed the reassurance that he wasn't alone in his use of call girls, and finally he had found someone who would break the Alex vow of silence. He was getting off as much on the voyeuristic gossip as he did on the sex. Lissa, in one fell indiscretion, had transformed herself from Jonah's whore into his confidante. She instantly saw that her biggest advantage over Alex as a madam would be that Lissa was out in the field, fucking the clients as Alex never had, never would, never could.

Lissa needed more and more clients, and Alex, either unsuspecting or indifferent to the threat to her business that Lissa wanted to be, kept playing into Lissa's hands. Lissa's next date was Bradley Diamond, the president of one of the major studios and a member of Hollywood's most exclusive club, the Yes Club of the big men in town who could green-light a motion picture. In an industry of rival baronies where each studio was its own fiefdom, Bradley Diamond was a king. And Madam Alex was his sexual Richelieu, his Mazarin. She always had something new and special for him. With his serious money and lawyerly mien, Bradley seemed all business, hardly the type to be a call-girl addict. But the intense pressures of his job and the knowledge that one flop, one *Ishtar*, one *Heaven's Gate*, and his head would roll faster than Marie Antoinette's, made him as horny as he was powerful, in dire need of explosive relief.

As a top entertainment lawyer, Bradley had represented the biggest stars. Then he was a seller. Now he had been hired onto the other side; now he was a buyer and all he thought about was buying two things, packages and pussy. The packages came from CAA. The pussy came from Alex.

Because of Bradley's high profile and picture-postcard wife and three children, the pussy had to be discreet. That's why Bradley eschewed the studio-proffered Mercedes and driver and drove his own Honda. That's why Bradley eschewed Armani and stuck with Brooks Brothers. A regular guy, people described him. Unpretentious, down-home, *haimish*. All that hominess gave Bradley the anonymous fifteen minutes he could blame on the traffic on the Ventura Freeway to detour into the Lazy Days Motel on Riverside.

Lissa was dressed in a very short, very tight Lycra dress, panty hose and no panties, and very high heels. The outfit wasn't odd. That she was standing on a coffee table was.

"Hi. I'm Bradley," the chief said as he locked the motel door behind him. "This place is like the Bates Motel. Sorry about that."

"What's the Bates Motel?" Lissa asked.

"The one in *Psycho*," Bradley said, and if Lissa hadn't known for certain that this was one of the lords of the cinema, she would have started sweating.

"You've got great legs," Bradley swooned, as he took off his thick glasses and gray suit jacket. "Excellent." He went right at them, saying nothing else, lifting her dress and munching right through her panty hose. She braced herself on the wall behind the table to avoid falling over. Bradley was really going at it, gnawing in a frenzy, beaver to beaver.

"Gentlemen prefer Hanes," Lissa quipped when he had finished. Bradley was too excited to get the joke. He fell back onto the bed, under a hideous dime-store oil of a Parisian waif. Lissa took off her dress. She threw away the shredded panty hose. She unzipped Bradley's trousers.

"Leave them on," Bradley said. "No time."

So Lissa took his erect penis and deep-throated it maybe five strokes, and he erupted. Studio head, she thought.

Any other call girl would have stopped there, because this was all Bradley Diamond ever wanted. It was a quick and easy five hundred dollars. Call girls rarely went above and beyond; to them, less was always more. But Lissa wasn't turning a trick. She was building a future. So as Bradley lolled in post-orgasmic bliss, she whipped down the Brooks trousers he didn't have time to take off, stuck her fingers into his anus, and gave him her trademark prostate massage, followed by a rim job that made him come in seconds. He was in a daze. He had never felt anything like it.

"I've never had *that* before," sighed the rumpled, academic former attorney. He had come twice in minutes; normally it was once a week. He made an immediate appointment to see Lissa again, three days later, en route to a lecture he was to give at a UCLA Film School seminar on European co-productions. Lissa added another convert to her list. Also, knowing the peccadilloes of one of the most pivotal men in the business gave her a sense of enormous leverage. Hollywood was not normally a town where knowledge was power. But Lissa's knowledge of Bradley's dark side gave her a power, a power to threaten and destroy, that, if she amassed enough of it, could make her a one-woman Doomsday Machine. Bradley assumed he was operating under Alex's protection, her guarantee of secrecy. He assumed too much. With each triumphant sexual encounter, Lissa Trapp was turning herself into a sexual Lethal Weapon.

Alex, still unaware of Lissa's evolving plan, fixed her up with movie stars. She also fixed her up with rock stars. Lissa met Ho Chih, a half-black, half-Vietnamese onetime abandoned child of an American G.I. in Saigon. Ho Chih, whose album *Atomic Blonde* went double platinum and whose life story was in development as a fifty-million-dollar Oliver Stone rock epic, lived in a style that rivaled Kublai Khan's, a secrecy that rivaled Phil Spector's, and a hypochondria and paranoia that rivaled Howard Hughes's.

"We can really fuck him," Lissa gloated to Nicky when Alex arranged the date. "What do you think the *Enquirer* will pay us?"

"What about *Vanity Fair?*" Nicky insisted, always pushing Lissa to think classier.

All their calculations were for naught. When Lissa arrived at Ho Chih's Mulholland Xanadu, his resident lawyer, in a pinstripe suit, met Lissa with a release in hand. Alex had told her to bring a copy of her most recent AIDS test; she never told her about the release, which warranted that if Lissa ever mentioned her encounter with Ho Chih to the press, or anyone else, she could be sued for more money than *Rolling Stone* could claim as its gross asset value.

For all these precautions, Lissa was surprised that Ho Chih never bothered to have sex with her. He didn't even touch her. Sitting in his mandarin robes, stroking his white Siamese cat, on a throne in the bedroom of his pagoda-like home, Ho Chih had arranged a twosome for Lissa with a statuesque black girl who turned out to be a transvestite with a massive cock that he insisted on trying to ram up Lissa's posterior.

"No way," Lissa shrieked. "My back door is closed to that thing."

"Racist cunt," the black switch-hitter snarled, pinning Lissa to the bed and choking her until she was so spent he rolled her over and tried to ram her again.

"Black bastard," Lissa shrieked, clawing his face. Blood dripped over Ho Chih's white satin sheets.

The little rock star had sat impassive for the entire bout. He never reached under his robes, never seemed to masturbate, never said anything. But when the fighting broke out, he began to smile.

Lissa went wild, pummeling, clawing, and kicking the transvestite, ripping at his/her balls, and then rushing at Ho Chih in a rage.

"You sick little gook fuck," Lissa assailed him. "I'm gonna rip your cock off. If you've got one."

Ho Chih's bodyguard intercepted Lissa before she could reach him. Locking her in a brutal vise, he carried her out of the bedroom. Her last sight was of Ho Chih walking over to the transvestite, who was writhing in agony on the bed. Lissa thought she saw Ho Chih taking off his robe, but she was too rattled to be sure. The lawyer, who waited for her at the exit, gave her a thousand dollars for her trouble.

"It's like a human cockfight," Lissa said.

"As it were," the lawyer replied.

"Is that what sick rich people do in Saigon?"

"I wouldn't know. Probably not anymore," the lawyer said.

"He's sick." Lissa, who had seen a lot of perverse behavior, paid her ultimate compliment: "He's whacked-out."

"He's Ho Chih," the lawyer said. "He's an original."

Lissa did much better, with fewer bruises, with Miles West, the cover-boy-handsome lead singer of Gila Monster, one of the biggest bands of the seventies. Miles had graduated from the cover of Crawdaddy to the cover of GQ. A former long-haired hippie freak, Miles was now a razor-cut gentleman. It was known as "the Bryan Ferry phase," in which coarse hellions became country squires, buying clothes, ranches, art. Buying women seemed to fit right in to this new acquisitiveness and status-seeking, and Alex was right at the top of the status pyramid.

"No, no. Move your arm further to left," Miles directed Lissa.

"My arm won't *go* any further."

Lissa was dressed in a Versace outfit that Miles had had in his woman's closet, which was bigger than Candy Spelling's. She was sprawled on the floor of his shower stall, her left arm reaching up, but not quite, to the shower handle, her right hand under her dress.

"Now don't move. Not an inch. You're dead. Completely dead. So when I turn the water on, you don't feel a thing."

Miles West, who had one of the city's finest photography collections, had a new hobby. He thought he was Deborah Turbeville, the artsy photographer whose *Vogue* shots of mannequins in showers had made her famous. Miles thought he could do better. After all, if he had made countless millions in music, why couldn't he do the same in art? He turned on the shower head, drenching and ruining the Versace, as well as Lissa's hair and makeup. She played dead. Miles snapped away, over, around, beside her, getting soaked himself.

"Yes. That's it. Perfect. Good. Good. Great." Miles finished his roll. Then he took off his jeans and his T-shirt and pulled Lissa's Versace all the way up and fucked her, without her moving an inch, because that would spoil the shot of the timed cameras he had set up.

"You make a super model, honey," Miles said when it was over and they were both drying their wet hair.

"Just an inch taller, and my life would be different," said the rail-thin Lissa, who had all the attributes of a star model—narcissism, vanity, bulimia, and a clothes fetish. If only she had been 5′ 8″. "If only," she mused. "But then I'd be in *Vogue* and not on your shower floor. Then you wouldn't have fucked me."

"Yeah, I would." Miles grinned. "I'd have found you one way or another." Miles had found his subject, the Dovima to his kinky Avedon. More important, he introduced Lissa to his manager, Art Vander, one of the Little Big Men of the record business. Art was one of the most voluble men in a cacophonous industry, especially in the presence of call girls. Fucking was little more than an excuse for him to talk. He was as open with hookers as he was with shrinks. Like others, he assumed there was a professional-patient privilege. With Lissa, he was chatting into the wrong box.

"When I was at USC I would have died to pork a chick like you, but you wouldn'ta pissed on me if I was a toilet and you had too much beer." Art described his college days to Lissa at her apartment. He had just come for a second time. He was going for three, trying to make up for what he had missed when he was a loser in the sixties.

"The only way I could even get *near* snatch was to deal drugs to the sorority houses. Boy, those were pussy palaces. Rich bitches. USC, University for Spoiled Children. Those cunts would have *two* cars, a T-bird and a Bug. They'd buy the drugs, but they *still* didn't notice me. I was a delivery boy, lower than a rat's ass."

"So what was your big break?" Lissa asked. She was a great listener, because she was always all ears for something she could use against her client someday. She played with Art's cock as they talked, gently feathering it with her fingers.

"There were these strung-out dopers I dealt to. They were a garage band, but they were too fucked up to play half the time. But they were good. I wasn't shit in school, 'cause all I did was listen to music, so I knew. I had an ear and I had an eye. And these were *dudes*, you know, lanky, druggy, dirty studs who didn't give a shit if they lived or died. Chicks dig that."

"Especially if they're spoiled USC sorority girls with two cars and four sets of divorced parents they hate," Lissa said.

"They were called the Four Freaks or some stupid shit. I came up with Gila Monster, and they dug that and they said, Be our manager, and I said, Maybe I'll at least get some spin-off trim. Moby Grape was coming to play at some bombed-out old speakeasy on Figueroa Street. And I knew Moby Grape, 'cause I had dealt them acid, and I knew that no way were they coming on before midnight. I made up some cheap posters that Gila Monster was the opening act, and nobody gave a shit. I mean, these freaks didn't have lawyers. Well, to make a long one short, Moby

Grape never even showed, typical. But Gila Monster was great, and the crowd was there, and they dug it, so all of a sudden I was a concert promoter and that was it."

"And the gates of Pussyland opened up," Lissa said, wrapping her long legs around Art's 5′ 4″ frame.

Art had built his coke dealership into a management company, then a record label, and now an entertainment conglomerate. He was one of the richest men, of any business, in Hollywood.

"But I sold myself short," Art lamented, after his third orgasm. "I never knew how big I was gonna be. I was insecure. I really fucked up and got married. I mean, she seemed good at the time. But, shit, now . . . Jesus! What have I done?"

Patti Vander, one of the young grandes dames of the rock aristocracy, was even smaller than Art. People called them "the voodoo dolls" because of their spooky diminutiveness. Patti was the daughter of a Beverly Hills shyster lawyer who had gotten Art and Gila Monster out of several scrapes with the DEA and the IRS, and had also ridden the Monster wave to become one of the biggest lawyers in the music business.

"So leave her," Lissa said, after nibbling Art's balls and bringing him up for an amazing fourth round.

"And give her half? It's all community property." Beverly Hills community property, at that, which *The Wall Street Journal* conservatively estimated at $600 million. "And her fucking father would take the rest."

"Why?"

"He's a fucking shakedown artist."

Lissa had read about the FBI's payola investigation and the bootleg-tape probe that Art was able to thumb his nose at. Lissa was curious to learn the truth of these matters. A few more of these sessions and Art would tell her, she was certain. Then she could *really* call the shots. When Art left, Lissa put on her favorite song, Madonna's "Material Girl." She did some coke, drank some Stoli, watched the sun glint off the GTE building far off in Santa Monica. Lissa *loved* L.A.

Lissa was meeting the men. But she couldn't be a one-woman bordello, madam and whores all in one. She needed talent, non-Alex talent.

She went out at night to look for it in the clubs. Cockatoo, the nitery of the moment, looked to Lissa like a gold mine for commercial sex. Cockatoo only sounded like a gay bar. It was the antithesis of one. Located on the Hollywood site of the old Don the Beachcomber, Cockatoo was a mock-tropical banana-tree version of New York's Nell's, a snobbish, nasty-doorman place for Hollywood's *belle*-est of the *belle*.

Cockatoo was hopping. There were more English and Australian accents than in an Earls Court pub, stunning actresses and models whose very presence in the club underscored how unfair Hollywood was. *Working* actresses and models wouldn't be here at midnight. Lissa was much more interested in the pretty girls than the pretty boys, the *nouveau* James Deans in torn T-shirts, ponytailed third assistant directors and moussed auxiliary cameramen. Not that Lissa was a lesbian, though she had no problem getting into that fantasy if the customer so demanded. It was simply that the pretty boys had no money, and at this stage of her life, Lissa was obsessed with money and nothing else. She had done the pretty boys back in high school; now they were boring. She was building her career. Like yuppies a decade or more older than she was, Lissa had decided to put romance on hold until her professional life was in order.

Cockatoo was a joke on all its habitués, a Central Casting fantasy of hip, happening Young Hollywood, a Seagram's ad for success that none of the players, for all their glorious appearance, actually had. Lissa knew that this juxtaposition of glittering fantasy and desperate reality was a fertile field for potential recruits. The English in L.A. were real whores, Lissa reflected. That there were so many Anglos floating about was a commentary on the depressed state of the British film industry, not to mention the British capacity for alcohol, usage of which among local Californians had dropped in the wake of the A.A.-ization of the film business. Here was a new generation of Jean Shrimptons and Julie Christies, lured to Hollywood with dreams of working for the London commercials directors who made it look so easy, Adrian Lyne and Ridley and Tony Scott. And Joan and Jackie Collins, who were washed-up in London, were now Hollywood institutions. These young club beauties thought that with their looks and their passport-to-everywhere British accents, Hollywood would be a piece of cake. If it was, they were certainly choking on it. These Cockatoo habitués, with little else to do but drink and pray for a break, were called Cockettes.

"They're all hookers," superstar Oliver Julian told superdirector Rawson Katz as they sat in a banquette snacking on lemongrass soup and steamed spinach and sorrel dumplings, drinking Suffering Bastards, and surveying the room.

"You think every girl's a hooker," Rawson said.

"Every girl *is* a hooker," Oliver replied. "Every one here. Look at that one." Oliver pointed to Lissa at the bar. "The skinny one in black. She works for Alex. I fucked her. Amazing. Her pussy muscles are stronger than Schwarzenegger's biceps. See the redhead and the blonde there. Alex girls. They're stylists."

"They look like models."

"Stylists. From Liverpool, luv, Mersey girls." Oliver mocked the Liverpudlian accent. "The really hot ones always turn out to be stylists, who are nothing but aging models and, hence, hookers. 'Stylist' is a big fucking euphemism."

"They're not hookers." Rawson was incredulous.

"I fucked them. I paid them. I swear," Oliver insisted. "That one, Sloane Ranger, yuppie bitch, deb of the year in London, some shit like that, picture in *Tatler*, I fucked her through Alex."

"Why give them a cent, man? Just fuck 'em. You and I are different, Ol. You think all women are whores. I think all women are fools. You don't give a bitch money for sex. You give her *nothing*. You fuck these bitches, and then you *fuck* 'em." Feminists often picketed Rawson's films, in which women characters rarely spoke and were usually raped and/or murdered. It was to no avail, because teenage boys liked women Rawson's way. Rawson, who was brutishly handsome, a beefier, younger Sean Connery, sans toupee, had been through three Asian wives. Only a geisha could endure his Oriental tortures.

"Hey, pal, you make me look like a feminist," Oliver said. Women loved Oliver as much as they hated Rawson. The slick-haired, sleepy-lidded, best-dressed star was one of the most charismatic, powerful actors in the business, even more so than his father, Rex Julian, a sex symbol of his generation. Oliver was, on the surface, an unlikely candidate to be among Alex's best customers. He was known for his steamy roles and his steamy affairs. Only Warren Beatty was reputed to have compiled a higher bed count with the city's desirable women. Then again, Warren didn't have a beautiful Venetian contessa's daughter for a wife, whom he was supposed to be home with. Wife or no wife, like the character Warren Beatty played in *Shampoo*, Oliver *had* to fuck *everything*.

"I *like* buying pussy," Oliver defended himself to the macho Rawson, Hollywood's poet laureate of violence and atrocity. "I grew up buying pussy. When my brothers and I turned sixteen, my dad gave us two birthday presents. One was a Corvette. The other was a trip to Alex."

"Him? Rex? He was the goddamn father of the year. I remember as a kid growing up in Kansas City, I always wanted a father like that. And he bought you whores."

"I *love* my dad," Oliver beamed.

"Fuckin' A." Rawson shook his head.

"Alex is great. She's the Old L.A., like the burgers at the Apple Pan or the chili at Chasen's. She's the way things ought to be. You should get into it. You buy Ferraris, you blow two hundred bucks at that sushi bar. Why is top pussy any different?"

"I would never pay to ball some bitch. I'd rather cut my dick off."

"Let's see. Lissa. Lissa. Hey!" Oliver called over to the bar and brought Lissa Trapp over to meet the only man in Hollywood who could steamroller a studio into committing thirty million to make a feature with serial killer Juan Corona as a leading and sympathetic character, "the Pancho Villa of migrant labor," as Rawson had pitched him. Tonight, Oliver and Rawson were meeting on Rawson's "art film" *Robber Baron*, about ruthless railway magnate Jay Gould's grandest of all attempted coups: cornering the gold market. It was, in Hollywood lingo, a "cocaine project," since one had to have drug-induced delusions of grandeur to take on a nonviolent period piece that could only be haunted by the specter of the failure of *The Last Tycoon*. But Oliver believed that the public would pay to see him in anything, and Jay Gould fit perfectly his swagger and endless arrogance.

"Rawson's never gone to a call girl," Oliver said, as unabashed at his own compulsions as Lissa was about hers.

Lissa made no secret about what she did for a living. "And I thought you were a big director," Lissa tweaked Rawson.

"He can't believe all these gorgeous ladies do it for money," Oliver went on.

"Can you believe *I* do it for money?" Lissa asked Rawson, who answered by lighting an expensive Havana cigar. "You just haven't found the right girl."

"Maybe he has," Oliver swooned, as the bamboo doors opened, Cece Da Gama entered Cockatoo, and Lissa Trapp had a jolt of inspiration. She would broker a deal selling Cece Da Gama, who insisted she didn't fuck for money, to Rawson Katz, who insisted he didn't pay for sex. If she could pull this off, it would definitely propel her into the major league of flesh peddlers.

"What *is* her story?" Oliver mused.

"The only thing more amazing than her looks is that she's not a star. Make her a star, Rawson."

"She has to fuck me to become a star," Rawson said, puffing on the Havana, struck near silent by Cece's Eurasian pulchritude.

"If she wouldn't fuck Roman, she wouldn't fuck Warren, she wouldn't fuck Jack, she wouldn't fuck *me*, goddamnit, why would she fuck you?"

"She's gotta fuck somebody," Rawson said intently.

Clarissa Da Gama had grown up in Scotland, her father a half-Jewish, half-Indian tailor from Goa, her mother a Glaswegian missionary. With her emerald eyes and shoot-the-moon cheekbones, she had the prettiest Anglo-Indian-hybrid look since Merle Oberon. Her only problem was that she was too short to be a big model, and too pure to be a big actress. Her mother had told her not to mix business with pleasure, not to trust the serpents who promised her roles in movies in return for rolls in the hay. Good daughter that she was, Cece listened to her mother, dating only nice non-show-business types and giving the Casting Couch Brigade a terrible time.

"She's a pain, won't do nudity, won't even flash her tits," Oliver said. "She even hates to kiss."

"You've seen her, haven't you?"

"No, not really?" Rawson said. "What's she been in?"

"She was in *An Apple a Day.*"

"Didn't see it."

"*Dime Store Romeo.*"

"Missed it."

"She's typecast as the star's bitch-goddess girlfriend, the one he sensibly dumps for someone sweet like Meg Ryan," Oliver said.

"She'll end up on *Falcon Crest* if she doesn't watch it," Rawson said.

In Lissa's mind, Cece was the perfect call-girl candidate, beautiful but unable to make her beauty pay enough. Lissa looked at the Cockettes at the bar. Like Oliver, she knew which ones had worked for Alex, the stylists and the failed stars who saw Alex as a solution, not a stigma. Here in the Wild West, across the world from England, these girls were liberated from any Victorian compunctions they might have had at home. What was there to be ashamed about? Actresses on their way up had done it, and actresses on their way down. The question was, how to get to Cece, who was several cuts above these others. She was slightly successful, a working actress, but not working enough. Lissa couldn't go and work Cece the way she'd recruit the others.

In the past, Lissa had found a number of girls for Alex at Cockatoo. She'd lead them into a conversation about money, usually by talking about some great apartment, some Moorish fantasy on Havenhurst that was just beyond the girl's reach. That would lead into a fiscal lament, whereupon Lissa would start talking, at first tentatively, about "this one thing you could do." Once the mark went for the bait, Lissa would go into high gear: "Alex is a status symbol," Lissa would say. "It's the thing to do in L.A." Lissa sold them. Like leasing an overpriced BMW or getting your breasts done. Alex could make a girl feel secure, and security, in this tenuous world of shifting fortunes and tectonic plates, was an enviable state of mind. Besides, Alex was so discreet that her girls could be confident, just as they were with their leased cars and their fake mammaries, that no one would know where their security was coming from.

It was easy for Lissa to sell Alex, because Alex was a long-going concern, an institution. Selling herself as a madam was much harder. How could she go up to Cece and say, "Rawson Katz will pay big bucks to fuck you"?

After several Suffering Bastards and several coke trips to the unisex bathrooms, that was precisely what Lissa did. And like the pushy jerk who gets a date with the ice-queen movie star by asking her out when everyone else is afraid to, and finds out that she sits home alone every night, Lissa, the pushy would-be madam, immediately got Cece's attention by her brash proposition.

"We should talk," Cece said, and retired with Lissa to a banquette. Lissa, who was totally brash, didn't mince words. "I'm a call girl, I work for Alex, and I've got a major shark on the hook for you. I can get you five big ones for one night, and that's just for openers."

"You know, I hate doing anyone in the business," Cece said.

Lissa was surprised. Cece's comment implied that she perhaps didn't hate doing someone outside the business. "Don't be old-fashioned," Lissa said. "Think of what he can do for your career. You're one hundred percent his type. Look at it as an introduction."

Once Cece was convinced of Lissa's bona fides, she took her even further aback. "Alex has been begging me to see Oliver Julian for the last year."

"Far out," Lissa marveled. "She's got all of us." Lissa was blown away at how discreet Alex was, how no one could hold a secret like Alex could. Cece had been working for Alex ever since Cece had realized she was going to be less than a star. The madam had met the actress through the Sloane Ranger hooker. The cardinal rule of the Alex-Cece liaison was that Alex would send her only to harvester moguls in Iowa, or sheikhs in Oman, or assorted dictators and political bigwigs who had more to lose than she had. The common ground was that none of these clients knew, or cared, anything about the movies. Alex had kept her word, shielding

Cece's secret even from top customers like Oliver, who would have matched the fees of sultans to have her. But just this week, Cece had lost out on a Joan Collins Brit viper role on a new television *Dallas* clone, and she was feeling particularly vulnerable. Three days later she called Lissa and said yes.

For five thousand dollars, Cece went on a date with Rawson Katz. They did all of his favorite things: shooting pistols at the Beverly Hills Gun Club, browsing through weapons manuals and independently published conspiracy theories at the Amok bookstore in Silverlake, eating blood-rare steaks at the Palm, and then topping off this macho bacchanal with the tamest, gentlest, most conventional sex Cece could have imagined.

Oliver Julian was so delighted that Rawson had joined the john club, that Rawson had finally paid to get laid, that Oliver forgot how much he wanted Cece himself. But by then it was too late. Rawson had fallen for Cece, and he took her totally off the market, writing a big part for Cece in a new movie. In this one, she didn't even get killed or raped, but got to kill a rapist. That was proof of how much Rawson respected her.

For all her brashness, Lissa got nothing beyond the thousand that she took as her discounted commission from Cece's first encounter with Rawson. If only she could have a piece of Cece's newly revived career, the way an agent would, just for that one introduction. She had hoped to have Cece as her own racehorse and Rawson as her power john, though that was not to be. As a consolation prize, she got Oliver Julian, who was furious that Alex placed more value on Cece's discretion than on his high-priced lust. Oliver's fury was something no one courted. He was the Last Angry Man, trashing restaurant kitchens that dared put butter on his steamed vegetables, shaving the head of a long-haired hairdresser who cut Oliver's hair too short, ripping the gate off a studio guardhouse when the uniformed attendant stopped him for too long. That Alex, his dear Madam Alex, would keep *any* secrets from him, much less keep Cece from him, was an act of lèse-majesté. He decided to assign his procuring to Lissa, whose gutsiness, not to mention tomboy body, he couldn't help but admire.

"Are you trying to become a madam?" Alex confronted Lissa when she learned of Oliver's defection.

"No, no, we were just goofing around. I was so high I had no idea what I was doing," Lissa lied to Alex.

"Do you know how much losing Oliver will cost me?" Alex went on. "He spends at least a hundred a year. That's forty out the window."

"Alex, don't worry. He loves me."

"That's what I'm worried about."

"Don't. He won't know where the girls come from. I'll just give him your girls and split the commission with you. That way all you lose is twenty." Lissa thought she was pulling another fast one. This way she would have access to all Alex's girls, and keep Alex, too. For the moment, while Alex was still useful. So she wasn't getting the full commission. She would, in time.

"Why are you causing this trouble?" Alex probed.

"Alex, I love you. You're my best friend." Lissa feigned hurt feelings. "I had no idea about Cece. Oliver has a violent temper. I can't help how he acts. Look, you take all the commissions, I don't want a cent. I'll just front for you."

"No, no," Alex said. "It's just one guy. Split the commissions."

"No way. You keep it all. He's your client. I feel terrible. I just want to help you out. I'd do anything for you."

"Don't play Joan of Arc with me. I know how greedy you are. How can I take money out of your hot little hands?"

"Just let me take ten percent and I'll be happy. Okay? Please, Alex, I love you so much."

Alex agreed, knowing full well she had a Judas in her midst. Lissa wasn't the first, though if it were up to Nicky and Lissa, she would be the last.

CHAPTER SEVEN

FOREIGN AFFAIRS

I'm Alex. Fly me. Who said you had to join the Navy to see the world? And who wants to be a stewardess? No, I sent my creatures all over the world, and always first-class. I should have had my own fleet and called it Trans Love Airways. Getting all these "take-out" requests from all over the globe was proof that I was doing something right. I remember when Liz Taylor had Chasen's send over their famous chili to the set of *Cleopatra* in Rome. I did for sex what Chasen's did for chili, and I think my sex was a lot better than Chasen's chili. That multinational moguls and powerful diplomats should want to import my creatures gave me as much, maybe more, of a thrill than catering to movie stars and superagents. I would have thought with all the beautiful girls everywhere, and all the beautiful whores, why go to all the trouble? I guess men love to shop by phone, even long-distance, and I did have that unique California dream girl that all these men fantasized about.

I know I'm in a minority, but I loved the Arabs, and not just because they spent so much. My Hollywood friends hated them. The Arabs' extravagance made it that much more expensive for the Hollywood set to get laid. Then again, these same Arabs made the homes in Beverly Hills and Bel Air shoot up in value by several millions, so the locals shouldn't complain. I've never had such loyal, good friends. Forget the stereotype. These weren't fat camel jockeys wearing sheets and fondling worry beads. My Arabs were cultured and elegant, Eton and Oxford, with great taste. If an OPEC man offered me ten thousand for the same girl a CAA man would only give two for, who do you *think* was going to get the prize?

A lot of my girls might have started out not knowing the difference between the Ritz in Paris and the Days Inn in Redondo Beach, but they learned fast. Just because they were gorgeous didn't mean they were surf-bunny airheads. I had some very, very smart creatures on my books, and the Arabs, more than anyone else, let these girls play out their Cinderella fantasies: travel, glamour, and big money to boot. Sheikh Charming, I'd call them, though to their enemies it was more like snake charming. But the others were just jealous. I don't care what anyone says, the Arabs were the last romantics, the last high rollers. The Hollywood crowd was a bunch of cheap tightwads by comparison. The Arabs, who had the reputation for haggling, never did, but you should see those studio heads. High rollers, ha! They're the ones who belong in the bazaar. And when it came to sex, the Arabs were a piece of cake—or should I say pie? Only the Japanese were easier. And I was very proud to do my part in correcting the balance of trade through my little *male*-order business.

The onion field of bald heads sprouting behind the wide seats of the British Airways 747 from Los Angeles to London gave Diana Harmon severe pause about the mission on which Alex had dispatched her.

Diana's anxiety was understandable. Here she was, working for Alex for the first time and being hurtled into space on a six-thousand-mile blind date with an Arab sheikh. All the bald pates took on a sinister aspect. Is this what first class was all about, Diana despaired, a claustrophobic flying club of dirty rich old men? And the sheikh? What was he going to be like? Diana hadn't even asked. She hadn't dared. She was terrified of Alex, who hated niggling questions about age and looks and habits and so forth. This sheikh was one of the richest men in the world, and Diana was going to make twenty thousand dollars for a week at the Dorchester in London, and how bad could that be? Incredibly bad, Diana fretted, but it was too late. The jumbo was making its turn over Palos Verdes, heading north by northeast to Vegas, to Canada, to the pole.

Diana squirmed in her huge recliner. She felt like a party crasher. In her faded jeans and baggy sweater, with her Eddie Bauer gym bag, she knew she didn't look like a first-class traveler, much less a twenty-thousand-dollar call girl. It was all so absurd, it had all happened so fast, just this afternoon; it was a surreal take on old game shows—*The Dating Game, Truth or Consequences, Queen for a Day*—to go from living with her parents in the Simi Valley to a London version of the *Arabian Nights* in less than twenty-four hours. Only in Hollywood. If only she had had the time to get some clothes. If only she had gotten some advance on the 20K. But she hadn't, and all she had been able to do was stop at the Panty Raid discount lingerie shop on Sepulveda en route to LAX and pick up some black lace bras and bikinis so she'd have *something* to offer the sheikh.

Then the Veuve Clicquot started to flow. And the beluga and blini were rolled out. And one Stoli Cristal led to another. And Faye Dunaway, all in black glasses and black leather, emerged from a seat in the front of the plane. And suddenly it sunk in that Diana's dream of flying to Europe first-class had just come true. The glamour of the voyage had transmuted Diana's shame over the price she was paying into pride over the price she was getting. Guilt trip had become adventure.

An unlikely call girl even on Alex's roster of unlikelies, Diana Harmon wasn't quite sure why or how she had been handed this plum assignment. With her long swan neck and sleek black hair and green cat eyes, she had occasionally been told she looked like Nefertiti. Maybe there was some pharaonic connection that would appeal to the sheikh, but Diana dismissed this as a stretch. Yes, she had full, beautiful breasts, but she was only 5' 4", and her ass and thighs needed enough work that she didn't even like to undress at the pool at the Y, to say nothing of the Sports Connection, where people came to judge and be judged. No, Diana was aware that Alex had chosen her not for her looks but for her brains. Diana, a Phi Beta Kappa from Columbia, was going to be Alex's whore of Mensa. It was a tribute to Alex's open-mindedness and to the breadth of her operation that she didn't choose her stalwarts solely by appearances. And it was a tribute to Diana, who couldn't get a date to her own senior prom, that a man who could have anything and anyone was going to pay twenty thousand dollars to have sex with her. In her current state, Diana needed all the tribute she could get.

The main reason Alex had chosen Diana was psychological. Diana was a Lissa substitute. Alex could sense that Lissa was slipping away, though she still had no idea of the treachery attendant to the slippage. Given her maternal nature, Alex liked having "daughters" whom she could guide and mold. Diana reminded her of Lissa. They looked somewhat alike, they were both lower-middle-class, and they were both ambitious. But Diana was educated, cultured, sophisticated in ways Lissa had no interest in being. Moreover, Diana was nice. Lissa was not nice at all, however much Alex always believed there was a loving girl inside her struggling to get out. Nor was Diana on drugs. That made her civilized and pliable. Alex could do lots with her, for her. Alex enjoyed playing Pygmalion with her girls, and Diana was hers for the molding.

Like a master criminal who had escaped from Alcatraz once only to wind up there again on a petty misdemeanor, Diana had escaped the numbing mediocrity of Southern California shopping-mall Valley life for the glitter of Manhattan, but was now marooned in a tract-house bedroom she had vowed never again to inhabit. Diana's father was a Czech émigré scientist who was so thrilled just to have escaped the Iron Curtain and communism that he never had come to grips with what capitalism was all about. He worked as the night pharmacist in a Thrifty Drug. Diana's mother was an elementary-school teacher from Chatsworth who was imbued with the Eisenhower-era ethic that husbands were supposed to be the breadwinners. She was therefore unable to take career action of her own when her husband failed to come under the spell of the American profit motive.

Both Diana and her sister were overachievers. Diana's sister had received a full scholarship to Harvard and Harvard Medical School, and was now doing her residency in neurosurgery at Mass General. Diana was the creative one, and had turned down scholarships to Yale and Princeton for one at Columbia so that she could go to New York, where she would figure out whether to be a famous painter or a famous singer or a famous novelist. What she had figured out first was that it was enormously expensive to be a bohemian. Her only classmates who could sustain their artistic pursuits seemed to do so at the expense of their wealthy families; the others became pre-law or pre-med.

From her freshman year onward, Diana grew increasingly resentful of the fiscal vagaries of life and parentage. Every stroll down Park or Madison made her furious at the good fortune of anyone with a trust fund, and just as furious at her own misfortune. Equating oblivion with the acceptance of a day job, Diana always worried about how she would survive in the real world and be able to pursue her muse. One answer came in her sophomore summer, when she stayed in New York to take a music course at Juilliard and took a part-time waitress position at the Three Guys Restaurant on Madison at Seventy-fifth, whose tony clientele of Sotheby's art people and *nouveau* society-in-a-rush denizens made it the Mortimer's of Greek diners.

"What is this pubic hair doing in my lemon chicken?" a handsome thirty-something banker Diana was waiting on demanded loudly, causing expensively coiffed heads to turn. The banker held up a kinky strand for Diana's inspection.

"It shows what a sexy place this is," Diana shot back, laughing at her own joke. "That's not a pubic hair."

"What is it, then? It's not parsley," the banker said, annoyed.

Diana examined the strand. "Do chickens have pubic hair? Maybe that's what it is, but it's not a human pubic hair."

"You're not funny."

"You're not serious," Diana shut him up, and whisked the plate of three-quarters-eaten chicken and roast potatoes off his table. A second later, she returned from the kitchen with the same plate and slid it down in front of the banker. "You can eat it and not grow a mons veneris in your throat," Diana told him. She couldn't control how offensive she sounded. This arrogant, snobbish guy was everything Diana hated about New York. "What do you expect for five ninety-five?"

"I don't expect a pubic-hair garni. I should go to the Board of Health."

"Eat this," Diana said, plopping down a box of Brillo in front of him. "Pubic hair! It's Brillo. Shows how clean we are here," she gloated.

Although she assumed she would be stiffed for the check, she got a hundred-dollar bill wrapped around the banker's business card from Salomon Brothers.

Intrigued with this young high roller, Diana called him. What she thought would be a date turned out to be a bizarre proposition. The banker, whose name was Amory, impressed by what he described as Diana's "snippy insouciance," wanted her to beat him for money, three hundred dollars for an hour of pain. Diana was flabbergasted at the request. She had had very little experience with men, or even boys, having been both too smart and too pudgy for Simi Valley tastes. Diana hadn't lost her virginity until after her high-school graduation, and when she had it was to a pimply fifteen-year-old gas-station attendant who had patched a flat tire on her mother's Honda. Afterward, having slimmed down to a shape that attracted male attention, Diana had only affairs, usually one-night stands, with teenagers with whom she had nothing in common. Fellow students, even the occasional professor who admired her wit and other charms to the point of making a pass, were doomed to withering disdain. To Diana there was no more fatal a disqualifier than being "too old," and for her too old began at twenty.

Consequently, Amory was not only too old, he was too rich. A preppy WASP, Amory lived in a Fifth Avenue co-op that he had inherited from his grandfather, who had been a wizard of Wall Street. Amory could have been an artist but chose instead to make even more money. In short, he was precisely the person Diana resented the most. Why not, she figured, actualize this contempt and earn money for it to boot, as it were?

Having prepared for her new role by watching a number of bondage-and-discipline videos, Diana met Amory at his apartment one afternoon after work. Without taking her clothes off, she ordered Amory to undress and get down on all fours. Then she spanked him with a riding crop he had brought from his sister-in-law's stable in New Jersey.

"You are pathetic, walking ectoplasmic pathos," Diana excoriated him. *Whack!*

"Without your inherited money, which you did nothing whatsoever to earn, you couldn't have gotten into Fairleigh Dickinson. You couldn't get a job at a Sabrett cart. You'd be homeless in Central Park." *Whack! Whack!* "No, they wouldn't even let you in Central Park. You couldn't get into Riverside Park. You're barely fit for Morningside Park. The rats would throw up on your flabby WASP flesh." *Whack! Whack! Whack!*

"Why do you hate me so much?" Amory gasped, his penis getting harder with each blow of the crop. "Why don't you like me?"

"Because you're weak. You're the end of your race. You're a genetic inbred loser, and when the money runs out, which it will, 'cause you squander it like this, you'll be poor and desperate and you'll starve to death on scraps from thrown-away Burger King bags." *Whack! Whack!*

"How will I survive? Won't you help me? I need you to save me," Amory sighed, more and more excited.

"Maybe you'll be a busboy at the Harvard Club, and then they'll fire you, and you'll have to go to Katz's Deli, and they'll really hate you there and the rabbi will come and circumcise you." *Whack!*

There were red welts all over his body. "Help me," he cried, and began to masturbate. He came on his priceless Persian carpet. Then he quickly sponged the rug dry, put on a new Savile Row jacket, gave Diana three hundreds, and went to the Knickerbocker Club for cocktails with some of his buddies from Groton and Harvard. He never took Diana out, never really asked her anything about herself. But he would call her every two or three weeks, and the drill was always the same. It was the easiest money she had ever dreamed of. She wished she had a way to make more of the same, but the opportunity did not repeat itself.

Back at Columbia, she finally fell in love with a classmate who was, curiously enough, her own age and I.Q. She also decided that what she really wanted to be was a film director, and she began taking classes with Milos Forman at the Columbia Film School. Diana fancied the idea of directing because she saw that there was a cult of youth in Hollywood, and thus an opportunity to get rich young. Besides, she loved giving orders. Books were becoming obsolete; the art market had collapsed; and who made a living as a singer besides rock stars? Directing seemed ideal, except for having to go back to L.A., but the L.A. of film directors was so different from the suburban-hell L.A. she had escaped that going back was really like going to another planet altogether. As a student she made a short film, *Spree*, about a shoplifter at Bloomingdale's, which earned her several awards. She also broke up with her boyfriend, began having terrible fights with her girlfriends, and was diagnosed as manic-depressive by the Columbia Health Society's psychiatrist and given lithium. Nonetheless, she graduated summa cum laude and prepared to take L.A. by storm.

L.A. ran true to form in that it was not impressed by Diana's education or her film or her wit or her anything. She shared an apartment in West Hollywood with two girls from Yale, who spent their days taking screenwriting seminars and pecking away on their laptops, and their nights with other hip Ivy League transplants dating Ivy League suits from the CAA mailroom, each of whom had dreams and boasts of becoming the next Mike Ovitz, gifted young men who in an earlier generation might have dreamed and boasted of becoming the next John Kennedy.

Diana dreamed of becoming the next Eric Rohmer. No one in Hollywood seemed to know who Eric Rohmer was, so she told them instead that Woody Allen was her model. Yet soon she realized that if she was going to play the Hollywood game she couldn't be a snob, or she'd be playing with herself. She and her roommates thus decided that they should get jobs "in the industry," that is, join the ranks of those uniquely Hollywood creatures known as "D girls." "She can't say yes, but she won't say no" is the line on D—that is, development—girls, who screen scripts, and field pitch ideas for producers and studio executives, and contribute mightily to Hollywood's being the only town on earth where you can die of encouragement. The word "development" here comes from the notion of R & D, that is, research and development. In Hollywood, most development is largely a public relations task of telling screenwriters how much you "love" their projects without actually ever paying them a cent. It is more like free love, and also akin to "Let's have lunch," which is Hollywood-speak for "Drop fucking dead."

Still, for a young woman like Diana, without the pedigree of a Jane Fonda or a Penny Marshall, being a development girl is the time-honored entry position for a would-be mogulette in the no-connection/all-ambition mode of Sherry Lansing and Dawn Steel. It's a great way to learn the business, and it's a great way to meet men. No one in town is as tuned in to the nuances of a writer's "eligibility" as a D girl, whose ultimate goal, short of running a studio, is to lure Steven Spielberg away from whomever he is married to at the moment. The problem for Diana was that so many D-girl positions are dispensed on nepotistic grounds—after all, this is Hollywood—that the competition for the meritocratic slots is extremely fierce. If you can't get the job based on "relationships," you are then forced to trade on your looks, and on certain despairing nights, Diana actually considered becoming a blonde. She agonized over whom she had to have sex with to get hired, a b-job for a d-job. But none of the men who interviewed her even made a pass, to say nothing of a proposition. Finally, instead of having to become a fake blonde, Diana was discovered by a real one, who became her mentor.

Tinka Thorsen was "Queen of the D's." A tall, rangy, Nebraskan Swede, she looked as if she'd been born to be on the other side of the cameras, but she was also considered too brainy to stake a career on something as ephemeral as *Sports Illustrated*-swimsuit-issue looks. Because brains were her thing, she was immediately taken with Diana and her summa and gave the younger woman a job as her assistant at Council Bluffs Productions, the company founded by Tinka's fellow midwesterner Dexter Haggard, the black star of the long-running series *Inner City*, who had joined fellow television actors Ron Howard, Danny DeVito, Rob Reiner, and Leonard Nimoy in the pantheon of bankable feature directors. Council Bluffs was what Hollywood called a "minimajor"; all the studios vied for its product, i.e., socially conscious family films with lots of heart. It was the very last place on earth where the deeply cynical Diana should have found herself. Her all-time favorite review was *The New Yorker*'s three-word take on *The Sound of Music*: "Not for diabetics." But Diana put on her Pollyanna face. She needed a job, and Council Bluffs was the hottest shop in town.

For a company with such ostensible heart, Diana found Council Bluffs completely lacking in soul. Dexter Haggard had bought a mansion on Lexington Road, the most expensive street in Beverly Hills, played golf at the ultra-WASP Los Angeles Country Club, had a smoked-chicken pizza named after him at Spago, and showed about as much affinity for the inner city as Ivana Trump. Council Bluffs' chief financial officer, a black accountant named Jamal King, spent much of his leisure time in Africa, not helping starving Somalis but big-game-hunting endangered species, or honing his marksmanship for such endeavors at the Beverly Hills Gun Club, where he and Sylvester Stallone would have bull's-eye contests. The company president, Hy Kleinwort, had gotten his job by being Dexter's tennis coach. Hy, who had been an all-American at UCLA, had now anointed himself a director, planning his debut with a thirty-million-dollar remake of the Tracy-Hepburn *Pat and Mike*, with Eddie Murphy as the sports trainer and Whitney Houston as a now singing gym teacher.

Diana felt that Hy had the most offensive sense of humor on earth. His self-styled parody of political correctness was to call Tinka, Diana, and all the other women workers "cunts." "Top of the morning, cunts," he would say on entering the office. "How are my cunts today?" It was as if Hy had *discovered* the word. Because Dexter was always out, either directing films or playing golf, Hy ran the show. All the ideas that the company would develop into scripts had to go through Hy, and thereby became "his" ideas. There were, for instance, three scripts commissioned about a UCLA playboy tennis star who (a) joins a street-smart black fraternity, (b) becomes a coach in a street-smart black junior high, and (c) marries a street-smart black woman bookie. Diana's task was simply to hear the ideas of the lower-echelon writers who were invited in to Council Bluffs to pitch their takes on Hy's concepts in hopes of landing the $300,000 script assignment. They never got them. Instead, after Diana reported these takes to Hy, he would present the best of them as "his" ideas to the "A"-list writers he personally courted and who would inevitably get the job.

Diana's other main task was to attend daily story meetings with Hy, Tinka, and other "creative executives" to talk about scripts in progress and packaging plans for the company's many projects. Diana usually had to bite her tongue to keep from lashing out, or gagging, but one time she couldn't control herself. Hy's newest "front-burner" project was a remake of *The Parent Trap* with Drew Barrymore in the Hayley Mills part as identical twins who reunite their divorcing parents. Hy felt that having two Drew Barrymores in the same movie was sheer genius. However, as insurance, he cast Robert Redford and Diana Ross as the parents. Diana thought it preposterous that Redford's aging blond genes could so dominate Ross's black ones, but her objection was met with intense derision from Hy. "It's a *comedy*," he snarled. "Not a biology lesson. Ivy League cunt, don't bust my chops." That afternoon, Tinka told Diana she was being let go, that Hy thought she was out of sync with the company "philosophy."

At first, Diana reveled in her firing. Free at last, from the hypocrisy, from the synthetic, from the system. But the blessing of freedom was counterbalanced with the curse of poverty. The only time in Hollywood you could get a job was when you had a job. Everyone loved to poach; no one wanted someone who needed something. Furthermore, Diana had the curse of Hy. To employ one of his discards—and word of his discarding traveled fast—would be a slap in his face. Hollywood never second-guessed a winner, which Council Bluffs would be until it had a flop.

Meanwhile, Diana hadn't been in the system long enough to have done enough favors to guarantee that she could fail upward. She wasn't a David Begelman, the former head of Columbia, whose "punishment" for being a convicted check forger was to be made head of MGM. At twenty-three, she was already Hollywood poison.

Unable to pay her rent, Diana accepted one ignominy, moving back to Simi Valley with her parents, and another, looking for "normal" jobs, that is, jobs outside the movies. She thought her student film might get her a quasi-artistic position as an advertising copywriter, but even the avant-garde Chiat/Day agency, which had the Nike account, found it "negative and antisocial." Diana knew they were right. She was a guerrilla warrior, a subversive, an artist. Artists weren't supposed to fit. Unfortunately, the only places that would give Diana any credit for her Ivy League education were those ultimate establishment capitalist tools— banks and oil companies. The Bank of America, for one, gladly offered to start her in their training program and give her a salary of thirty-five thousand dollars a year. Her parents, who had pushed her on the interview, were thrilled. Diana, on the other hand, believed that if she accepted the position she would be signing a death warrant on her dreams as well as her humanity.

This was when she went to the Castle. The Castle was a bondage parlor that advertised in the local porno tabloids that filled the often jimmied dispensers on the shady side of the Pavilions supermarket, where Diana was pacing one afternoon, contemplating her bleak future while her mother was shopping for taco shells and cat litter. The paper Diana noticed was the L.A. X . . . Press. On the cover was a silicone Juno named Wendy Whoppers. Inside was some editorial copy; an article on star divorce lawyer and palimony expert Marvin Mitchelson; a profile of the local rock band Sacred Reich; an investigative piece on the infiltration of a Cambodian-run Donut King in a Sepulveda mini-mall by Jamaican drug dealers (the L.A. melting pot gone seriously awry); an "Erotic Dining" food column with no reference to food but many hints on how to be picked up at the bars of the Biltmore and the Hollywood Roosevelt; and a horoscope. It was a measure of how terminally bored and depressed Diana was that she actually read the paper.

She was particularly riveted by the endless pages of ads. There were full-color pages of naked blondes fondling each other to promote phone sex: "1-800-926-MUFF"; "Pussy Party"; "Chicks with Dicks—Chat with Live Transsexuals 1-900-505-TSTS. Only $1.98 a minute." There were pages of Oriental massage parlors, and more pages of "actual photos" of beautiful "models" and "escorts" with their home numbers: "Kimberly: ex–Playmate of the Month—tan, toned, and tight, for generous discreet gentlemen. 10-minute callback"; "Freaky Blondes"; "California Beach Blonde with lactating nipples. Must-see"; "French Maid"; "Greek Thrills"; "Bi Aussie Girls." Diana wondered if all these Playmates and models and aerobics instructresses were real, all offering themselves for money. She was mesmerized by the ads. She couldn't put the X . . . *Press* down.

Then she saw it. "Pain for Gain" was in big Gothic letters. The ad was a full quarter page in the "Specialties" section: "If you're so smart and so gorgeous, how come you're not rich? Exploit your rage. No sex guaranteed. B & D. S & M. Infantilism, Fetishism, X-Dressing. Work out your anger. Earn Big Bucks. The Castle."

The Castle was located in a plain, taped-over-windowed storefront between an electrolysis parlor and a Lebanese deli on Sherman Way in North Hollywood, not far from Disney and NBC. The manager was a bleached-blond Persian man in his thirties wearing an orange Members Only windbreaker. He deflated Diana, who thought she looked nastily chic in her Melrose Avenue black leather outfit. "I need to see your I.D.," he said. Once he made sure she was past the age of consent, he gave her a tour of the premises. The manager led Diana into a deep labyrinth of stockades, manacles, stretching devices, even an iron maiden, which Diana joked must be there for decor, though the Persian did not laugh. There was another room, called the Romper Room, which was outfitted with a large cradle. Pacifiers were strewn about on tables, and there was Flintstones wallpaper. Then there was a shower room painted black and hung with enema bottles. The fetish room had more outfits than Western Costume, everything from Tom Mix to Tinker Bell. The price for these fantasies was $100 an hour. Diana would get $30 of this, plus any tips, which, the Persian promised her, were anywhere from $25 to $100. A quick conservative calculation based on $55 an hour for five hours yielded $275 a day, or $1,375 for a five-day week, or $71,500 a year, which was over twice what she'd earn at the Bank of America. "And you never have to undress, you never let them touch you," the Persian assured her, sensing he had a fish on the hook. "And it's all totally legal."

Unfortunately for the Persian, his spiel was broken by the arrival of the two afternoon dominatrices, one a chubby black girl named Aretha, the other a skinny, pimply white girl named Robin. Robin had with her a copy of *Tiger Beat*, while Aretha had a tub of Kentucky Fried Chicken to munch on between sessions. Diana felt mortified that she had sunk so low as to come here. She fled through the stockades into the comforting smoggy haze of Valley daylight.

The next weekend, in the much more salubrious climes of Sunset Plaza, Diana had a lunch with Tinka Thorsen, who expressed that rarest of Hollywood emotions, remorse, for Hy's brutal termination of Diana's celluloid future. They were drinking wine and eating salads at Le Petit Four, L.A.'s version of a sidewalk café on the Cannes Croisette at festival time. Again, Diana felt like the stranger at the party, though Tinka was trying to bring her back in, giving her a list of possible D-girl openings with producers who despised Hy and hence might sympathize with Diana. Still, Tinka conceded that every possibility was a long shot. In her despair, Diana told Tinka about her visit to the Castle, and about her collegiate S & M experiences with Amory.

Somehow, Tinka wasn't shocked. "If I had known that, I could have introduced you to this famous madam."

"How do you know a madam?"

"I was developing this script, like *Klute* but set in Beverly Hills."

"For Council Bluffs?"

"For Joel Silver," Tinka said. "I could have introduced you to Alex." Tinka then went on to describe the supermadam at some length.

"But I'm not a hooker," Diana insisted, standing up for an honor that she insisted had been preserved because her "client" had never actually penetrated her. "I never had sex with him."

"He had sex with you."

"Not with me. With himself."

"He wouldn't have had it unless you were there. You got him off."

"It's different."

"You took money for a sex act. Look, it's fine. I'm not judging you. But don't try to split hairs. You've done it. You've crossed the Rubicon. And since you have, and if you can, you can make a lot of money with Alex. I can introduce you. I promise you won't get grossed out by the other girls there."

"Stop it, Tinka. It's not a possibility. I'm not a whore."

"We're all whores," Tinka sighed, looking around at all the blondes scoping out the Eurotrash and the Eurotrash rating all the blondes, circling, staring, moving in for the kill. "This is a city of whores."

Alex was the most intimidating person Diana had ever met. Lying in her muumuu in her priceless antique bed in her antique-filled mansion working the bank of phones, feeding live shrimp to her cats, she struck Diana as a cross between Buddha and Blofeld, the James Bond villain who fed goldfish to his cat. Although Alex was all charm and sweetness, Diana, who had never felt more paranoid, didn't trust a bit of it. The fresh chamomile tea from the garden, the wonderful cookies from the Ivy—Diana worried that she might be drugged. The big blondes wafting through the house, blondes Diana was sure she recognized from billboards and magazines and rock videos, only added to her insecurity. She felt short, fat, ugly, absurd.

Yet Alex managed to put her at ease. Without being at all inquisitorial, she brought Diana out, getting her to talk about her family, her ambition to direct films, her self-perception as an "artist."

"We can't let you keep hours," Alex said, all understanding.

"I should've been born rich," Diana sighed.

"We'll just have to compensate," Alex said, reassuringly, and Diana slowly began to think that maybe there was indeed a way out of her doldrums. So she wouldn't be a film executive. Who cared? She could take her time, write a great script, hold an auction with herself irrevocably attached as director, and have Hy Kleinwort begging for it. And he'd never get it. Stop the Hester Prynne self-loathing, she told herself. This was a calculated trade-off. This "fuck-me" money was also "fuck-you" money.

There was no talk at all about business other than Alex's curiosity over whether Diana had recently had an AIDS test. Diana told Alex she had had three.

"I'm a hypochondriac," Diana said. Alex seemed pleased, though still curious as to the love life that had triggered Diana's concern. Diana sheepishly confessed her continued passion—though "passion" was far too strong a word—for young "dudes"—though "dudes" was too cool a word for her one location scout, two gaffers, one nerdy USC screenwriting student, and one clerk at Blockbuster Video she had had sex with, once each, in the last six months. "It's mostly guilt and hypochondria," she assured Alex. "I don't really think these guys got around all that much." Diana was abashed that she couldn't claim to have been partying with the Brat Pack. Diana was fucking goofy gaffers. Alex's girls fucked movie stars. What was she doing here? Why was Alex being so nice to her?

"Don't you like sex?" Alex asked her.

"I don't hate it, but . . . it's not a big deal."

"I know," Alex said, which sounded odd, coming from her, but totally sincere. And then, out of the blue, Alex offered Diana the $20,000 trip to London. Tinka had told her she might get a $1,000 trick. That sounded like a fortune. But $20,000? This was winning the lottery. Diana tried to stay calm. She couldn't hide her excitement. Only when Alex mentioned the name of the client did Diana's face fall. Every windfall had its cost.

Sheikh Fuad. The mere name made her gag. Diana had the typical American knee-jerk antipathy toward Arabs.

"You're too bright to be prejudiced," Alex told Diana.

"All I think of are terrorists," Diana conceded. "Dark guys with big mustaches and bombs."

"Try thinking of mathematics and the beautiful mosques and the art. Think of the civilization they created."

"That was then, this is now."

"I'm not sending you to Arafat," Alex said. "I deal in princes. They're a million times more elegant than what passes for class in Hollywood. These are the barbarians, not the Arabs. You'll see. Wait till you meet my people. I love Middle Easterners, of a certain level. They're my best customers. They're my friends. You better be nice to them," Alex told her, and Diana knew it wasn't idle chatter. "No S & M. Be a little lady."

"I promise," Diana said.

"If you do behave, the sky's the limit for you," Alex said. "I have this other girl, Lissa, who reminds me a little of you, and some of my Arabs liked her a lot. But she was awful to them. Awful. She would've done Hitler if the price were right. But Arabs . . . whole different story. That Lissa, she's so ignorant. Don't be like that," Alex said, hoping her maternal hope that Diana would turn out better than Lissa had. Alex was lonesome for a new girl to be her confidante, and Diana had the brains to be the one.

Alex first started doing business with the Arabs at the beginning of their oil boom in 1972. Before then, she had been strictly Hollywood and *Fortune* 500. However, because of her contacts in the *Fortune* set, she was always looking for investment opportunities. One of these opportunities was selling American steel to the oil emirates, which were on a high-rise building spree with all their petrodollars. She met an Englishman named Walton, a ruddy soldier-of-fortune type who lived in Bahrain and acted as a purchasing agent for one of the ruling families there. As a loss leader for her hoped-for steel deal, Alex sent Walton and his prince pals, who were at the Beverly Hills Hotel to visit Disneyland and Knott's Berry Farm, a complement of her California Girls. Her gift turned out to be a great hit and a huge mistake. The Bahrainis lost all interest in buying anything from Alex except sex. Bahrain led to Abu Dhabi and Kuwait, and blonde fever engulfed the ruling houses of the Gulf and eventually the entire Mideast. Alex's house of mirth became their California Mecca, and Alex was invited to bring and/or send her charges to New York, London, Geneva, Paris, wherever the princes and sheikhs and their courtiers were encamped. In a three-year-period, Alex herself, who hated to leave her house, made over thirty-six trips to London alone, where she was ensconced at Claridges and the Dorchester, bedecked with jewels, laden with antiques, art, cars, whatever the Arabs could bestow upon her for bestowing upon them the best of American beauty.

Alex told Diana the story of how she had sent Kit Langan, who was probably the most famous actress ever to work for Alex, on one of these London Arab jaunts. "And she never had sex with anyone," Alex cackled.

"How'd she pull that off?"

"Let me tell you," Alex said, and launched into another of her stories, delighted to have such an intelligent listener.

Kit Langan was the Elizabeth Taylor of her generation, minus the husbands, the huge breasts, and the weight problem. Kit had been a child star, a teen star, an adult star. She was the quintessence of brains and class. Just having her in a picture gave it prestige. That she was considered one of the top romantic leads in the business was a testimony to her thespian skills, for Kit was a hard-core lesbian. This was understandable when one found out that Kit's mother, Rawn, was a madam, a minor madam in the Valley whom Alex had known from her earliest days in the business. They had come of age together, and Alex shared Rawn's pride in watching Kit grow up and prosper.

But prosperity for child stars when Kit was coming of age was quite different from prosperity as Macaulay Culkin would come to redefine it. Rawn couldn't give up her phones and survive as a stage mother. Thus when Alex proposed that Rawn send Kit, then age sixteen, to London to see Sheikh Abdul Raman, one of the richest oilmen in the world, Rawn wasn't at all horrified or insulted. She was grateful for the deal. It wasn't that heinous a deal. The sheikh was an old, sick man. He adored watching American television, and that's where he'd first seen Kit. He'd become a fan, and followed her career for five years. When Alex learned of the sheikh's interest and told him that she knew Kit well, the sheikh said it would give him the greatest pleasure in his sure-to-end-soon life if he could meet Kit in person. Since Alex had made a small fortune giving pleasure to the sheikh and his many friends and retainers, she saw no reason to stop now. The sheikh flew Alex, Rawn, and Kit over together, put them up in adjoining suites at the Dorchester, bought them jewels and antiques and clothes, and gave them fifty thousand dollars to boot, all for having dinner in his grand Georgian home for five nights.

"All Kit had to give him was a cheek kiss hello and good-bye," Alex said. "But after all, she *was* an actress, and she was sweet, in her way. She held the poor man's shaky hand all through coffee and dessert, and she cuddled with him when we watched a tape of that stupid movie she won the Oscar for, where she played the blind dog trainer."

"*Puppy Love.* No shame."

"I loved it. Two madams and a minor flying overseas to meet an Arab billionaire. I half expected Scotland Yard and Interpol to meet us at the airport. But it was as innocent as a trip to Westminster Abbey."

"What happened to the sheikh?"

"He died three months later."

"A happy man."

"Happier."

"Do you ever talk to Kit?" Diana asked.

"Never. Once she went off to Princeton, I never heard from her, or her mother, again."

"Didn't that hurt your feelings?"

"She was in the national spotlight. Her publicist would have killed her," Alex said. "I understand."

"The official line on her mom is that she's her 'business manager.' "

"She is." Alex chuckled.

"Do you ever feel like Broadway Danny Rose?" Diana asked. "When people like Kit get famous and . . ."

"And dump me?" Alex completed the thought. "I'm not naïve. Looking for gratitude in this business is praying for snow in Death Valley. All I expect is my forty percent, nothing more. If I make an introduction that makes them famous, God bless them. What hurts me is when they fail."

"And most fail?"

"Most disappear."

Alex went back to talking about her Arabs.

Diana was dazzled by the way Alex reeled off names of princes, emirs, sheikhs, ministers, Egyptians, Jordanians, Syrians, Saudis, but to her they were still just Arabs—dark, scary rich people who had made it too expensive for normal people to stay in luxury hotels in Europe. To have sex with one of them seemed inconceivable.

"Fuad is divine. Thirty-five, very international."

"So is Arafat."

"I warned you."

"Just joking."

"You have a lot in common."

"Not our bank accounts."

"He went to Columbia, like you. He went to the business school, after Oxford."

"The B-school guys were geeks." Diana was feeling more at home. She let her own personality come out, and Alex enjoyed that.

"But those gaffers you slept with weren't geeks. They were Gary Cooper, right?"

"You win," Diana said. "But why would he like *me?*"

"Fuad likes bright girls. So don't act stupid with your ageist bullshit. I warn you. What you want is to take control, I know you, that's why you go for these little morons. But this is about letting go of control."

"I understand," Diana said. "I won't act out."

"Fuad has a wonderful art collection in his summer home in Cap-Ferrat, all the great Impressionists. He has horses at Longchamp. And this is for you: He's gotten interested in movies."

"Why?" Diana's interest piqued.

"He saw how well that *nouveau riche* Dodi Fayed did producing *Chariots of Fire,* so he figured, if Dodi could do it, why not? He loves it out here, probably because I take such good care of him," Alex exulted. "He wants to spend more time in L.A. Movies would give him the excuse."

"Maybe I could get him to back my movie," Diana reflected.

"It's as close to big money as you'll ever get," Alex tantalized her. "If he likes you, anything's possible."

"And I could tell Hollywood to stick it." Diana was already planning her Oscar speech.

She accepted the mission. She hadn't even asked what Fuad looked like, or what he wanted to do with her. Somehow such questions seemed rude and inappropriate. The very fact of Alex's recommendation had to stand for itself. Diana had seen nothing but charm and friendliness; still, she had heard Alex on the phone being hard and peremptory. They were just random phrases—"Then she's out." "Enough." "Forget it."—though they were delivered with a heavier, darker weight. Diana, who knew she was playing way outside her league, had no desire to incur Alex's wrath.

The liveried chauffeur who met Diana's flight at Terminal 4 at Heathrow knew exactly who she was. He took her gym bag, not as if it contained a dead skunk but rather as if it were Hermès's finest leather, and led Diana out of the terminal to a waiting racing-green Bentley. The back windows were smoked, and there was a divider between the front and back seats. There was no sight-seeing and no dialogue. Diana opened the electric-powered window. It was a bitter cold and wet March day. She hadn't even thought about the weather; no one in L.A. ever did. She saw the black Austin cabs going down the wrong side of the motorway. She saw a billboard, sponsored by the British Dairy Council, depicting a cow that said, "Scream for Cream." Yes, she was really in England. Diana closed the window of the Bentley and closed her eyes.

"Welcome to the Dorchester," said the tall doorman in a green felt top hat and gold-braided uniform. Diana had been to London twice when she lived in Paris, staying at five-pound-a-night student B & B hostels in Bayswater, so she was totally unprepared for the gilded Art Deco opulence of the Dorchester, the headquarters of Noël Coward, Marlene Dietrich, Judy Garland, and Elizabeth Taylor, who recuperated there from the pneumonia she contracted in Rome while shooting *Cleopatra* and whose 1960s romance with Richard Burton was played out in adjoining suites overlooking Hyde Park. The Beatles held court here after receiving their OBEs, but by the Thatcherite eighties, the hotel was Mecca on Park Lane, the residence of Arab oil sheikhs and their blond harems. Diana never dreamed she would be part of this scene. Yet here she was.

A morning-coated reception clerk took Diana's passport and showed her to her room. Along the plush-carpeted broad hallways, she saw three wiry Oriental men in dark Ray-Bans, black leather jackets, and white patent-leather Gucci loafers. Diana gave the clerk a puzzled look.

"They're bodyguards," the clerk said, sotto voce.

"For the head of Sony or something?"

"No, for several of our Middle Eastern guests, actually. They say the Japanese make the best bodyguards."

Not sure she would be sleeping more or less soundly with the Yakuza outside her door, Diana surveyed her "junior suite," which had a view over the Georgian town houses of Mayfair. A chilled bottle of champagne and a basket of fruit awaited her. A card inside the door listed the rate at £475 pounds (about $750). When Diana opened the closet, she saw several designer dresses, which at first she thought had been left by a previous guest. She quickly figured out that they were not only her size but had been shortened accordingly. There was an evening coat and a Burberry trench coat and high heels to go with the dresses. This wasn't a game show anymore; this was *The Twilight Zone.*

Just as Diana was about to have an anxiety attack over the lack of instructions on what she was to do, the phone rang. A smooth Italian-accented voice that did not identify itself welcomed Diana to London, inquired as to her well-being and to the fit of her clothes, and said he would meet her in the lobby at ten o'clock to bring her to "dinner." Twice he suggested that she relax in a hot bath, which reminded Diana of Alex's explanation for the Arabs' demand for her charges. Shipping California Girls halfway across the world seemed to Diana like carrying coals to Newcastle, what with all the local beauties, not to mention those across the Channel. But it was the bath, Alex told her, that made the difference. "They think European girls are dirty," Alex said. "With the English, they have to drop a shilling just to get hot water. And the French with their bidets. They may clean their pussies, but what about the rest?" It seemed ironic to Diana that the Arabs, of all people, would have a cleanliness fetish. The Swiss, maybe, but the Arabs? Oh well, she thought. If she couldn't be tall or blond or Californian, she could at least be clean. Not the ugly American, but the spotless American. For once, a cultural stereotype—the American sanitation complex and germophobia, the Taped Motel Toilet Seat syndrome—was working to her benefit.

Diana soaked for an hour in the huge porcelain tub, then got dressed in her Panty Raid lingerie, a black Chanel, and Maud Frizon pumps. In her last year in Hollywood, she had never gotten so dressed up. In fact, she had never even tried on a Chanel. She felt grown-up, glamorous, sexy. And nervous beyond belief. She opened the complimentary bottle of Cordon Rouge in the ice bucket, turned on British MTV, and nearly finished the entire thing.

The grand hall of the Dorchester was lined with two rows of faux-marble columns that gave it the look of a lush Roman bath. Overwhelming the occasional British couple nibbling on smoked-salmon sandwiches were clusters of Arab men in pinstripes sipping tea and fondling worry beads on the low sofas. Diana, whose mind was both drunk and racing, walked the hall as if it were the gauntlet of a seraglio, each leering dark man a potential buyer. None of them was her buyer. She felt completely alone, adrift, waiting for someone she had no image of, the ultimate blind date.

When she heard the word "Diana" and turned around to see a dashing young man with wavy hair and the glint and panache of a young Marcello Mastroianni, she felt that her sheikh was her true Prince Charming. He could have been a model in an Armani ad, except he looked much warmer and more open. She wasn't sure whether to call him "Sheikh," or "Prince," or whatever. She decided to get personal. "Fuad." She put out her hand. He kissed it. "Mario," the man said, and her heart sank. Mario was Fuad's "personal assistant," which proved to mean his chief procurer. Nor was he Italian, though he had certainly spent his time there buying clothes and getting his hair cut and scouting the modeling agencies. Mario was Lebanese, as all the great procurers for Mideast royalty have historically been, and he had the charm of a Levantine trader. That his trade was flesh required him to be all the more charming.

Every Arab sheikh worth his petrodollars had his Lebanese pimp, who was in practice his man Friday, arranging not only women but chartered jets, skiing weekends, restaurant reservations, theater tickets, papal audiences, and the like. Mario was quite young for the trade; like butlers, procurers tended to be older, wiser types. Mario compensated for his youth with his pimpish pedigree. His grandfather had been an *aide-de-chambre* of King Farouk, and his uncle had been the Shah of Iran's man in Paris. Mario himself was so arresting that Sigourney Weaver, who was entering the Dorchester, gave him a second look as he was escorting Diana out. If Mario didn't have a rendezvous, he might well have tried to pick up the actress for his master. Any woman was fair game, and, as required by his profession, Mario was impervious to rejection. Besides, it was easier to approach women with the sheikh's hat in his hand than his own, though often the women were frankly disappointed that Mario was not trading in his own account. Still, Mario never committed the breach of duty of subordinating his principal to his own interest. He never "tested" girls intended for Fuad.

Diana was jarred when Mario opened the door of the Bentley to reveal a chorus line of long legs and a cacophony of French. In the backseat were three very dark and very tall Scheherazades, all dressed similarly to Diana in black Chanel outfits. They all glared daggers at Diana. Mario introduced them as Jasmine, Fatma, and Nevine, "guests" of Fuad's who had just arrived from Paris. When Mario presented Diana to them as a "guest" from Los Angeles, the girls all began babbling in French, assuming that Diana could not understand them. Diana responded in French, and the girls switched to Arabic. Diana suddenly felt less like a Cinderella than a harem slave. As the other girls twittered on, the only words Diana could comprehend were "Manolo Blahnik," "Bruce Oldfield," and "Rifat Ozbek," the names of English shoe designers and couturiers.

She stared out at the empty streets of rain-swept Mayfair, a prisoner of the Bentley.

The restaurant they were taken to was Wilton's, on Jermyn Street. It seemed an odd choice for a sheikh and his harem, Diana thought, but she had no idea what an Anglophile Fuad was. Wilton's was the most "English"—and expensively so—of any traditional restaurant in London. It was as clubby as the real clubs like White's and Boodle's in nearby St. James's, except that it had better food. Wilton's was, in effect, a club for the clubless, *nouveau chic* art dealers and wine merchants and other West End nabobs long on pretention and short on lineage. It was a great favorite of Anglophiliac Hollywood types, one of whom, the American-in-London literary agent Ed Victor, Diana recognized from a meeting she had sat in on when someone at Council Bluffs was briefly interested in acquiring one of the Jackie Collins novels Victor represented. Diana was mortified. She stared so hard at the agent that she stepped on the heel of one of the Arab girls' Chanel pumps, nearly tripping her over a silver roast-beef trolley.

Luckily, Victor was too intent on the deal making at hand at his table to look up. The maître d' rounded the corner and led the group to a large booth with velvet curtains. Waiting for the girls were Fuad and Hosni Samma, the global arms dealer, who seemed to know the three Scheherazades. He kissed them warmly and spoke to them in animated French. Samma was fat and cuddly, the kind of character who would break the bank in Monte Carlo in a 1950s movie. As for Fuad, Diana had expected Mecca. What she got was Eton. A tiny, delicate man in his thirties with razor-cut thinning hair, Fuad wore an elegant Savile Row suit and handmade shoes. He spoke like Winston Churchill. Diana was completely intimidated. What could he want with her? He seemed totally the young statesman, hardly the type to order up sex parties from all over the globe.

Nervously reaching for small talk, Diana broke the ice. "I think we went to the same school."

"Did we now?" Fuad replied.

"Columbia."

"Oh, yes. My MBA. The West Point of capitalism. It was a grisly experience there. And you? Were you at Barnard?"

"No, Columbia," Diana said. "The men's part."

"It's fully integrated now?"

"Well, it's coed," Diana answered, struggling to keep the conversation going. "Did you live in a dorm when you went there?"

All of a sudden, Fuad, Mario, and Samma broke into wild paroxysms of laughter. In Arabic, Samma let the other girls in on the joke. Eventually they explained it to Diana. When Fuad went to Columbia, he had bought a multimillion-dollar landmark town house on East Seventieth Street between Park and Lexington, perhaps the most beautiful and expensive block in Manhattan. The idea that Fuad could live in a dormitory was as ludicrous as the image of Queen Elizabeth in Guess? jeans. Diana forced herself to laugh along, but she knew that rather than being in on the joke, she *was* the joke.

For all his wealth and polish, Fuad wasn't Saudi royalty. He was royalty adjacent. The word "sheikh" did not necessarily denote nobility but was rather an honorific for a distinguished citizen. Fuad's father had been an Egyptian doctor to the Saudi royal family, a gastroenterologist whom the royals flew in so often from Cairo to treat their *crises de foie* that they finally set him up in Riyadh. Fuad fused his Western education and his capitalistic ambitions with his palace connections to become the middleman on many construction deals American and English companies wanted to do in the Middle East. Fuad was a facilitator, even a fixer, but never of planes, never of guns, never of chemical weapons, just of nice things like industrial parks, schools, resorts. Everyone liked Fuad. He was above reproach. He had a family in Cairo that he took to his home in Cap-Ferrat for the summer, and when he was with them he was a devoted father. Nevertheless, like the true Middle Easterner that he was, Fuad had a harem mentality.

Yet he was not a stereotypical sexist pig. To Diana he was all charm and courtesy. Over an endless procession of British fruits of the sea— including Scotch salmon and Dover sole—all washed down by Evian for Fuad, who was a devout Moslem, and champagne for the rest, Fuad quizzed Diana about California suburbia and about Hollywood. By the end of the meal, she felt very important, the center of attention, much to the dismay of the three Arab goddesses. They glared at Diana throughout.

After dinner, the ensemble proceeded to Annabel's, at Berkeley Square, for decades London's most exclusive private nightclub. The people there looked as if they had stepped out of the pages of the *Tatler,* or the royal enclosure at Ascot, and Diana felt self-conscious being part of this very un-English desert caravan. Nevertheless, the entire club bowed and scraped to Fuad and Samma as if they were visiting royalty. This time, however, the seating was much more haremesque. Diana and the three Arab girls were seated at a banquette behind that of Samma and Fuad, who literally held court to the various and sundry suppliants and well-wishers. The Arab girls talked about shoes in Arabic and French, smoked endless cigarettes, ran up a small fortune in champagne tabs, and did nothing to include Diana in their revelry.

Just as Diana was about to zone out into terminal boredom, who should appear at Fuad's table but Lowell Landesman, a brash Hollywood sore thumb on this velvet glove of British exclusivity. Straight out of Brooklyn, with an obvious hair transplant worse than Frank Sinatra's, Lowell still dressed like a sharpie from his glory days in the 1960s, when he was the hottest thing to emerge from the William Morris mail room. Whatever his visual limitations, he wasn't aware of them. Lowell had a unique knack of always being seen in all the right places at all the right times, places in which he had absolutely no right or reason to be. From Carnaval in Rio to the Kentucky Derby, from the Union Club in New York to the Circolo della Caccia in Rome, from Little Nell's in Aspen to the Oriental in Bangkok, Lowell Landesman was always there. Why? He was looking for money. Now in his early sixties but not even close to slowing down, Lowell was famous for having produced over forty major studio films. Not one of them had ever made back its investment. His secret was assembling star packages and always being one movie ahead of his next flop. Hollywood believed in stars, and Lowell milked this idolatry for all it was worth. A King Midas in reverse, he could turn anyone from Marlon Brando to Arnold Schwarzenegger into box-office poison. But Lowell understood stars like no one else did. He knew that what they all wanted to do was act, i.e., play someone they were totally not.

A case in point was the "hot" project Lowell was here to pitch to Fuad. "It was so hot I snapped it up before it was in galleys," Lowell said. "Listen to the title: MC^2. Fantastic, isn't it?" He was referring to the new biography of Albert Einstein, the film rights of which he had bought without reading a word. Then again, Lowell wasn't a reader. He was a seller.

"Tom Cruise is dying, literally dying, to play Einstein. And Carmel Lane, you know her?"

"The megamodel." Fuad nodded.

"Fuad, you're on top of it." Lowell winked. "Carmel would make her debut as Einstein's wife. Hot, huh? Plus, get this, did you know Einstein was into music?"

"He played the violin, didn't he?" Fuad said.

"Mr. Biography!" Lowell flattered him. "That violin was only slightly less important to him than his slide rule, so who do I have to do the music, only the biggest band in the world. U2. Can you see it, U2, MC^2. It's the biggest package of all time. Fuad, you saw *Top Gun*, didn't you?"

"I must confess it was rather silly. It was the only movie I ever saw that made me airsick."

"Those vomit bags were full of money," Lowell said. "Do you know how big that was? Three hundred million worldwide, and this is better. *Top Gun. Top Brain.* It's Cruise. It's class. It's a love story. It's perfect. Tom Cruise *is* Albert Einstein!"

"So what do you need me for, Lowell?" Fuad asked.

"To keep the studio from taking all the profits. I want us to own the negative. I want to finance the movie without the studio. Let them distribute, *c'est tout!* Fuad, all I need is forty. I'll give you back two hundred, at least. You have my word."

"That's a big return, Lowell."

"I'm a big producer, Fuad. I want you with me. I want to see you blow Dodi away."

Diana hung on every word of Lowell's honeyed pitch, the sheer audacity of it all. She had never heard anyone drop so many names—Desmond Guinness, Queen Noor, Jane Fonda, Conrad Black, Michael Caine, Prince Rainier, Jack Lang, Jehan Sadat, Henry Kissinger, the Aga Khan, all Lowell's "dearest personal friends." Lowell used the names to varnish himself with respectability, and he always managed to insert some little detail about each one that indicated that the relationship had not been fabricated from the pages of *People* or *Vanity Fair*. Further, the fact that he had made forty films, albeit disasters, enabled him to lure people like Fuad into the Hollywood Casbah. Lowell's marks didn't read the *Variety* box-office charts. All they knew was names, and Lowell certainly had those. Diana wanted to jump in and warn Fuad about Lowell's track record, though that had never stopped Lowell from getting rich investors, all of whom had been cured of their infatuation with Hollywood after their honeymoon with Lowell. Lowell was the Manolete of hype. Diana couldn't stop herself, much as she wanted to, from being impressed.

Lowell must have spotted this. Even though Fuad did not introduce any of his girls to any of his visitors, Lowell managed to bump into Diana as she was coming out of the powder room, and somehow extracted from her that she was from California and was also in the film business. Here was a Hollywood legend, a man who could get more mileage out of failure than others from success, and Diana knew she would probably never have another chance to meet him. Her embarrassment about her current assignment notwithstanding, she wanted to connect with him as a co-conspirator. After all, weren't they both after the same thing? Fuad's money.

"You were a D girl? Things are looking up in Hollywood."

"I hated it."

"So did I. Can't live there."

"I love your project. Sheer genius."

"You don't think it's too highbrow?" Lowell expressed a rare sentiment of doubt.

"Not with Tom Cruise. He'll make I.Q. sexy."

"Where are you staying?" Lowell asked.

"The Dorchester."

Lowell raised an impressed eyebrow, but he was too polite to pursue how the room tab was being paid. "Can I take you for drinks?"

"Why not?" Diana didn't see this as a meaningless "Let's have lunch." She would have never gotten this close to this legend as a mere scribe in a story meeting.

"Maybe we can cook up something. Tell Fuad you love the project."

"I think it's great for him," Diana said, bluffing that she had a degree of influence over the sheikh. "Call me." She shook Lowell's hand. She suspected that Lowell knew what her game was here, just as she knew his. There was honor among thieves.

The games finally began for Diana around two-thirty in the morning when the Bentley brought her and the three Arab girls back to the hotel. Fuad, who traveled in a separate car, an antique Rolls, had stayed behind at Annabel's, and Diana thought she was off the hook, at least for to-night. It was not the case. Mario told her she could go to her room, but suggested that she keep her clothes on, as Fuad would want to see her when he returned. Diana watched MTV for the next hour. Then Mario called and invited Diana up to Fuad's penthouse quarters.

The suite was overwhelming, almost surreal. The effect was that of an enchanted forest. There were endless papier-mâché branches and gilt leaves, and door handles in the shape of birds on twigs. There was a *Sleeping Beauty* room, and a *Magic Flute* room, and there was a bedroom with locked doors, where, Mario informed Diana, Fuad was "entertain-ing" Fatma and Nevine. He added that she and Jasmine, who was al-ready in the suite when Diana arrived, would be next.

"I've never done this before," Diana said in French to Jasmine, trying to create some connection.

"Why do all you Americans have to pretend that you are virgins?" Jas-mine snapped back.

"I swear. I have no idea."

"Please." Jasmine rolled her eyes.

Alert to Diana's anxiety, Mario returned with a Valium and a bottle of champagne. "It isn't brain surgery," he assured her. "Smile," he said to

Jasmine, who gave in and forced one, mumbling something to Mario in Arabic. He replied with what sounded like a threat, after which Jasmine's personality totally shifted. She assured Diana how easy their task would be and told her just to follow her lead.

Fuad finally ushered the girls into his candlelit bedroom, a floral Disneyland of forest creatures and fairies. Classical music was playing. He was wearing a white Dorchester bathrobe, and sat back in a gold brocade armchair to watch Diana and Jasmine undressing each other. Jasmine led the way, unzipping Diana's Chanel and cueing Diana that with each item Jasmine removed, it then became Diana's turn to remove one of Jasmine's, dress for dress, black slip for black slip.

"*Belle*," Diana said, admiring Jasmine in her very French demi-bra and garter belt and silk stockings. She felt short and dumpy compared to the towering, sleek, elegant Jasmine. Then Jasmine leaned over and kissed her, and because Jasmine was so beautiful, and had been so nasty, this display of affection, charade though it may have been, had a voluptuously hypnotic effect on Diana. They kissed again, and fell back onto the vast bed.

Fuad sat in the chair impassively, watching Jasmine unsnap Diana's bra and bury her face in Diana's perfect cleavage. "*Vous êtes belle*," Jasmine moaned, and Diana wanted to believe her. They continued to remove each other's lingerie. Diana rolled down Jasmine's stockings, undid her garter belt, and felt rather inelegant by comparison in her panty hose. She felt even less elegant after she slid off Jasmine's silk lace bikini panties. Jasmine's mons veneris was completely shaven. Diana didn't want Jasmine to see the Panty Raid ten-dollar specials under her panty hose, much less see how hairy she was. She felt like a slob, although Jasmine was doing everything in her power to make her feel like a queen, whispering French and Arabic sweet nothings in Diana's ears, sliding her long fingers down Diana's panty hose, feathering her vagina, teasing her clitoris, getting Diana something she never thought she could be: excited.

Then Fuad called time-out. "I think we need a bath," he said. A bath was the very last thing on Diana's mind at this point. But the bath, she remembered, was why she was there. Fuad showed them into the master bathroom, as large and ornate as a Roman nymphaeum. A bubble bath was waiting. Fuad took another armchair and watched Diana take off her tights and panties and ease into the suds. The tub was less a demonstration of erotica than of sanitation. Each woman would rise up and be soaped and scrubbed by the other, with Diana following Jasmine's lead. Although he was still showing no emotion, it was clear that soap was Fuad's thing, and Diana and Jasmine gave it to him, careful to keep their heads above water, their hair dry, and their makeup intact. All Diana could think about was the old Bobby Darin song "Splish Splash," and the lyric "Rub-a-dub, I was relaxin' in the tub." She struggled to keep from giggling. "Aah," she moaned and groaned.

Fuad stood up and motioned Jasmine out of the bath. He went to the medicine cabinet and took out a large jar, from which he scooped some red cream. He began massaging it all over Jasmine's glistening wet body, rubbing it between her legs, concentrating on her pussy, turning her around, probing his creamed fingers inside her, front and back. Jasmine moaned with ecstasy, though she made no attempt to undo Fuad's robe, to engage him in the pleasure she seemed to be getting from him. Watching from the bath, Diana assumed that the cream was some sort of powerful aphrodisiac. Finished with a very spent Jasmine, Fuad sent her into the bedroom. "Your turn." He waved Diana over. She quickly realized what a superb actress Jasmine was. The cream was a burning astringent, hardly an emollient of pleasure.

"What is it?" she asked Fuad.

"A special disinfectant from Kiehl's pharmacy in New York, very effective. Kills everything." It became difficult for Diana to match Jasmine's multiple orgasms. She felt she was less in a seraglio than in a hospital, less with a lover than with a gynecologist. Fuad was the Howard Hughes of the Middle East. He was beyond paranoia about disease.

Diana worried that her ill-concealed discomfort would turn Fuad off as much as she was turned off. Instead, Fuad began breathing more heavily, actually sweating. The man who had been so in control all evening was now losing it. His robe fell open. His small penis was erect. He gave the jar of disinfectant cream to Diana and gasped instructions on how to rub it over his body. "But don't touch me there," he muttered, pointing to his genitals. Diana couldn't believe she was turning him on.

"Quickly, quickly," Fuad urged.

Fuad led Diana back to the bed, where Jasmine was masturbating with an ivory vibrator decorated with carved camels at its base. Fuad got into bed next to her and pulled Diana in with them to make a sandwich. Before Diana had the chance to worry about Fuad's not wearing a condom, the point became moot. She felt something wet and sticky all over her thigh. The slight friction with her body had been all that was necessary to get Fuad off. "Yes, nice" was all he said. Without any afterglow, he was off to the shower, back in his robe, applauding Jasmine and Diana for a "very stimulating evening." In the hallway en route to their rooms, Diana thanked Jasmine for her help.

"Don't thank me. Thank Alex," Jasmine said.

The next morning, Mario woke up a very hungover Diana to tell her how much Fuad had liked her and that he wanted to see her again in his suite right before lunch. He wanted her to dress in a new Versace outfit she would find in her closet. This time it would be only the two of them. Otherwise the routine would be the same. Strip, bath, bed. Mario reminded her to bathe first, even though she was going to be bathing again shortly. By one o'clock, Mario still hadn't called to summon her to the suite. By two, getting impatient, Diana called him. Fuad had had to go out to meet some British cabinet minister, Mario apologized. But he would be back shortly, and "needed" to see Diana. Mario asked her to wait in the room. It turned out to be waiting for Godot. Fuad got back to the Dorchester at four, then had to rush out for tea. "Right back" meant three more hours, at which point he had an unexpected brief meeting, which took two more hours and forced a cancellation of the pre-dinner quickie. Dinner, to which Diana had originally been invited, ended up transpiring at a Pall Mall club to which women could not go, so she had to eat room-service food alone in her Versace gear. At one A.M., Fuad finally returned. Mario asked her to take another bath, so that she would be "fresh." Diana cheated and used the bidet. She finally saw Fuad at two, and the entire session lasted no more than a half hour, the sex part mere seconds, as he came when she accidentally touched his penis while rubbing him down with disinfectant. Rather than showing any disappointment, or trying to get it up again, Fuad was completely elated. "Superb," he complimented Diana. "Excellent." Then he sent her back to her room, promising to see her in the morning.

Morning proved to be three A.M. some twenty-five hours later, after another endless day of dressing, this time in Armani, and waiting from one delay through the next. Diana was the prisoner of the Dorchester. She wanted to go out, explore London, go to museums, anything. Every hour, though, Mario would ring up, making sure she was on call for Fuad's imminent arrival. It was like being stranded at an airport waiting for a flight that will never take off, constantly being "handled" by reservations clerks who promised you everything and never even gave you Arpège. Although Alex had told Diana that Fuad would appreciate her for her brains, he barely spent enough time with her to enjoy her body, much less her mind. On the third night, there was still no sex, only the slightest friction. This time Fuad made it to the bed, though not much further. It was easy money, obscenely easy. It wasn't even like domination. All Diana was really required to do for the twenty thousand dollars was bathe, dress, and wait.

This was becoming the longest week of Diana's life, even if it was the most lucrative. When Mario called on the fourth day, saying that Fuad had had to go to a conference in Scotland that would last until the following afternoon, Diana rejoiced in her freedom. She rejoiced even more when Mario's call was followed by Lowell Landesman's inviting her to lunch at the San Lorenzo.

The airy, multi-tiered Italian restaurant behind Harrods was to London what Mortimer's was to New York and the late Ma Maison had been to Los Angeles. Diana had read that it was Princess Di's favorite restaurant. She saw rock stars—Bryan Ferry, Eric Clapton, David Gilmour of Pink Floyd—all of whom Lowell knew and kissed on both cheeks. Lowell seemed to know more people than the maître d'—socialites, art dealers, photographers, clothing manufacturers. He introduced Diana to all of them as "a filmmaker in from L.A.," which sounded very grand and made Diana feel a part of this in-crowd.

Lowell was all charm, so polite that he never even mentioned Fuad and what Diana was doing with him. He did want to know everything else about her, and once he found out, he suggested that she should come to work as his development girl in Los Angeles. Lowell didn't have one, as he divided his time between London and New York. "I can't take the Coast anymore," he said. Hollywood had gotten too corporate, too young. He talked about paying Diana fifty thousand a year, plus making her associate producer of any projects she brought in, if she would work for him. But what about her writing, her directing?, she wondered.

"You gotta build up favors first. I'm making you a buyer. Buyers buy from buyers, not sellers."

After lunch, Lowell drove her to his flat in Cheyne Walk in his racing-green Aston Martin DB-5. His car, his clothes, his furniture, were all Swinging London of the sixties. A David Bailey photograph of Lowell with Jean Shrimpton dominated one wall of the flat; aside from the bad hair transplant, he hadn't changed at all. Lowell poured the champagne along with the stories, and Diana came under his spell, believing that she could be a player in the very exclusive game of Hollywood, that Lowell Landesman had discovered her and was going to be her mentor, even her messiah. She also assumed he was going to make a pass at her at any second.

"I want you to go out with John Novachek tonight," Lowell said, catching Diana completely off guard. Novachek was in London rehearsing a play. Lowell proposed to fix Diana up on a blind date, a goodwill gesture to bring the actor around on a film to which Lowell was trying to attach him. "He'll love you," Lowell flattered her.

Diana wasn't sure whether to take honor or offense. John Novachek was one of her least favorite actors, as far as wanting to go out with was concerned. She liked pretty boys, kids. Novachek was too old, too bald, too weird, too scary—and furthermore, what was she supposed to *do* on this date?

"You meet him in his flat off Redcliffe Square," Lowell said.

"And go to dinner?"

"Whatever he wants to do."

"Is this a date or a trick?" Diana asked, flat out.

"It's business. I want you to work for me."

"As a D girl or a B-girl?"

Lowell chuckled. He hadn't mentioned Fuad, but now he brought it up, albeit obliquely. "He's a movie star. Broads love him. You're flexible. You're a realist."

"You want me to go over and fuck John Novachek for you."

"For us. We're going to be a team."

"And who else will I have to fuck?"

"Whoever. All these nerdy young film-school kids, the new Spielbergs, they're all ours for a piece of smart ass. A good working girl who knows how to fuck the right guys can rule this business. Look at the ones who do. I will tell you who the right guys are. I'll tell you who and I'll tell you when and I'll tell you when to cut it off, and if you listen to me, you can leave Sherry and Dawn and Stacey and Gail Ann and all these girls in the dust."

"But I don't want to be a hooker," Diana said.

"We're all hookers," Lowell echoed Tinka.

"I can't do it."

"You are doing it. You're doing it great. You're in the majors, baby. What are you talking about? You're big-time. Besides, now you're fucking for money. I'm talking about your future."

Diana burst into tears. Being Fuad's whore was one thing. Being Lowell's whore was another, because that was her future, and if the only way she could have it, to play with a master player like Lowell, was to be his sexual hit girl, what kind of future was it?

Then Geena Davis's agent called Lowell from ICM, and then it was Debra Winger's agent from CAA, and then Mike Nichols's office was on the line. And Diana realized that it was a better, more exciting, and more glamorous future than anything else she could expect, and that she was fortunate to be in actual striking distance of what to all the *People* readers in the country was nothing more than a Hollywood fantasy. As Lowell began talking to someone about letting Madonna direct, Diana dried her eyes and sat next to him on the black leather couch overlooking the graceful Albert Bridge across the Thames. She thought about Jasmine and Fuad and how far she had come during the last three days, and she unzipped Lowell's bespoke Tommy Nutter fly and gave him a blow job the likes of which, a week before, she couldn't have imagined bestowing upon anyone less young or less cute than Rob Lowe.

The Hollywood grapevine had had it that Lowell was gay, that the three icy socialites he had married were networking tools, not sex objects. The way Lowell had proposed selling her into bondage to John Novachek as lagniappe on a deal had made Diana suspect the same. How could one of the ultimate Hollywood producers be eschewing the casting couch? Yet Lowell responded to her instantly. Although he could never come, he was a skilled and endless lover. His silver tongue was an instrument of pleasure, not merely of hype. They stayed in Lowell's circular bed for hours, their lovemaking interrupted only by two calls from CAA. That Lowell screened all the rest, including ones from Paul Newman and Shirley MacLaine, made Diana feel special, even exalted. Even John Novachek went by the boards, though Diana wasn't sure whether that was a function of Lowell's ardor for her or of the fact that Lowell was unable to reach him.

They broke to drive out to Fulham for Thai food. Then it was back for more sex. Although Diana was a bit distressed that she couldn't bring Lowell to a climax, she wrote it off to his age. Lowell had no problem maintaining his erection, which stood, literally, in contrast to his otherwise sagging physique. Nonetheless, Diana wasn't acting out her own arousal. She wasn't fucking a father figure. She was fucking Paramount and Columbia. And Fox. And Universal.

And the whole star system. Diana listened to Lowell's stories about sex in Hollywood, how he got girls for Darryl Zanuck, boys for Cary Grant. His tales made Sammy Glick seem naïve. Lowell told her of his intrigue with Grace Kelly, who, he said, slept with everyone except Hitchcock, who wanted her the most and who got especially piqued when even Lowell, as a Young Turk, got lucky on a slow night on the *Rear Window* set at Paramount. Lowell told Diana about Sharon Tate, and how he helped discover her. There were tall tales of Cannes festivals, Oscar nights, of locations from *El Cid* to *River Kwai*, of starlets found and lost. And here was Diana, with Lowell's head between her legs, his tongue of a thousand stars. Grace. Sharon. Diana. This was Cinderella time indeed, the courtesan of a sheikh in London, the consort of a king of Hollywood.

Lowell talked about Diana staying on awhile in London, maybe flying over with him to Paris to see his friends Polanski and Depardieu, eat at his friend Alain Senderens's Lucas Carton, make love at al-Fayeds's Ritz. Of course, Diana's assignment had to be completed before they did anything else. Lowell respected the twenty thousand, he applauded it. Dropping her off at the Dorchester in his Aston Martin, he told her he'd see her in three days. "Ciao, babe," he said, roaring off to Park Lane. Diana felt like Audrey Hepburn in *Love in the Afternoon*, very sophisticated, very privileged, giddy, happy.

Diana asked for her key at the concierge's desk.

"But you've already checked out," the Jeeves-like clerk said to her.

"Checked out? There's some mistake."

"Not at all. We have your bags. The bill's been taken care of."

What was going on? Diana said she wanted to go back to her room. The front desk politely refused. Diana spotted the three Asian bodyguards in sunglasses around the desk. Were they there for her? It was all so ominous. Diana left the concierge, went to reception. Again, the well-mannered stonewalling. She was out.

She called Mario's room on the house phone. There was no answer. She called Fuad. Nothing. She called Lowell. Machine. She left an urgent message. Then she called Alex. It was the middle of the night in Los Angeles. Alex picked up, right away. She was wide-awake.

"How can you be so stupid?" Alex scolded Diana. "How?"

"What did I do?" Diana asked.

"You were there for Fuad," Alex said gravely.

"I still am. He was away."

"You were on his dime, his time. You don't fuck another man when you're there for Fuad. It's incredibly insulting. He's your host."

"Who said I fucked anybody? I just had lunch . . ." Diana sputtered.

"You fucked Lowell Landesman. Don't lie to me."

"How do you know what I did?"

"We know everything."

"Alex, I'm here. I like Fuad. He liked me. We were doing great."

"He did like you. That makes it even worse."

"Come on. I'm not like his girlfriend," Diana insisted.

"That's exactly what you were. You really screwed this up. Why? Did Lowell promise he was going to give you a job?" Alex bore down on her.

"Alex, I'm sorry."

"Go to Heathrow. British Airways. I'll wire you a ticket so you can get home."

"But the twenty—"

"Please."

"I saw him three nights. I came all the way here. I should get—"

"Nothing. You really fucked up. You're lucky to get a ticket home, which I have to go out of pocket for. You've insulted these people. These are my friends. You stupid little opportunist." Alex slammed down the phone. This was one more daughter she would have to disinherit. Alex had wanted so much to build a relationship with Diana; she was deeply disappointed it wasn't to be.

Diana didn't want to go back to Los Angeles. She didn't really know what she wanted; this reversal was so precipitous. Wandering out of the hotel in a daze, she walked the glorious streets of Mayfair and was nearly run over twice because she looked left when she should have looked right. No, she told herself, Lowell would take care of her. She had lost the twenty, but she had gotten back her career.

She returned to the Dorchester, to the stares and askance glances of the staff. She might as well have been wearing a scarlet A. She checked at the concierge's desk for messages. There were none. She called Lowell again.

"Sigourney?" he answered the phone.

"No, it's me," Diana said. "You won't believe this nightmare."

"I know all about it," Lowell said. "Bad news."

"Can I come over now?"

"No."

"Meetings?"

"No. Just no."

"What?" Diana was shocked.

"It's a bad idea, babe. It's not going to happen. I'm in enough shit myself." Lowell explained how badly he needed Fuad to bankroll the Einstein project. "I could lose Cruise, I could lose the book, the whole thing. I had no idea how hot he was on you. I shoulda never let you come on to me like you did."

Diana was horrified. Lowell, her mentor, her ticket to the stars, was bailing out on her. "What about working together?" She groped desperately for a lifeline.

"These people have a very strict code of honor."

"But what about you?"

"They blame the chick, babe. That's their culture. I gotta face reality. I like you, you're great, you'll have a big life, but you're a hot potato now. I need the deal, babe. That's entertainment."

CHAPTER EIGHT

STAR WARS

*A*madam's greatest asset is her client list. The obsession Lissa Trapp had with getting mine showed how valuable my list was. She came after it so hard, so maliciously, so relentlessly. She was like one of those terrifying velociraptor dinosaurs in *Jurassic Park*, or the monster in *Alien*. She just kept coming. My poor clients. She had to have them. Clients. Who were my clients? That's all anyone wants to know. Names. Name names. It's like Senator McCarthy. If I did name names, the same thing might happen to the stars as happened to the Hollywood Ten, or however many they were. They'd stop being stars. Instead, they'd be sick men who paid to have sex. America is hypocritical. In this country, everything is for sale: senators, judges, the White House. Look at the BCCI scandal. You can buy cabinet members, but you can't buy pussy, or love, or sex, or whatever you want to call it. No, buying pussy is un-American. But things are getting better. The Gennifer Flowers thing couldn't stop Bill Clinton. And look how the public loves hooker movies—*Pretty Woman, Indecent Proposal,* although I think the million was way out of line, six figures out of line, even for one of my clients, and even for Demi Moore.

Who, who, you keep asking? *Everybody!* Listen, I was amazed myself at the people I had. The most famous, the richest, the handsomest, I couldn't believe it. What did they need *me* for? But they did. Take the stars. No matter how cool and self-assured they seem up on the big screen, actors are the most insecure people on earth, especially in the bedroom. Warren Beatty may have known how to trade on his celebrity to get laid, but I can't imagine Kevin Costner going up to the bar at the Olive to some starlet and saying, "I'm Kevin Costner and you've just hit the jackpot in sex lotto." Stars can't do that. They don't even go out anymore. It's too crazy out there. They're pretty much scared of women. And if you saw the women in Hollywood, you'd be scared, too. They lure you in with their Alaia dresses and their Sports Connection bodies, and then they kick you in the balls with feminism. No star wants to have a fling and then read in the *Star* the next week how small his cock is or how fast he comes. And they surely don't want their wives to read it. So they called me.

I don't care if a star is typecast as Jesus—once he takes the beard off, he's just a guy, and guys can't help but be horny. Think about our saintly president JFK. Hollywood is the horniest place on earth. And the most repressed. And certainly the most two-faced. Pussy is like smog here; it's in the air. The women are amazing, and they're right out there with it, all the right stuff. But there's no such thing as free love. Everything has a price, everything is a deal. Sex is a negotiation, just like buying a house. The girls drive a tough bargain. They've got the beauty, for sure, but, if you want it, you've got to promise them a career, or a lifetime. Compared to that, I was cheap at my price.

I did a huge business with the stars. I did an even bigger business with the studios and the agencies. I felt sorry for those poor guys, making nothing but glossy T-and-A movies and television and then having to bullshit the world with family values and socially redeeming this and that. These players, these power brokers, are aroused all the time, yet all they do is drive around in their Mercedeses and make deals on their car phones or stuff their faces with boring food at Mortons and make deals that make no sense because the place is so noisy they can't possibly hear what the other guy is saying. How much pleasure do they get out of any of it? There's so much aggression—fuck you, fuck him, fuck this, fuck that, no fucking way—no wonder they want to do some *real* fucking. And their wives are all too busy at the Beverly Center to pay much attention to them. So who were they gonna call? Ghostbusters?

This town is sensory overload. Hollywood is all about sex, but in reality it's the biggest tease on earth. It's show time, all right, all show and no go, a giant jerk-off. These guys end up getting off by paying Michelle Pfeiffer five million dollars to be in their movies, and then calling me for two thousand wanting to arrange a *real* fuck with someone who looks exactly like her. Hollywood is the world capital of arrested development. The "Players" are about as mature as the juvenile delinquents they make their blockbusters for. I'm not so sure how many of them could get it for nothing. All I do know is that when it came down to sex, *real live sex*, I was the one person in this come-on town who, as they say, put out. No wonder everybody wanted my number. No wonder Lissa wanted to take it over.

At thirty-eight, Zack Davis had it all. By Hollywood standards, he was a star, having created a long-running TV series, *Urban Professionals*, and directed two hit movies, and CAA was at his beck and call. By general American standards, too, he was a star: attractive, Harvard-educated, a beautiful Century City lawyer wife, two perfect children, a gracious New England–style home in Brentwood, a ranch in Montana. Despite all these trappings of success, however, when measured by the yardstick of American manhood Zack Davis was a dismal failure. Why? Because he committed an act that, at least in this country, is an admission of inadequacy, of self-loathing, of being anything but the winner all the other indicia said he was. Zack Davis went to prostitutes. He paid for sex. He did it all the time.

Today at the Fox commissary, Zack was having lunch with a senior executive who was trying to lure him onto the lot with an overall deal— features, TV, a fat discretionary fund to acquire scripts, salaries for a v.p. and three D girls, and his own Tudor bungalow, not a converted trailer like so many of his peers had. Where Zack was concerned, the main reason to come to Fox was that its commissary had the only decent food on any lot, specifically the Chinese chicken salad and the gazpacho. Its menu was very health-conscious, listing the fat and cholesterol and caloric content of each dish. He liked that. He also liked Melanie Braun, the executive who was giving him the hard sell. Specifically, he liked her ankles and thighs and the way she crossed her legs and the slit in the skirt of her slightly risqué business suit. If she had been really smart, she would have taken him back to her Santa Fe–style office overlooking the *Hello, Dolly!* set, closed the blinds, and fucked him on her tasteful cowhide couch. Then he would have signed with Fox. It would have never occurred to Melanie, who was not above giving her all for her studio. She had given it before, but Zack Davis was Mr. Normal, far above such carnal pitches.

So they talked gross points and first refusal, and Zack turned his fantasy to Kathleen Turner, crossing her big, powerful legs across the room. She had gained weight since *Body Heat*, and Zack suggested that she might have used a body double in that scorcher. Melanie assured him she hadn't, still not picking up on Zack's libidinousness. All Zack could think about was sex. He coveted Rosanna Arquette, sitting by the window, cute and pert. She had the best tits in Hollywood (Mimi Rogers had the biggest), and Zack thought about pressing himself between them and exploding into Rosanna's lush, big lips. And there was Sally Field. He coveted her too. She was the Flying Nun, and that turned him on. The idea of piercing the veil, exposing the façade, stripping the stars naked, got Zack really going. The stars were packing the place today. There was Farrah Fawcett, with that amazing Texas hair, and Melanie

Griffith, whose phony-sounding voice was real, and, wow, there was Jane Fonda, Miss Hanoi Peace Jane Fonda, Miss Perfect Body Workout. Zack had been dying for Jane Fonda ever since her Roger Vadim days. But that was when Zack was just another horny, brainy guy in Cambridge. Now he knew the star. Now he could cast her. Now he could fuck her. But not really, because he was the perfect family man, above sport fucking, above affairs. Zack was a class act. People looked up to him. He hated it.

The commissary was pure show time, Silicone Valley, and Zack was totally turned on by the star power and tinsel of it all and by the fact that Fox was courting him and would have sucked his cock if only they knew that that was *precisely* what Zack wanted them to do. All the female stars, plus Melanie Braun, had given Zack a terrible hard-on, so massive that he had to push it down under the table before he could excuse himself and cross the room and wave hello to Mel Gibson and Mel Brooks on his way to the pay phone to call Madam Alex for some desperately needed help.

"Rescue me," Zack said to Alex.

"Who do you want? When do you want her?"

"I want Jane Fonda and I want her now."

"Who's your second choice?"

"Anyone. No, make it an actress. But above all make it fast. I'm in the Fox commissary surrounded with celebrity pussy, and it's driving me nuts."

"You saw Lynn Armstrong last week. How was she?"

"Fine, but I want big, fake tits today. I want a plastic actress. Somebody who *looks* like she'll make it one day. Gotta be an actress."

"I've got a great one. Just started working again. Just split from her rich boyfriend. She's an actress, but I'm not sure how famous she's going to be. But she's fabulous-looking. Blond. She was in *Playboy*."

"What month?"

"Zack!"

"What about her breasts?"

"She's an actress," Alex said. "Let me call her. Hold on. She's in *Playboy*. That says it, doesn't it?"

Zack watched Farrah Fawcett walk out. He nearly had a spontaneous orgasm. Alex *had* to come through, he prayed. Otherwise he wouldn't be able to write a word.

Alex got back on the line. "You're in luck." She gave him a name, Missy, and an address near MacArthur Park.

"I could die," Zack fretted. "Is she a junkie or something, living *there?*"

"She's an actress. Now shut your trap and get down there. She's waiting for you."

Alex kept her fingers crossed that the date would work. Zack was a valuable customer. She couldn't risk losing him, not now. In the six months since Lissa Trapp had gone on her own to see Sir John, Lissa, backed by her Svengali, Nicky Kroll, was making a major power play to steal Alex's best clients. Sir John, Oliver Julian, Art Vander, many of the big spenders were being picked off one by one, in the most heinous ways. Alex rued that she was bedridden and sick, that she didn't have the body of a whippet and the morals of a snake to go out there, head-to-head with Lissa, the daughter she never had. Ah well, she figured, all was fair in love and whores. How could she expect anything other than foul play? But *this* foul? All Alex could do was what she had always done: top quality, top service. She hoped it would be enough.

Zack roared onto Pico Boulevard in his Mustang convertible. Zack drove a Mustang because it was the all-American thing to do, because Disney's Jeff Katzenberg, who more than anyone else in Hollywood determined what America would see, also drove this most American of cars and gave it a certain reverse chic. Not that Zack was in any way beholden to Katzenberg, whose movies he derided as $7.50 television. But Zack had made his fortune as one of the voices of his yuppie generation, and he wanted to be its courage as well. For him, *not* driving a BMW represented true courage. To yuppies, driving any new car to the no-man's-land neighborhood near MacArthur Park would be considered true courage, if not insanity. But this was where Alex had dispatched Zack, and, as she would say, an erection knows no fear.

Zack's wife, Caitlin, was the source of all his yuppie material, the personification of the BMW, a fusion of *L.A. Law* and *thirtysomething* who as a super-ambitious trophy Wellesley girl had rejected Zack at the same time Harvard Law School did, and took him back only after he had won his first Emmy. Capitalizing on his unrequited college crush, Caitlin, a rising entertainment lawyer, first made Zack a client, making him a lover only after she had wrung an engagement ring out of him. Having wanted the elusive Caitlin for so long, Zack, when he finally got her, found the experience a bit anticlimactic. The climaxes got fewer and fewer, and the body that Caitlin had used for so long as a bargaining chip proved much less exciting unwrapped than Zack's perfervid imagination had rendered it. The only thing that kept their marital sex going for as long as it did was Caitlin's continued distaste for it. Her resistance was the one thing that was provocative to Zack. By the second child, the sex was gone. Everyone lusted for Caitlin, the classiest female lawyer in the business, everyone except her husband, who regarded her as a trophy not worth having won.

With her clients, her deals, her kids, her charities, Caitlin rarely thought about sex, and she figured that by allowing Zack his "Saturday-night special" after an evening of Cystic Fibrosis or Heal the Bay or Patch the Ozone and rubber chicken at the Beverly Hilton ballroom, she was standing by her man and keeping him satisfied. Zack often pretended to be horny on weekday evenings and deeply frustrated when Caitlin had a power breakfast at the Polo Lounge the next morning and couldn't take the time to fool around. It was all a charade. Zack had met Alex through a star friend with an equally perfect wife. Zack didn't hate Caitlin. He didn't want a divorce. She was a great wife, a star wife, the mother of his children. He just didn't care about fucking her.

He did care about fucking. He loved the thrill, the suspense of going to a strange house or apartment, having the door open and seeing a beauty, of talking to her and being intimate with her. To Zack, an Alex girl was the perfect blind date, the type he always dreamed about, love at first sight. He didn't see the girls as whores, any more than he saw himself as a john. It was a fix-up. The money was administrative, a dating fee. Zack didn't have ego problems. He had been on the television shows, *Entertainment Tonight* and *Letterman*. He had been written up in *People* and *Vanity Fair*. When those doors opened, he knew that the women were as excited to see him as he was to see them. The American stereotype of the john was the blubbery traveling salesman having to pay for something he could never otherwise get. Zack could get anyone, but he wanted to stay married. Marriage was part of his mystique, part of his bankability. In the baldest terms, Zack wanted to have his pussy and eat it, too.

He drove his Mustang past the glorious Art Deco cathedral of consumerism that was Bullocks Wilshire, where no one shopped anymore, past the massive brick Fifth Avenue–style apartment blocks, where no one lived anymore, past the pharaonic Elks temple on the west end of the park that had become a once-a-week nightclub called Power Tools for the Charlie Sheen crowd but where no one went anymore either.

Zack was actually enjoying the adventure, his own excursion into this sexual heart of darkness. Missy's building actually had something Los Angeles generally lacked, which was charm. The complex was called the Gaylord, after Gaylord Wilshire, whose unpaved road through his orange groves turned out to have oil underneath it and became L.A.'s most fashionable thoroughfare, its highway to heaven. The Spanish Colonial complex, built in the roaring twenties, reminded Zack of Nathanael West's San Bernardino Arms in *The Day of the Locust*. There was an unkempt yet verdant courtyard around a wishing well. Zack climbed a white stucco staircase and rang a bell that didn't work. He knocked several times. He despaired that he might have been stood up. Hookers were the most unreliable people on earth. A bigger deal, some drugs, a cute guy, and they were gone. Appointments meant nothing, nor did reprisal. Alex could cut them off, but Lissa or some other madam would always take them on. Zack walked back downstairs and tried to peer into the closed windows, but the foliage was too thick. He went back up and knocked again, to no avail. He tried to listen for sounds through the door, but the clangs and drills of the nearby subway construction drowned everything out. As he was about to give up, the door flew open, and there was Missy, a strawberry-blond vision, glistening with beads of water, wrapped in a white towel. Zack couldn't have been more aroused if Jane Fonda or Rosanna Arquette had met him at the door.

"I'm *so* sorry," Missy gushed, all southern charm. "I was in the shower, and it was so nice and wet and . . . I got carried away."

Zack could only speculate lasciviously on what she meant by that.

"This place is awful, it's like Watts," Missy apologized some more. "I'm so sorry you had to come down here."

"It's all right. It's got a lot of charm."

"You're so polite." Missy stroked Zack's arm, sending a spark through him. "Just think, two months ago I was living on Bellagio, just down the hill from Elizabeth Taylor."

"You were?"

"I'll tell you all about it, as soon as I get dressed." Missy stroked his arm again.

Don't get dressed, Zack despaired, but Missy's effusive courtesy prevented him from tearing her towel off and ravishing her on the bare hardwood floor. Because Zack, of course, was a polite guy, and in his mind this was a date and Missy wasn't a whore and he wasn't a john. "Take your time," he said.

"Here. I'll give you some great bourbon," she said, and poured some vintage sour mash into what had been a peanut-butter jar.

"You're very southern," Zack said. "Great accent." He meant, Great body, I'm dying to have it.

"Social Circle, Georgia," Missy drawled

"I bet you were the homecoming queen."

Missy ruffled Zack's hair. "Alex told me you were smart. Now just make yourself at home. I *wish* this was a home . . ."

Zack sat on the tattered cotton couch in the empty high-ceilinged living room with its grand fireplace and listened to a Steely Dan CD. Missy went into the bedroom, the door of which managed to stay open just enough to flash some provocative moments of Missy dropping her towel, trying on several colors of panties, pouring her striking breasts into a breezy sundress. These were lightning glimpses, and Zack was so polite he was almost ashamed to be peeking.

Missy emerged, the personification of summer, dressed for an Easter egg hunt or a garden party.

"We should be drinking mint juleps on some plantation lawn. You look great," Zack said, wanting to rip the dress right off.

Missy sat next to Zack on the couch. "I just wanted to say what a big fan I am of your work. I never missed an episode of *Urban Pros*. And I cry every time I see *No Regrets*. You must be the most sensitive guy in Hollywood."

Only my cock, Zack wanted to say. "I write from the heart."

Another barrage of compliments, and after a while and a few more bourbons, Zack wanted to kiss Missy and run away with her and not simply fuck her.

They talked and talked. Missy told him about being homecoming queen in high school and Honor Court at Georgia Southern and how she was "discovered" to appear in a College Girls of the Deep South photo spread in *Playboy*. "I thought it was the greatest thing that could ever happen to somebody. Look what being in *Playboy* did for Kim Basinger—Prince, her own town, a big star."

"What did you look like in *Playboy*? Were you naked?"

"I'm embarrassed to tell you."

"Tell me."

"Well, I wasn't completely naked. I had a Georgia Southern sweatshirt on and . . . I can't say."

"Say."

"I was holding the school mascot, this pet bulldog, between my legs."

The *Playboy* shot did get Missy to Hollywood. It even got her a Playmate of the Month centerfold. With some gentlemanly prodding, Zack got Missy to show it to him. "Excellent picture," Zack said, barely able to control himself.

Looking at the provocative layout, Zack also got to find out that

Missy's favorite food was hush puppies and that her favorite book was *The Other Side of Midnight,* and that her favorite actor was Warren Beatty and her biggest turnoff was garlic breath and that her secret fantasy was to walk naked through the Omni in Atlanta.

Playboy was where Missy and Kim Basinger parted company. "Kim got to be a James Bond girl. I did some cheap Korean martial arts films down in Little Tokyo." She also got to live for a while at the Playboy Mansion.

"You must have met a lot of celebrities there," Zack said.

"Jack Carter, Shecky Greene, and Jim Brown," Missy reeled off the short list. Like most Playmates and Mansion girls, Missy tried everything—acting classes, tarot readings, psychics, breast implants—but the parts she was offered got worse and worse. Missy starred in one porno film, *Penis Envy,* and then found her way to Alex through another centerfold.

"Alex's was the only place being in *Playboy* gave me any clout," Missy told Zack. "Especially to the Arabs and the Japanese"—to whom the pictures were worth more than a thousand words; they were worth thousands of extra dollars. In the Middle East and in Japan, *Playboy*'s luster had not tarnished. It was still the bible of masculinity. "A pinup is a goddess to those guys."

It works for me, too, Zack felt like saying. "It's a really interesting cultural phenomenon, this deification of tabloid figures."

"All those big words," Missy said, slapping Zack's knee. "So I changed my goal from being Hollywood star to being Hollywood wife. I thought one of these foreigners who worshiped me would marry me. Smart girl, huh?" Missy described her succession of kept situations, a Filipino banker, an Abu Dhabi oil trader, several Persian businessmen who owned prime real estate in the Valley. But the Filipino and the Arab both had wives at home, and the Persians used her up and tossed her away. Missy was around too briefly to claim palimony. "Because I had met them through Alex, how could I be a pal?" At twenty-seven, Missy knew her time was running out. "The end of my rainbow has taken me to MacArthur Park. I can't be Miss July forever."

Zack wanted to cry. He also wanted to go down on her. What he did was talk some more, about his Georgia girlfriend at Harvard and their trip to Savannah. Zack talked because he was nervous, as nervous as on a high-school first date. When he could stand it no more, he leaned over and kissed Missy. And like on a high-school first date, she shied away.

"Zack, I feel really funny about this," Missy said. "You see, I feel like I kinda know you, and I really like you, and I'd hate for you to think of me *like that*, you know?"

"I wouldn't think of you *like that*," Zack said, his anxiety mounting at what Missy might be getting at.

"So I think we should just be friends," Missy said, dropping the bombshell.

"You mean," Zack sputtered, "you mean, we're not going to *do* anything?"

"I'd rather have your respect," Missy said.

Come on, you're a *whore*, Zack thought. What is this? I'm here to fuck you for a thousand dollars. What respect is worth that, from someone who'll never talk to you again? But Zack was way too polite to articulate these ideas. Besides, he reminded himself, she *wasn't* a whore, and he *wasn't* a john, and he *did* like her and would surely see her again. He usually saw all of Alex's girls at least three times before the thrill of novelty wore off. Missy could take even longer. Above all, he *did like* her. "You've *got* my respect. I really *like* you," he insisted, and tried to kiss her again. This time she let his lips brush hers before she pulled away.

"I don't want to get hurt," Missy said, tears in her eyes. "Can't we just be friends?"

Zack sank back onto the couch in despair. "Sure," he sighed. "Whatever you want." And then they got into a discussion about the desperation of Missy's life, of the shattered dreams and lost opportunities, and during the hour Zack had planned to spend going down on her and fucking her as a substitute for Rosanna and Jane and Sally and all the other stars he lusted for in the Fox commissary, instead he spent that hour listening to a life of pain and loss. At the end of that hour, rather than leaving her with a thousand dollars, he was in for two thousand, to help her get out of MacArthur Park and into the apartment she wanted on

Barrington in Brentwood, blocks away from where Zack lived, north of Sunset.

Zack was about to leave, his horniness having become pride about being a good Samaritan, lust transformed into compassion. It was a pure Hollywood ending. Jeff Katzenberg would have loved it, even though it would have never occurred to Zack to write anything so syrupy. As he turned to leave, however, Missy gave him a thank-you kiss that lasted a split second too long to be merely a platonic demonstration of gratitude. It evolved into the hottest gratitude Zack had ever received, wild, animalistic sex on the floor of the Gaylord that was proof to him forever that virtue was more than its own reward.

Six months and thirty thousand dollars later, Zack had made the down payment on Missy's new Santa Monica condo and was eagerly fucking her twice a week. Eventually, the sex did wear off, though not the friendship, which was all Alex's idea to begin with. Fully aware of Zack's erotic response to resistance, Alex had suggested the entire bit about keeping Zack waiting, wearing the towel, leaving the door cracked, saying, "Let's be friends." Missy's first reaction to Alex's gambit was to say, "You're crazy." She couldn't afford to roll the dice in her precarious fiscal state. Alex provided a net for this high-wire act she had set up: If, for any reason, Zack walked, Alex would guarantee Missy her fee. All Alex got out of Missy's windfall was her first four hundred. If a client saw a girl again, on his own, without Alex arranging the date, the girl took all. That was the business, with its presumption that men wanted infinite variety, and that if a girl could get a man to see her again, she should reap the benefit of her effective charms. Alex's task was to consistently come up with new girls, and she had thrived at it. That is, until Lissa Trapp had begun her juggernaut. Now Alex had to take chances like the one she took today, to provide that something extra that would keep her clients under her spell.

The main reason Lissa was doing so well in pilfering Alex's book was that she was willing to cheat, to stop at nothing. Just that week, Lissa had added Johnny Berman to her roster. Johnny, who was famous for portraying Mafia bosses and deranged gangsters, was a pussycat as a client, as shy with the girls as a cost accountant. The closest Johnny had ever gotten to the mob before he came to Hollywood was when he served Meyer Lansky a corned-beef sandwich at Johnny's father's deli in Miami Beach. It was nothing but a fantasy to be a "made man," and Johnny's good luck in Hollywood enabled him to play out his dreams to the hilt. Johnny decided he was the new Bugsy Siegel, minus the crime. He went to Vegas, he went to Santa Anita, he had his bookie, he hung out with guys and dolls. A lot of the dolls came from Alex.

So good was Johnny Berman at playing the high roller in his personal life that his entire career nearly went up his nose. When he went into rehab, all his addictions had to go, including the call girls. "Just don't tempt me with your ladies, and don't let me tempt you," Johnny put his request to Alex, and Alex honored his request, despite Johnny's several efforts to cancel the arrangement.

Not Lissa, who knew Johnny liked to frequent Nicky Blair's, a Vegas-in-Hollywood hangout on the Sunset Strip, the only restaurant in the city that gave a wardrobe credit on its menu: "Mr. Blair's wardrobe by Rick Pallack" (Pallack was a Sherman Oaks haberdasher). The last temptation of Johnny Berman had arrived at Nicky Blair's in twin Alaia black microdresses and the spikiest of heels. Lissa had with her her Valley girl soulless sister, Marti Gold, whom she had seduced away from Alex with coke and a lowered commission. Here they were, the blonde and the brunette, the Jewish and the ersatz-Jewish supersirens who wanted to sing their song so that Johnny Berman would crash and burn on their sexy shoals.

"Ladies, ladies, I'm trying to be good. Help me," Johnny begged off when the two temptresses flanked him at the bar. He had fucked Lissa once, in his bad days, and it was hard not to want to again.

"We want to help you, Johnny. We want you to feel good again. You haven't felt good for a long time, have you?"

"I'm married now, Lissa, I'm square."

"Have you?" Lissa pressed him, pressing her pointy, hard nipples against Johnny's arm.

"Where is your wife?" Marti asked, crossing her bronze legs square in Johnny's face. She wasn't wearing panties.

"She's in New York. Visiting her folks."

"Old times, Johnny," Lissa urged him. "I want you. You were hot."

"I can't. I've been sober for six months."

"You'll stay sober. It wasn't the sex that fucked you up, Johnny. It was the coke," Lissa said.

"It's not the sex, it's the hookers," Johnny said. "I'm trying to be a family man."

Lissa and Marti looked at each other and laughed dubiously. Marti leaned over and whispered in Johnny's ear, "I've been dying to fuck you since I was in junior high. Don't you want to see me sucking your cock while Lissa's sucking my cunt? We can get real crazy together. I'm a fan, Johnny. A huge fan. This is no act."

Johnny looked at Marti's fabled thighs, smelled her musky perfume. Lissa ran her finger up the inside of his thigh, increasing the pressure as she stopped just short of his groin. "Not many men can make me come," she took her turn whispering to Johnny. "You should see Marti's tits. You should see her body. She was an Olympic gymnast. Think of what we can do to her. You and me, Johnny. You're a man. Be one."

Johnny shook his head and stood up. Everybody in the room was watching the big star, the Mafia boss of bosses. They expected him to be with goddesses like these. He always had been. "Pussy," he said under his breath, and began walking out. "Let's do it." He motioned to Lissa and Marti and gave in to the inevitable.

Not that Lissa was above using coke to snatch a client. That was how she stole Travis Watson, another on-screen wiseguy, who had drifted into Hollywood, from Texas, as a stuntman. Where Johnny Berman's dream was to become Bugsy Siegel, Travis Watson's was to become Noël Coward, or at least a straight Noël Coward. Graduating in films from crazed cowboys to crazed hippies to crazed mobsters, Travis graduated in life from ten-gallon hats to dashikis to five-thousand-dollar Gianni Versace suits. He graduated in women from Woodstock love children to socialite heiresses and, on the side, to Alex girls. Why? Because he was a Hollywood star and could afford the luxury. Travis basked in luxury.

"That's called *Sarah Siddons as the Tragic Muse,* by Reynolds, but Lawrence painted her, too." Courtney Van Ness was with Travis Watson at a black-tie party at the Huntington Art Gallery in San Marino.

"She looks much better in the Reynolds," Travis observed.

"You've got a good eye," Courtney said. She was wearing discreet décolletage, which made her a sexy standout in this sedate, WASPy crowd of Pasadena aristocrats milling through the former estate of Gilded Age railroad tycoon Henry Huntington. Aside from Ronald Reagan, Travis was the only actor in the house. He liked that.

"I do have a good eye." Travis gazed down her dress and saw a flash of nipple.

"Reynolds made all his society subjects look better than they did in real life. That's why he got all the work."

"Whore," Travis said.

Courtney gave him a look. Travis just laughed.

"I like this one the best." Travis pointed to Lawrence's *Pinkie.*

"You would," Courtney said, admiring the budding teenage aristocratic English girl of the early 1800s. Then she leaned over to Travis so that no one could hear her. "I shaved myself completely, just for you, so I'll be just like her."

Travis clicked champagne flutes with Courtney, the naughtiest glint in his eye. "Forever young."

"Let's go out to the Japanese Garden. We can fuck in the Teahouse of the August Moon," Courtney said.

Travis ran his hand along Courtney's ass, then he yanked it away when a tall, very distinguished man came up and kissed Courtney hello.

"Travis Watson, meet Otis Chandler," Courtney said. Chandler was the chairman of the *L.A. Times.* To a social climber like Travis, shaking hands with him was almost as good as screwing Courtney. In any case, it got him even hornier for her.

"I want to see you naked right now," Travis said. He and Courtney made their way through the legion of tuxedoed aristos out onto the

Gatsby-like grand terrace, where a jazz band played "Running Wild." They danced a Charleston, drank more champagne, and then walked through the fabled Huntington Gardens by the light of the full moon, through the cactuses and the roses to the moon gate and the arched Japanese bridge over the *koi* pond, where they kissed and Travis picked Courtney up and sat her on a railing and went down on her, before culminating the encounter in the sixteenth-century teahouse beside the Zen garden. Who was to stop them? This was a private party, for L.A. high society. The Huntington was theirs. Courtney was his. Tonight Travis was his own greatest fantasy; he was an aristocrat.

Lissa Trapp had learned well her lessons from Alex about how to traffic in fantasy. It annoyed Alex to no end that this was one fantasy she should have orchestrated. But Lissa had gotten to Courtney Van Ness first, because she was able to motivate the flaky Brooke Kuhn in the only way Brooke could be motivated, by getting her the highest-quality cocaine. Because Alex refused to deal in drugs, her motivational arsenal was limited. Lissa's knew no limits. Having met Brooke at Alex's, Lissa cultivated her by getting her higher and higher, and soon she drew Courtney into her cocaine sisterhood, after which it was a piece of cake, or coke, for Lissa to turn her out. Not only did Alex lose Courtney, who was making a superb blue-chip call girl, to Lissa, who insisted on exclusivity with all her girls, but Alex also lost Brooke, who was so embarrassed that she had let Alex down in the Sir John episode that she did the Hollywood thing: Whenever you say no to a project or break a promise, you simply avoid the person you have disappointed, until you need that person again. Right now, Lissa was fulfilling Brooke's needs, which centered on her nostrils.

In Nicky Kroll, Lissa had a wonderful mentor for her depredations. All Lissa wanted was Alex's business. Nicky wanted Alex. He wanted her destroyed. "If we don't destroy her, she'll come back and destroy us," he warned Lissa again and again. It wasn't only Alex whom Nicky wanted. Nicky was a nihilist. He was perfectly happy to see the world, which he would never rule, go up in smoke.

Nicky had just come back from the Beverly Center, where he had slashed the tires of the Rolls Corniche of Mrs. Chaim Ben Ami, the wife of the North African jeans mogul whom Nicky had used to lure Lori Schwartz, the rebellious rich Valley girl, away from Alex. Having been dumped by UCLA hoopster Juwan Jefferson in favor of a top black model who was on the rebound from one of the Lakers, Lori decided the next best way to drive her parents to despair was to sell her body to a sixty-year-old Algerian who had built his EX-tasy jeans empire on the half-broken backs of near slave labor. Chaim's suggestive erotic ads, featuring a Brooke Shields look-alike, denim-clad legs spread open, zipper slightly unzipped, inviting the viewer to "come into ecstasy," had built him an empire worth several hundred million. At Nicky's coke-aided urging, Lori decided she should marry Chaim.

The situation was loaded. Chaim was married to a dumpy wife he hadn't slept with for years, and had children. But for all his corruption in business, he was an Orthodox Jew who flatly refused to get a divorce. On the other hand, Lori was the dream Jewess Chaim had always wanted, as well as his fountain of sexual youth. He was totally addicted to her. And Lori, nice Jewish Valley Princess that she was, vowed that she wouldn't see Chaim anymore unless he married her, no matter how much he paid her. It was a vow she continually broke, while Chaim one day promised to leave his wife, Yetta, and the next day changed his mind. And Yetta, traditional Orthodox wife that she was, stood by her man, notwithstanding the slashed tires, the decapitated chicken in the Neiman-Marcus shoe box, the video of Chaim and Lori having a ménage à trois with a black stud whom Nicky had lined up for them.

"Okay, pull out, enough," Chaim had ordered the stud, who instantly obeyed the command, removing his foot-long shaft from Lori, who was spread-eagled on the bed of the Beverly Wilshire suite Chaim kept for such afternoon ménages.

"But I'm coming," Lori whined.

"You're coming with me," Chaim barked. The handsome black man stepped aside as the little fat man with the fringe of white hair that looked like a laurel wreath waddled to the bed and plopped between Lori's long tan legs.

"Thanks a lot," Lori pouted.

"You prefer the *schvartze?*"

"I was coming."

"Keep coming."

"I can't," Lori whined. "You're selfish."

"Selfish? I bought him for you."

"Then let me finish with him," Lori insisted.

The stud stood in the corner, cock still huge and hard, freaked out by the domestic scene he was watching.

"You can only get off on *schvartzes*, can't you? Why can't you get off on me?"

"Why can't you leave Yetta?"

"Don't bring that up."

"I'm outta here." Lori shoved Chaim off her and wrapped herself in a Pratesi sheet. "I'm not your whore anymore."

"Maybe if I had a big black dick!" Chaim shouted.

"Dream on," Lori mocked him.

"You cunt!"

"Don't you *dare* call me that," Lori shouted, hurling an ashtray at him. She missed, but the ashtray shattered a full-length mirror.

"You little bitch. You coulda killed me." Chaim lunged at her, ripping off the Pratesi sheet, throwing her to the carpet, trying to fuck her again.

"Rape! Rape!" Lori screamed.

The black stud came to the rescue, pulling the two apart. "Hey, man, leave the lady alone."

"You cocksucking *schvartze* faggot, I'm *paying* you!" Chaim swung at him, oblivious to the foot differential between them. Chaim had not gotten to the pinnacle of the most ruthless business short of munitions by being afraid of anyone.

Lori locked herself in the bathroom.

"Open the fucking door!" Chaim pounded on it. "I want to fuck you. I'm paying you a thousand a day and I want my money's worth, you whore."

"Fuck him, you're paying him," Lori shouted from behind the door. "Fuck him. Let him fuck you. It's good. It's real good!"

Chaim grabbed a chair and rammed it into the bathroom door, shattering another mirror and breaking the chair's legs. He hurled a lamp at the door, then started kicking the door in.

"Hey, man, cool it, you're gonna have a heart attack," the black stud warned him.

"Shut up!" Chaim swung at him. He pounded the door till the hinges were about to pop off. He didn't hear the rapping at the door of the suite. "Let me in. I love you. I love you."

"Then leave her."

"I will. I will. Just open the door. I love you."

"Mister Ben Ami, please," the hotel manager, backed by three security guards, pleaded with him. What a sight, a naked old white man, a naked young black man, and a beautiful naked girl destroying an enormously expensive suite.

"I'll pay for the suite."

"But our other guests," the manager remonstrated.

"I'll buy the guests. I'll buy the fucking hotel!"

Chaim and Lori were barred from further trysts at the Beverly Wilshire. They were also barred at the Biltmore, Checkers, the Bel Air, and the Mondrian. They were running out of deluxe hotels. Still, the beat went on, with Nicky and Lissa fueling the flames and collecting huge commissions for Lori, who needed their support and was willing to pay for it. Yetta hung in there. She wouldn't let Chaim go. If she had to get off on something, it was her own martyrdom. "I pray for you every day," she wrote to Lori.

Nicky hated any competition, not just Alex. One of Lissa's biggest rivals, albeit without trying to compete, was Judy Breitling, whose one-woman business had grown exponentially since Rex Fried's bachelor party. She was so completely booked that her regular clients had to wait longer to see her, sometimes two weeks or more, than an out-of-towner would have to wait to get a table at Spago. If only she could clone herself,

Judy sometimes thought, because there was just so much money one girl could make. For Judy, that was about $350,000 a year, seeing three $500 guys a day, five days a week, with a month's vacation.

"I don't want to make a million, not that way," Judy told Lissa, who called her and invited her to lunch at the Ivy and made her an offer Lissa couldn't believe Judy would refuse.

"You can see a lot fewer guys," Lissa said. "Fewer guys and more money."

"But I *like* my guys. I *want* to see them. I'm not interested in being a madam."

"You've got such a great book. Why waste it? Each guy could see five, ten, fifteen new girls every six months, you rake forty off each introduction, you do nothing. It's like Amway, a big pyramid."

"Most of my guys only see me."

"Do you really believe that?" Lissa was dubious.

"I do."

"And you don't think they want to see new girls?"

"They seem perfectly happy," Judy said, so self-contained that Lissa wanted to splat her in the face with her Key lime pie. "These aren't typical johns."

"Hey, they're buying you. We could trade them out. They're johns, all right. You're being too possessive, you're like a wife."

"No, I'm like a friend," Judy said, getting a little insulted by Lissa's pushy tone. "I don't want to be Alex. I don't want to run girls. I don't want to drive myself crazy."

"I can run the girls. I can be Alex. All you have to do is turn your guys on to me, lay back, and let me bring you money. You'd be a fool not to go for it," Lissa made one last push.

"I guess I'm a fool," Judy said, reaching for the check and paying it.

"You'll be sorry," Lissa said, with a false smile as the valet parker brought Judy her new baby Maserati. "Bitch," Lissa added when Judy drove away, her mind racing with ways to fix this prissy little Mary Sunshine.

Lissa had reason to be jealous; Judy had become the paid sweetheart of Young Hollywood. She was the particular darling of the agencies, and particularly of the colossus AA, Amalgamated Artists.

"Should I wear my new Brazilian *tanga* or the garter belt and the crotchless panties?" Judy asked the three Young Turks from AA who were spending their business lunch at her apartment.

"The *tanga*," David said. "You've got the tan for it."

"No, the garters. You can see the *tanga* on any beach," Marty objected.

Armin made the Solomonic decision. "Wear the *tanga* with the beach boy and the garters with the pervert, and I'll go last and decide which one I want."

These guys, who did Schwarzenegger and Stallone deals together, rafted down the Snake River together, and climbed the Rockies together, all now got undressed together and prepared to watch as each of them would fuck Judy. AA's hallmark was its teamwork and cultlike spirit. This was another way for the rising stars to combine efficiency and camaraderie.

Judy went into her dressing room and put on her red *tanga*, the stringlike bikini that left nothing to the imagination except the color of her pubic hair. She emerged and walked up the stairs of her Hollywood duplex, filled with newly bought antiques and rare movie posters. David was waiting for her, naked under the covers. Marty and Armin were sitting at far ends of the room in their undershorts. Judy put on "The Girl from Ipanema" and took the plunge with David.

"Take the damn suit off," Armin urged, as Judy was giving David head.

"I like the suit," David shot back. "*You* take it off."

Judy ran her tongue up and down David's straining shaft. "Do something, anything," Armin razzed him. But Judy, whose blow jobs were considered the smoothest and best anyone who ever had them had ever had the privilege of enjoying, had rendered David helpless under her lingual assault. He flailed upward to stroke her thighs, to pull the string. He came before he could make it. Judy swallowed it. The two agents cheered, and the third agent smiled. This was for the greater glory of AA. This wasn't homoerotic, they insisted to themselves in their inner voices. This was *teamwork*.

Judy was so busy that she was extremely loath to take on new clients. Martin Jaffee was an exception. His cultivated British accent on the phone inspired confidence. His references, Rex Fried and the lawyer Peter Greene, were impeccable. His approach was simpatico. "I'm an English playwright. I write about love affairs and heartbreak, and they've brought me out here to write *The Exterminator* for Dolph Lundgren. I'm completely blocked. I miss my kids. I'm completely depressed. Rex and Peter thought you might help. They absolutely raved about you."

Judy rarely got weird calls. Her clients guarded her number too closely. Still, she was cautious. She called Rex to check Martin Jaffee out. It was Friday afternoon. Rex and Sindee had gone to Sun Valley. Peter Greene was in Tokyo negotiating with Sony. Judy didn't know Dolph Lundgren. She called the Writers Guild. Yes, there was a Martin Jaffee who lived in London. She called the Shangri-la in Santa Monica, where all the hip writers stayed, and sure enough, Martin Jaffee was there, just as he said. Bookie Feinstein, who was supposed to see her tonight, had just canceled. Spielberg wanted to meet him. "Come on over," she told Martin Jaffee. "Let's see if we can cheer you up."

Martin Jaffee looked like a young Michael Caine and sounded like a young Rex Harrison. He arrived with a bouquet of roses and a bottle of expensive champagne. "You're very kind to take in this orphan from the storm," he said.

Judy was wearing a mandarin robe Fox's Jeff Simon had bought her when he paid to have her meet him on a business trip to Hong Kong. Incense was burning in the apartment, soft jazz was playing.

"You're even more beautiful than Rex and Peter said," Martin commented admiringly. "You're very kind to have me."

"My pleasure," Judy said, taken with him.

"The pleasure is mine, I assure you," Martin said.

They relaxed, drank the champagne, and smoked a little pot Judy always kept on hand to relax her often wound-up guests. Martin showed her pictures of his children.

"This is Amanda, and this is Cyril."

"Pretty names. Pretty kids."

"I love them, as you can imagine. I wish they were here. We could take them to Disneyland together. I bet you're good with kids." Martin placed his hand lightly on her leg. "Of all ages."

"That's what they say." Judy smiled at him. "Does your wife work?"

"She did. She was a wonderful schoolteacher."

"She stay home now with your kids?"

"She passed away two years ago, I'm afraid."

"Oh, I'm so sorry. It must be so hard . . ."

"My mother is a big help. She stays with them while I'm gone. But it is hard. Being a writer is lonely to begin with, and I'm not very good at dating."

"You shouldn't have any trouble."

"You're terribly sweet. And terribly attractive." Martin kissed her, and Judy opened her mouth to him.

"Shall we go upstairs?" She led him by the hand to her boudoir, undressed him as he undid the buttons of her robe.

"I hate light," Martin said, flicking off the switch of the one lamp.

"As you like it," Judy said. "I like it. I like you."

Martin kissed Judy down the length of her body, his tongue searching every crease and fold. Judy gasped with pleasure. She tried to return the favor, but Martin lightly pushed her head away from his penis.

"Let's wait. I'm too excited," he begged off. "I want to come inside you."

Judy reached inside her nightstand and into the box of lubricated condoms she kept at the ready. She tore open the packet and began to roll the rubber onto Martin's cock. He held her hand. "Please."

"We should," Judy whispered.

"I hate those things."

"Me, too, but . . ."

"I want to feel you."

"I want to feel you," Judy echoed.

Martin kissed her deeply. "Trust me. I trust you."

Judy stopped for a moment. She thought about Martin, and his lovely children. Here was someone with everything to live for. He was Rex's friend, Peter's friend, he was English. He was okay. She let the condom fall to the floor. She let him glide inside her.

They fucked for almost an hour, wild, powerful sex, not the kind the AA boys had.

"I thought you were about to come," Judy said, as Martin turned her over for yet one more position.

"Second wind," Martin told her. "I don't want to let go."

"Don't," Judy begged him.

Judy came, multiple times. And finally Martin came, and after he did Judy tried to take his cock into her mouth.

"Let me do this. It feels wonderful after you've come. I want every drop," she urged him.

But Martin declined, disappearing into the shower and then getting back into his clothes.

He explained his rush to depart. "I want to call my kids before Mummy takes them to the Heath."

"Call from here," Judy suggested. She wanted him to stay. She liked him.

Martin considered the invitation. "I'd better not. I'd feel funny. This is the first time, you know." He gave her five hundred-dollar bills. It was one of the odd times Judy felt bad about taking the money. It distanced her from Martin. She didn't want distance this time.

"I hope I see you again."

"You will. I'm here for two weeks. Maybe even tomorrow night, if Dolph doesn't need me."

"That would be great," Judy said. "Call me."

Martin didn't call Saturday. Or Sunday. On Monday, Judy called the Shangri-la to make sure she hadn't said or done something wrong. Here was a vulnerable man. She was vulnerable, too. She liked him. Maybe there was a future here. But Martin Jaffee had checked out, with no forwarding address. She called Rex Fried on the lot, to find out where Martin was. Rex Fried had never heard of him. Judy was rattled. A few days later, Peter Greene came back from Tokyo.

"Sure, I know Martin Jaffee. I represent him."

Judy felt relieved.

"But I never gave him your number. I wouldn't unless I called you first. Odd."

"What does he look like?"

"Sort of, say, a young Dom DeLuise. Roly-poly. Teddy bear."

"Not blond hair?"

"Not *any* hair."

The phone went dead. Judy was freaked out. Who *was* this man? Why did he fool her? She calmed down, wrote it off. He paid, he was nice, the only thing that was damaged was her ego.

Or so she thought. Two weeks later, Judy began to get muscle aches in her legs. Maybe she was working out too hard. That weekend she was supposed to run a marathon, but the muscle pains forced her to drop out. Then she got a fever, and urination became painful, burning, like peeing razor blades. She went to her gynecologist.

The doctor gave her the diagnosis. "You've got a particularly virulent case of genital herpes. Nasty." The doctor knew what Judy did for a living. "You should always require a condom."

"I know, I know," Judy said, hating herself for trusting, for caring.

"You're lucky you went this long without something like this," the doctor said.

The herpes outbreaks continued for several months, and Judy, who had a conscience, had to cancel thousands upon thousands of dollars' worth of appointments, never knowing what to say, how to explain. Her only relief was that her AIDS test, six weeks later, was negative. She was glad she had her MBA to fall back on.

Martin Jaffee was a figment of Nicky Kroll's genius. Martin, in reality, was an English con man, an actor named Alfie Leitch, even more failed and bitter than Nicky was as an also-ran producer. Having followed some brief runs in the West End with several terms at Brixton Prison for theft, fraud, and narcotics, Alfie had come to Hollywood, where his good looks and mellifluous voice landed him jobs as a Ferrari salesman and as a tony maître d' in faux-Brit clubs. All the jobs came to naught but petty theft and failed embezzlement, and Alfie became a tony drug dealer. Beverly Hills people preferred buying their coke from men with Etonian accents rather than Colombian ones. Alfie's only unqualified success was with women. He sometimes hired himself out as a gigolo to aging Valley *nouveau riche* dowagers for long weekends in Puerto Vallarta. Alfie could score with almost anyone, until they found out what a corrupt, evil fraud he was. He had scored so many times that he had one of the worst cases of herpes a stud could have. His cock was a mass of scars and tiny sores, hence his avoidance of Judy's oral offering and his insistence on the dark. Yes, Alfie could always score once, and once for this venereal Typhoid Mary was enough for Nicky to knock Judy Breitling right out of the competition on Lissa's quest to be Madam 90210. He gave Alfie two grand for his trouble. "I did it for you," Nicky told Lissa exultantly, and even Lissa was a bit horrified.

Whenever possible, Lissa preferred to accentuate the positive. A madam's success was measured by the new girls—new girls of quality— she could offer, and Lissa could usually get new girls without having to destroy old ones. "I'm the CAA of the sex business," she would boast, "and Alex is the William Morris." The analogy was apt. Creative Artists Agency had been founded by Mike Ovitz, Ron Meyer, and several other renegades too impatient to wait their turn at the then all-powerful William Morris Talent Agency. One by one, the CAA upstarts picked off the William Morris superstars, because the upstarts were younger, hipper, more flexible, and more energetic than the Hollywood establishment that Morris represented. Unlike Alex, who sat on her laurels and played oracle in her Doheny Olympus, Lissa *was* one of the girls she was recruiting. She was their age, or younger. She shopped with them, did drugs with them, fucked with them. She could "relate" to the girls, their hair problems, their plastic surgery, their cars, their rock-and-roll no-good boyfriends, their astral and psychic needs.

With Lissa breathing down her neck, Alex couldn't coast on her reputation alone, not with Lissa and Nicky scouring the nightclubs, the Beverly Center, the rock concerts, even the high schools, for new talent, as well as stealing customers left and right.

Alex had to talk to Lissa. This was no easy task, as Lissa changed her phone number, on average, once a week, and avoided Alex the way an agent would sidestep a client for whom he couldn't get a job. Finally, Alex found her.

"Lissa, what's come over you? Why are you doing this?"

"You fucked me, Alex," began Lissa's tommy-gun complaint. At Nicky's prompting, she had had months to work out an elaborate rationale. "You sent me to shit people, you took all the money, you never let me go to Europe, you back-streeted me with the WASPs, you kept me away from the Arabs, you thought I was stupid and ugly and coarse, you *used* me, Alex. Fuck you!"

"Lissa, are you possessed? You know how much I cared for you!"

"I was just another forty percent. You sucked my blood. You were ashamed of me. You would never introduce me to Brooke Kuhn. You would *never* introduce me to Sir John. Well, fuck you, 'cause they're all *mine*. I'm big now, Alex, and you're *finished*. You're just a pathetic old lady. You're old and you're sick and you're *through*! And *I* am the *one*. I am the queen!"

"If you can't stop the coke, you're going to be dead at twenty-one," Alex warned her, genuinely concerned at Lissa's ranting megalomania.

"I'll *bury* you! I've got the studios, Alex. I've got the stars. I've got the girls. I've got it all. You're finished, Alex. Fuck you and your fucking cats!"

There was no logic, no reason, no way to bring Lissa back. Alex realized what she had to do. If Lissa was fighting with venom and jealousy, Alex would fight back with love.

In the months coinciding with Lissa's onslaught, Alex left her house only for elaborate medical tests that her doctors couldn't bring to her. Her diabetes was bad; her heart was worse. But when she heard about the dire straits of one of her legendary racehorses, Cathy McQueen, she pulled herself together to see if she could help. The last place on earth Alex expected to find her $300,000-a-year creature was at the Pio-Pico Convalescent Center in El Monte, a Latino low-rider exurb of Los Angeles off the San Bernardino Freeway. Alex sat in the backseat of her BMW as her driver sped through the smog and industrial waste east of downtown through the little Hong Kong of Asian flight capital.

Old men in wheelchairs, young, sunken drug casualties, raving Charles Manson types blissed on Prozac, Squeaky Frommes staring into mirrors—they were all, like Cathy McQueen, wards of the county locked in this barred and wired coed snake pit. It was a mighty slip for this former star of the Ice Capades.

"Alex, my God!" Cathy shrieked when Alex showed up, unannounced, in the Formica recreation ward where Cathy was eating her morning snack of Oreos and Pepsi. "I'm so fat" was the first thing she could say. "Don't look at me."

"You're still beautiful," Alex said, hugging her, playfully squeezing the rolls of fat around what had once been a wasp waist. "More to love," Alex cackled, though she was heartbroken at where Cathy had ended up. Alex gave Cathy a gift box from Neiman-Marcus. Inside was a high-style leather motorcycle jacket by Moschino. "That's to wear when you ride your Harley to jump the fence, like Steve McQueen in *The Great Escape*," Alex said. "We're gonna get you out of here."

"But I don't want to get out," Cathy said, totally surprising Alex. "I've got a great scam cooking," she whispered.

Cathy explained how she had been arrested for sexual battery at a West Hollywood lesbian nightclub called Sahara. "You know me, I always hated eating pussy. I was just there to score some Ecstasy, and this bull dyke got a little too frisky, so it was self-defense."

"Why didn't you call me? I'd have gotten you Tony or Richard," Alex said, referring to her own bar of criminal-lawyer friends.

"I didn't *want* a lawyer. Listen to what a deal this is. All I have to do is stay three more months in this nuthouse and the county'll give me eight hundred dollars a month, plus three hundred child support, *for life*. Not to mention food stamps. Tell me, is that a deal or is that a deal?"

Alex didn't know what to say. "This is new math for me. . . . What child?"

"God, that's right. It's been almost four years. Fidel."

"Fidel?"

"He's two now. You'll love him."

"Who's the father?"

"Unmentionable scum. As is my mother. She took custody of Fidel, says I'm an unfit mother. I mean, *she* should talk. She won't even let me *see* my baby, much less raise him. I've got to deal with that when I get out. Oh well. But, Alex, don't you see the beauty of this?"

Alex looked around at the shattered inmates, moping, screaming, masturbating. "I must be missing something."

"It's great," Cathy said, all smiles. "It's money for nothing. Just like hooking."

"We've got a lot of talking to do," Alex said. "Now get dressed. We're going out."

"They won't let me out."

"I got you a day pass."

"How'd ya pull that off?"

And Alex gave her that enigmatic smile.

"I forgot," Cathy said, and kissed her.

Twenty pounds overweight, Cathy stuffed herself into her one remaining black Chanel suit and put on what she knew was too much makeup, but she had to cover up her bad complexion, which she blamed on the greasy prison slop. Normally, Cathy was a dead ringer for JoBeth Williams, or at least the rangy, naked JoBeth Williams of *Kramer vs. Kramer*, Dustin Hoffman's first post-abandonment fling, the smart all-American brunette of the perfect ass and perfect legs. Cathy was exactly that, a head cheerleader and straight-A student in Mission Viejo in all-American Orange County.

Still there was a dark side, Both of her parents were alcoholics, bad Irish drunks. Her father worked as a shoe repairer. Her mother barely got out of bed. They never encouraged Cathy, never praised her. She was completely self-created. She worked as a baby-sitter to pay for her skating lessons. At fourteen, she was raped in her own home by the Sparkletts water delivery man. She had seen her father's penis before, but she had no idea penises could get hard and go in and out of her. She never told her parents what had happened. They either wouldn't care or, worse, would blame her for it.

When she graduated from high school, she turned down a scholarship to UCLA to join the Ice Capades and see the world. She wanted to get farther away from her family than Westwood, and the idea of becoming the next Peggy Fleming was highly romantic. Cathy didn't become Peggy Fleming, but in her three years on ice on the road, she had a lot of romance. She discovered that she loved sex, and that men loved her. She came back to Los Angeles with dreams of becoming a movie star. Her well-scrubbed looks quickly landed her a commercials agent, and she made a good living doing ring-around-the-collar-type detergent and diaper ads, perfect-housewife stuff. But the commercials were erratic, and she did odd jobs, a nearly-nude ice-skating video wearing a G-string with Hans Brinker emblazoned on the crotch, a stint as a Bunny at the Playboy Club in Century City. She also discovered cocaine, and thrown into a depression by the death of her high-school best friend, she saw coke as a way out. It only dragged her down deeper, though, and she became an addict, an all-American girl-next-door coke addict.

Cathy moved into an apartment in Hollywood, which she shared with several other high-school friends. One of them worked for a call-girl ring operated by a beautiful cousin of a famous star. Cathy went with her friend to a party in a bungalow at the Beverly Hills Hotel for seven Arabs in robes. There were four girls in all. Cathy, high on coke, went into a bedroom with one of the Arabs, pulled up his robe, and had two minutes of sex, after which the star's cousin paid her $150. Money for nothing. Cathy was hooked on hooking.

After an abortive trip to Cannes to promote a D-grade film called *Bikini Dreams* in which she starred, Cathy accepted that she was not going to be the next Marilyn Monroe, or JoBeth Williams, or anyone. She went to work for Alex, whom she met through the owner of a big auto-leasing concern who gave her a car in return for a series of blow jobs. Alex did a makeover on her, changing her hair, nails, skin, clothes, with the idea to make her look less sexy, more "demure." That accomplished, Alex sent her off to Paris for a five-thousand-dollar weekend with an Arab arms dealer. Back in Hollywood, Cathy met a lot of stars, and had only two bad experiences, but deciding that neither the film business nor the town was right for her, she asked Alex to send her to London. There, Alex introduced her to Alex's then correspondent madam Pauline, who insisted that Cathy buy a fur coat before Pauline would send her out on dates. Cathy fell in love with one of Pauline's johns, a rich Israeli jewelry dealer off Bond Street, who was also a coke addict. She eventually fled the Israeli, but not the coke, moving to New York and working for Alex's correspondent Manhattan madam Jackie, starting out on East End Avenue and winding up in the Cokeland of Washington Heights as the drug mistress of a junior runner for the Medellín cartel and the mother of his child. When their tenement was burned down by members of a rival Cuban drug gang, Cathy found herself in the street with nothing but her baby and the fur coat she had bought to turn tricks for Pauline.

Alex had taken Cathy on a shopping spree at the West Covina Fashion mall. Alex wanted to get her some decent food, but the best that was available was the California Crisp Salad Bar.

"Gross," Cathy muttered, refusing it and insisting on a chili burger and chili fries.

"You can be so gorgeous," Alex chided her. "Why eat that junk?"

"I'm living a junk life. Why spoil the mood?"

Alex was frustrated with Cathy's blithe self-destruction. "All you had to do was call me when you came back to L.A."

"I was too strung out. You wouldn't have touched me. Besides, I had decided to bag hooking. I became an agent."

"What kind of agent? A CAA agent?"

"Yeah. CAA. Con Artists Agency." Cathy was always quick. "It was called Celebrity Management Limited. It was limited, all right. We would find girls who wanted to be actresses and models and we'd charge them five grand to develop their career. What a joke. I got half the fee for every sucker I signed up."

"And you found people? It's so bogus."

"L.A. is filled with desperate people," Cathy said. "I was a great closer."

"What did the parents do when nothing happened for the girls?"

"They just ate it. No, I was doing great there, till the cops shut it down."

"For fraud?"

"No, for coke," Cathy said. "Geez. Look at that girl. I'll get her for you." Before Alex could stop her, Cathy had cornered a perfect girl, an almond-eyed, Subcontinental dark temple goddess, snatching her at the frozen-yogurt counter and lassoing her back to Alex.

"Shalimar, this is Alex. She can make you a star, just like she did Shakira Caine."

Before Alex could say that she had never met Shakira Caine, Cathy went on with her hype. "Did you ever see *Jewel in the Crown?*" Shalimar nodded. "You can be in a miniseries. You can be famous. You can meet rich men—"

Alex cut Cathy off. "Are you Indian?"

"Pakistani," Shalimar said.

"You could be a model," Alex said.

"I know," Shalimar said. "Ford and Elite have already asked me."

"We're toast," Cathy scoffed. "They've beat us to her."

"Did you apply to them?" Alex asked her.

"No, they found me."

"Where?"

"Right here. They have scouts. But my mom wouldn't let me. We're devout Muslims. She didn't want my pictures taken."

"Excellent," Cathy said gleefully. "What kinda guys do you like?"

Alex cut Cathy off again. "Shalimar, how old are you?"

"Fifteen."

Alex fished into her pocketbook and handed Shalimar a twenty.

"Wow!" Shalimar said.

"Go have fun, and study hard in school," Alex told her, and sent her away.

"Are you crazy?" Cathy said, puzzled.

"Are *you* crazy?" Alex parried.

"Think of what you could've made on *that*. She would've done it. I had her for you."

"Cathy, I don't want to join you at Pio-Pico. I value my freedom."

Eventually, Alex taught Cathy to revalue hers. Alex got Cathy released into her care, with Cathy getting to keep the welfare money. Alex put Cathy on a diet, cleaned up her complexion, and turned her into a race-horse once again, starting her out with the sexaholic star writer Walter Burke, who flipped for the made-over Cathy.

Alex also took pity on Diana Harmon, who, after her abortive trip to London, had sunk into the deepest depression, marooned in her parents' tract house in the Simi Valley, working for an answering service because she didn't have the stomach to go out and face anybody.

"I can't believe you're calling me," Diana said.

"I was too hard on you," Alex apologized. "It was only your first as-signment, and you were halfway around the world, and—what can I say?—I'm sorry. Do you want to try it again?"

"Not with any Arabs," Diana said.

"What about another aging stud producer? You were great with Low-ell Landesman."

"Up to a point."

"You won't even have to go to that point with this one," Alex said.

This one was one of Alex's once top clients, Carlos Wynburg, to whom Alex had made the mistake of introducing Lissa Trapp. Carlos was a six-figure-a-year spender, and Alex, now pressed to the wall by Lissa, got the inspiration that she could win Carlos back by sending him the right girl. All it took was one, and the client was yours. Until the next right one came along. Alex flayed herself for not having thought of Diana sooner, but she had been so put off by Diana's career move in London that she had put her completely out of mind. Now that Alex was scram-bling, her mind opened up. In the sweepstakes of which producer had used the most call girls, Carlos Wynburg, a former studio head, would have won the Cock d'Or award. Having been married to three major movie stars and slept with most of the rest, Carlos was incredibly jaded. He couldn't get it up anymore, but he wanted the call girls to keep on coming, even if he couldn't.

Diana Harmon thought Carlos Wynburg was much more frightening than Lowell Landesman. He had had several face-lifts, and had the slicked-back hair of a Valentino, courtesy of Grecian Formula. He wore a terry-cloth robe with his own crest on the pocket. He was trying, at sixty-something, to look like the young matinée idol who had been discovered by Joan Crawford as a lifeguard at the Beverly Hills Hotel pool. He had an odd, phony accent, somewhere between Mayfair and Oyster Bay, which left him between the Azores and the Bermuda Triangle.

Carlos showed Diana his Oscars, his wall of photos of himself with statesmen and stars, the rich and even more famous, the framed pictures of his three star ex-wives. "She was cheating on me the night of the premiere," Carlos said wearily, too weary for rancor. "The biggest night of my life and she was fucking someone else. God, how I loved her."

"Maybe it wasn't you. Maybe it was the movie. She knew it was going to bomb." The movie was *Battery Park*, about a gang of laid-off brokers who tried to blow up the New York Stock Exchange. It was a disaster.

"I *am* my movies," Carlos said.

That all Carlos's movies since the seventies had been disasters may have explained his state of mind. Without asking Diana a single question about herself, Carlos went on to show her his Picassos. He did some lines, played some Vivaldi, and took Diana into the Olympic-size Jacuzzi. He talked about his upcoming movie, *Shrinking Violet*, starring Savannah Parkinson, another girl he'd discovered through Alex.

"I've got this hot sports-club pool scene where she's wearing a patchwork tank suit with a black crotch. The audience'll think it's pubic hair. You know what *trompe l'oeil* is, baby?"

"I lived in Paris," Diana said.

"It's gonna go through the roof. They're gonna think they're seeing pussy," Carlos said, never asking Diana about Paris. Even though he and

Diana were naked in the roiling pool, he made no attempt to touch her or comment on her naked body. He just went on about himself.

Next it was on to his surreal master bedroom, with its Henry Moore sculptures and Dalí prints. As Alex had told her he would, Carlos had Diana lie on her side on the Frette-sheeted superbed, where he proceeded to give Diana a rim job. The first one she had ever had, it made her very uncomfortable.

"Why do you like this?" Diana couldn't stop herself from asking.

"Because it's the only mystery left for me," Carlos said.

And then Diana snapped. She jumped off the bed. "I *am* an asshole," she said. "I'm crazy. I'm a Phi Beta Kappa Columbia graduate and I'm taking money to let a famous producer I used to dream about making a movie for lick out my butt? You kiss my ass, but you won't even ask me who I am. This is insane. You're degrading yourself, I'm degrading myself. We're in Hollywood. You're the king. I'm talented. We should be making movies, good movies, not eating shit. I'm sorry, but this is not for me!"

"Darling, you can't go," Carlos said, racing her to the door.

"Oh, yeah, I can."

"I do want to get to know you."

"Not that way."

"I've got a better way."

"No way."

"But, baby, something very special has just happened, and it hasn't happened in a long time."

"What?" Diana snapped.

"My cock is getting hard."

Carlos Wynburg thus became Diana's mentor, getting her a development deal at Columbia to write a script. He also came back into Alex's fold.

The other big prize Lissa wanted to grab was superjohn Jock Palfrey. This time Alex's salvation was heaven-sent. Charity Rose was the twenty-year-old, 6′ 2″ blond daughter of Hawaiian missionaries on the leper-colony island of Molokai. Charity had already lived more than most women three times her age. On a Baptist teenage Royal Ambassador tour of Japan, she had disappeared and been presumed dead. Actually, she had been abducted by Yakuza procurers and taken into white slavery, forced to work in a *torko*, a Turkish bath massage and sex parlor in a remote gambling spa in the mountains of Hokkaido. After three months she escaped. But Charity never became the missionary her parents wanted her to be, unless one includes the missionary work she did on her back in the Okura Hotel with the clients she would meet at "Meliryn," the hostess club in Asakusa that employed only Monroe-type blondes from Australia and the States.

By the time Charity decided to move to L.A., she already had met Alex through a bigwig at Matsushita. (Because Japanese stuck with brand names, Lissa never stood a chance to take over that part of Alex's business.) Charity's first stop on the Alex trail was Jock Palfrey, who immediately invested a fortune with Alex to try to take Charity off the market. Ann, the Denver divorcee who Alex hoped would be Jock's salvation, hadn't worked. Despite her makeover, she was still too meek, too depressed from her failed marriage. Charity, on the other hand, brought her family's missionary zeal to her work. She infused her sin with Christian values, and in her company Jock Palfrey was, in more ways than one, born again, to Alex's delight and to Lissa's chagrin. The Big One was off her hook.

"She's fighting back," Nicky said disgustedly.

"So what. Competition's good for business. This is America," Lissa said.

"I am *not* an American," Nicky averred.

They were at the Malibu Country Mart, L.A.'s only pretty shopping center, an outdoor clapboard affair of expensive shops, with the surf roaring on one side and the mountains looming on the other. They weren't here for the shops or the scenery. Sipping their peach protein shakes from John's Garden health bar, they were scouting for talent. The Malibu Country Mart had the largest concentration of beautiful kept women in the world. They lived nearby, in the Colony or the Cove Colony or at Broad Beach, in multimillion-dollar sand castles with their star and mogul sugar daddies, and they were bored out of their minds. So during the day, while the stars and moguls were at the studios, the kept ladies would drive to the mart in their providers' Rollses and Ferraris, eat chocolate chip cookies, and shop. A lot of these kept ladies had been call girls, and a lot would be call girls again, as soon as their tours of duty ran out. Lissa and Nicky were here scouting for talent, searching for hookers on the rebound.

Staring at all the perfect blondes, Lissa reflected, "We'll never corner the market, no way. But look how far we've gotten."

"Don't you want to be Number One?" Nicky asked.

"Sure."

"Well, as long as she exists, we're not going to be Number One, and unless we're Number One we'll never get the Japanese, because they only go to the top, and we'll never get the Arabs—"

"Who wants the Arabs?"

"I do. I want them all. I want the Jock Palfreys. I want the L.A. Country Club. I want the big downtown law firms. I want aerospace. We can't count on these Hollywood assholes."

"The others are boring." Lissa drained her peach shake.

"It's business. We have to be big. We have to grow. I want to go back to Europe. I want to export these California blondes."

"No problem. This is the dream job, to be a six-figure call girl. There's nothing else they can do to get so rich, so quick, so young. They're ours, Nicky."

"Not until she's out."

"Alex'll never be out. Not until she's dead."

"So?" Nicky gazed his Svengali gaze at Lissa. "What's the problem?"

Before Nicky and Lissa could take out the contract on Alex, another force intervened, namely the L.A.P.D. They assumed that Alex owned the L.A.P.D. She had been operating so long, at so high a level, and so openly, at least in the top circles, yet she had never been bothered by the IRS, she had never gone to jail. There had been one big bust, back in 1982, though it was a bigger bust for the police, who had mysteriously dropped the charges. Besides, Nicky and Lissa could hardly sic the cops on Alex, not with their drugs, and hot goods, and underage hookers. That would be the guilty dog barking.

No, Nicky and Lissa were preparing for drastic measures. Little did they know that the L.A.P.D., *politia ex machina*, would beat them to the coup.

CHAPTER NINE

BUSTING

*T*he only way most vice cops can have an orgasm is when they bust someone. That's why they do it. It doesn't make them bad people, any more than film agents are, when the only way they can get off is by closing a deal. It's a fact of life. There are a lot of great vice cops. Some of my best friends are vice cops. And a few of my worst enemies. And the problem is, after twenty years of dealing with them, I'm still not sure who's who.

I'm a law-and-order person. I support my local police. I damn well better, because when I see what's going on out on our streets, these deceptively beautiful streets, I get scared. Riots, gangs, drug wars, carjackings, you name it. Expensive call girls may not be the solution, but they're definitely not the problem. If I had ever thought I was doing anything bad, morally bad, I wouldn't have done it. I was a very strict Catholic, a good girl, and I'm still a good girl. Not like Mae West said: "I used to be Snow White, but I drifted."

In Manila, where I grew up, prostitution was normal. In Europe, it's normal. In Japan, it's normal. There's no stigma. I'm not even sure it has such a stigma here anymore, but I will say one thing: Busting is the most fun some cops can ever have. Yet because of the "arrangement" I had with the L.A.P.D., I never believed they could have so much fun at my expense.

I never informed on my clients. That was a privileged professional relationship, like doctor-patient, lawyer-client. Madam-client. It's certainly professional, the oldest client relationship there is. But I heard a lot, through these clients and, even more, through my creatures. Remember Art Linkletter's *Kids Say the Darndest Things?* Well, call girls *hear* the darndest things. If I could make the world a safer or better place by passing that on, that was my civic duty. So when the L.A.P.D., my boys, the cops I cared about, some of whose lives I helped save, turned on me and tried to ruin my life and destroy my career, I got to learn, in a multimillion-dollar lesson, what the game of "Good Cop–Bad Cop" was all about.

It was an open-and-shut case. This time they were really going to get her. This time she was going to be closed down, once and forever. They had nabbed the Big One. Leading the chase was a pretty young L.A.P.D. officer named Patricia Corso. A graduate of Michigan State and the Los Angeles Police Academy Vice School, Corso had been on the force since 1981. In 1987, after working in the Hollywood Vice Division, she was promoted to the L.A.P.D.'s Administrative Vice Division, where her primary assignment was the investigation of pimping, pandering, and prostitution on a much higher level than the hot-pants streetwalkers who pounded the sidewalk stars of Hollywood Boulevard. The first, main, and prime target of Corso's new beat was Alex Adams, she of the infinite aka's: Alex Fleming, Elizabeth Adams, Betty Joan Jensen, Betty Jean Scott Adamson, Betty Elsa Adamson, Betty Elsa Doerfel, Betty Elsa Jensen, Betty Elsa Fleming, Betty Alexander. By any other name, everyone knew who she was: Madam 90210.

The L.A.P.D.'s Trojan Horse was Alex's handyman, David Wells, who had begun doing odd jobs at Alex's Doheny Drive estate in November 1987. According to the affidavit Corso filed on behalf of Ad Vice to secure the search warrant that was designed to bring Alex down, Wells was something of a man Friday for Alex, cooking, driving, shopping, and cleaning. Establishing the case that Alex was a madam, Corso stated that Wells, Corso's "confidential informant," overheard Alex discussing issues with numerous "young females" that could only point to one profession.

> They discussed personal hygiene relating to sexual activity with Alex's male clients, the use of condoms, and the large amounts of money made by the females by having sex with those clients. On one specific occasion, Alex had a conversation with a female that the informant knew was a prostitute regarding her income for that year. Alex asked the prostitute what she did with the $90,000 that the prostitute had earned from "fucking" her clients. Alex also told the prostitute that the "Arabs" were disappointed that she could not rejoin them on another cruise to the Carribean [sic] because she had gotten pregnant. The informant also observed young females arrive at Alex's house and give Alex money. From the conversation that he overheard, he realized that the money was from some prostitution activity that had occurred on a previous day. Specifically, Alex would ask the young female how long she had been with the gentleman and then Alex would pay her accordingly. The informant also said that cab drivers would deliver money from prostitutes directly to Alex's home.

Not only was Alex in the skin trade, Wells told Corso, she was also dealing in drugs, he said.

> On three occasions during the month of December, 1987, the informant, along with a prostitute drove Alex to a house located at 8973 Lloyd Place, West Hollywood. Alex told the informant that she rented the house

on Lloyd Place for $1,600.00 a month and she used it to store antiques. The prostitute told the informant that each time he drove Alex to the house on Lloyd Place, Alex would remove cocaine from a safe located in one of the bedrooms. On one occasion, the informant observed Alex giving the prostitute some cocaine after Alex had weighed it and told her (prostitute) to put it in her purse. The informant then drove Alex and the prostitute to Alex's residence (1654 North Doheny Drive). Once inside the house, Alex took the cocaine from the prostitute and handed it to one of two Lebonese [sic] looking men. One of the men said to Alex, "$1600.00 right?" And Alex said "yes." The man then handed Alex a large amount of money and she placed it in her pocket.

Wells had more and more information for Corso. In December, he told her how Alex had importuned him for "new, young females to work as prostitutes." Alex said she "preferred very young looking brunettes that appeared to be 18 years or younger and who were not hardened prostitutes." Alex suggested that Wells could find such youthful candidates down Doheny at the nearby Rainbow on the Sunset Strip. The club was a smoky teenybopper bar and burger boîte with red vinyl banquettes and a small disco room up a steep flight of steps that showcased the microskirted assets of the party dolls to the lecherous rockers, roadies, and A & R scouts who made the Rainbow their local hangout.

Wells said Alex promised him a hundred-dollar finder's fee for each girl he introduced to her. He made a quick three hundred. On each occasion, he overheard Alex tell each girl that she "would see wealthy clients, locally and some from abroad," and that she "would be paid a lot of money to please her clients."

In February 1988, Corso testified to the magistrate of the L.A. Municipal Court, where she sought her warrant, that she had directed Wells to set up a meeting between Alex and a Detective McElroy, an undercover police officer, who would be posing as a potential candidate. After a cordial meeting in Alex's bedroom, the undercover detective left, with Alex supposedly having told her that she could work for Alex and that Alex would be calling her. It turned out to be a Hollywood promise, a "Let's have lunch" sort of brush-off. Alex told Wells that the candidate was too old. Her cutoff age was twenty-five. Nevertheless, Wells reported that Alex gave him his hundred-dollar finder's fee for his efforts. Wells said that he would "make it up to her" by bringing her another, younger female.

The new female was Officer Rae Berwick, a beautiful blonde, 5' 5", 115 pounds, who was twenty-one "but looked as though she was 17 or 18." This was precisely the Alex type. In late February, Officer Berwick, posing as Renee Nelson, went to visit Alex. She had a listening device secreted in her handbag. Patricia Corso was parked down Doheny Drive recording the following key conversation, which Corso believed would be the coup de grâce for Alex and her empire of sex.

OFFICER: Hi, your house is beautiful.

ALEX: Thank you. (*Alex motioned for "Renee" to sit down.*)

OFFICER: Here?

ALEX: So, have you ever done this before?

OFFICER: No.

ALEX: Are you scared out of your wits?

OFFICER: Yeah.

ALEX: Most girls are, it's just like going on a date but you get paid for it. The people are very nice, I know them very well. It's a 60/40 split, you always bring the money the next day and you never give your number or take numbers and I want you to dress in a certain way because they like you to be very elegant and you need to get a haircut and a weave.

OFFICER: Okay.

ALEX: And, um, that's it. If you ever get busted, and I don't think you would from my guys, but if you ever did, it's better to not say anything and just call me and I'll have the lawyers—

OFFICER: Do . . . The 60/40, do you get the 40 or the 60?

ALEX: I get the 40.

OFFICER: Okay, and, do they pay me there?

ALEX: Yeah.

OFFICER: Okay, and, I'm embarrassed. Um, like, what do they expect though? You know, like . . .

ALEX: The same old stuff.

OFFICER: Well, you know, normal?

ALEX: Nothing fancy, and it's better for you to always carry condoms with you.

OFFICER: Okay, so it's all pretty much straight, like straight lays and stuff like that?

ALEX: Uh-hum, no fancy—

OFFICER: No what?

ALEX: No fancy anything.

OFFICER: Okay.

ALEX: It's very easy. Where do you live?

OFFICER: Well, right now I'm staying with my father in Baldwin Park but I want to get out of there. I just don't have a job or anything right now.

ALEX: Do you have a car?

OFFICER: Yeah, well, I'm using my dad's.

ALEX: Well, how do you get out at night?

OFFICER: Well, he's real, you know, he kind of doesn't want me there 'cause he has girlfriends and stuff, you know.

ALEX: Uh-hum.

OFFICER: And my mom doesn't want me at her place 'cause she lives with some guy.

ALEX: How old are you?

OFFICER: 21, I'll be 22 in October.

ALEX: You should have your own place.

OFFICER: Yeah.

ALEX: What's your phone number? What's your name, first of all? What's your last name?

OFFICER: Renee . . . Nelson. Okay, it's 808 area code, [555–5555].

ALEX: Here's mine. (*Alex handed "Renee" her telephone number.*)

OFFICER: Okay.

ALEX: I'll send you to people and they'll fix you up and then you'll return me whatever I lay out for you.

OFFICER: Okay.

ALEX: And, uh, you have to dress nicely, what size are you?

OFFICER: A 10, 9/10.

ALEX: I'll tell you what you have to do. Come here before you go on a date. And I'll show you how I want you to dress. So that's it. When do you want to start?

OFFICER: As soon as possible.

ALEX: As soon as they start calling. Okay. I want you to get a passport.

OFFICER: Okay, the passport, what is that for?

ALEX: To travel. Most of my clients like to get the girls where they are, which is abroad, like Europe. You know, Paris, Geneva, you get to see the world, that's nice.

OFFICER: Wow!

ALEX: And I want pictures of you. I want just face shots. Let me see your boobs. I need to see, open up, I want to see if you need a boob job or what.

OFFICER: Oh, I'm so embarrassed.

ALEX: Well, don't be embarrassed, this is very important, because—

OFFICER: But my boobs are nice, they're firm.

ALEX: Well, then, let me see them, because I don't want them calling me up and saying, Did you see her like this?, or Did you see her? They always ask me, you know, so I have to know what I'm talking about.

OFFICER: I just feel so uncomfortable.

ALEX: Don't be shy with me, you're a woman.

OFFICER: I know, but . . . See?

ALEX: No, I can't see anything. Take your bra off.

OFFICER: Oh, I don't want to.

ALEX: Darling, you have to show me because I don't want them telling me later that it was bad or whatever is wrong with it. If there's anything wrong with it, we'll fix it.

OFFICER: There's nothing wrong with them, though. Most men say they love them, I think they're beautiful.

ALEX: You can't be shy because I know they're going to ask you to expose yourself to them.

OFFICER: Well, I know that.

ALEX: You have to be very sure of yourself.

OFFICER: Okay.

ALEX: But that's all. Pretty face, you need a facial, hair weave, new hairdo. And you'll make lots of money, you never made money like this in your life.

OFFICER: No, how much do you make?

ALEX: Well, there's three prices. For two hours it's $300.00, for four hours it's $500.00, and for all night it's a thousand.

OFFICER: Just for the normal stuff?

ALEX: And you can't tell me you won't do it, because you have to do what I tell you, whatever price . . . and, um, after you get more polished and more well dressed then you start to have in the thousands.

OFFICER: $40,000.00???

ALEX: No, no, in the thousands.

OFFICER: Oh.

ALEX: You need a lot of polishing to get there because they are very fussy, they're older, they're all from Saudi Arabia and they want their girls very well groomed and very elegant and very young. You just have to go with it.

OFFICER: I just haven't had the money.

ALEX: You can't be shy, and, uh, always be very honest. Tell me everything so I can protect you, because we are working together. Other girls have tried to charge things to the rooms, you don't do that.

OFFICER: Okay.

ALEX: If they say, You can go downstairs and have a facial, then you can go downstairs and have a facial, but don't go shopping and charge it to the room because they will call me and tell me. So that's it.

OFFICER: Okay.

ALEX: Come over here where I can see you better. How do you know David?

OFFICER: Well, I met him a long time ago, like four years ago, 'cause my mom goes to his mom's a lot. We used to be close but she has this boyfriend.

ALEX: Were you ever his girlfriend?

OFFICER: No, just friends. Just talking to him and sometimes he tells me his problems and I'd tell him mine.

ALEX: He's a nice guy.

OFFICER: Yeah, he's real nice.

ALEX: You're very pretty, I'll show you how to do your face and your eyebrows but don't you touch them.

OFFICER: No, I won't do, I have to do that first.

ALEX: No, I'll call you if anything happens.

OFFICER: Oh.

ALEX: You have to know about feminine hygiene, you have to clean yourself before and after. They're very conscious of smell.

OFFICER: Do I always use a condom?

ALEX: It's preferable for your sake.

OFFICER: They don't mind.

ALEX: No, because they know that they have to.

OFFICER: Oh, okay.

ALEX: And that's it.

OFFICER: So you'll just call.

ALEX: Yeah.

OFFICER: Okay.

Following up on this meeting a few days later, Officer Berwick ("Renee"), who was a bit anxious at her refusal to take off her bra, called Alex to ask if her looks were really acceptable. Alex told her "that she was very happy but she ["Renee"] needed some work and then she'd be pretty."

According to Corso, Alex called Berwick on March 6 with a job offer. If she had a passport, Alex said, Alex would send her to the Bahamas. On March 7, before Berwick could begin to try to stonewall Alex by telling her how hard it was to get a passport, Alex told her that a passport was no longer necessary and that Alex would instead send her to New York in a few days. But Berwick and Corso were impatient. Corso had Berwick ask Alex if there was any job she could do before the New York trip. Alex told her to phone back before nine that night. Berwick made the call, and Alex said she might have a customer for her at nine-thirty. But the last thing Berwick wanted to do was be called upon to "put out." That would blow the case they were making. Berwick made up an excuse that she would be busy that night, but would be available the next day.

At six that day, Berwick called again. Alex had two questions. The first was about Berwick's still unseen breasts. Did she have "big boobs"?, Berwick said Alex queried her, and Berwick adroitly parried the question by indicating that she was appropriately "built." The other question was whether Berwick wanted to make a thousand dollars by going to San Diego that evening. She would have to fly down by nine and take a taxi to the client, who would pay her the thousand and reimburse her for her travel expenses. Berwick called Alex back, pretending there was no early flight to San Diego. Alex, who knew the flight schedules by heart, called her on this, pointing out which flight to take. Berwick's fallback was that she was having her period. "Well, you can't go until you're finished, because they don't like that," Alex said over the phone (the call was being recorded by the police). "So when you've finished, call me."

The recordings were enough to convince Patricia Corso that she could nail Alex on pandering charges. And there was more. The informant, David Wells, lived in a downtown loft apartment on East Third Street with a twenty-one-year-old girl named Helena Roe. The apartment itself was owned by a Doctor Jean Bre, who lived in the Korean district of Western Avenue. The doctor stored expensive art and antiques in the apartment, which Wells told Alex about. Alex told Wells and his roommate, Roe, that she would buy some of the items from them. Eventually, Wells said, Alex paid him and Roe a thousand dollars for twelve items stolen from Dr. Bre's loft, including jade figurines, a Miró print, a Limoges bowl, and a 9mm Browning automatic, and stored the items in her house on Lloyd Place.

On March 9, after Officer Berwick ("Renee") had used her period to avoid her San Diego assignation, Patricia Corso and other Administrative Vice officers began staking out both of Alex's houses, the one on Doheny and the one on Lloyd Place. At the Lloyd Place house, they observed Alex and a "white male" remove several items wrapped in white sheets and one item that wasn't wrapped, a tall Oriental statue. Alex took the items to her Doheny house, where detectives continually observed "numerous young females" arrive, stay a short time, then leave. The detectives also saw an "Arabic-looking male" driving a Checker Cab arrive at the Doheny house and give some "U.S. currency" to a female outside the house, who then went back inside.

Based on all this, Patricia Corso and her colleagues at Administrative Vice were ready to make their move. Alex was clearly a madam, Corso told the magistrate.

Alex was a madam, to be sure. She was *the* madam. In that, Patricia Corso was completely correct. But the rest of the case was complete Keystone Kops, and did as much to inspire confidence in the local criminal-justice system as the first Rodney King trial and the ensuing debacle. On March 10, a huge force of around thirty police officers assembled on Doheny Drive. It was dinnertime, and they might have expected Alex's house to be packed with starlet/harlots and famous stars and moguls, plus a few Arab sheikhs for good measure, in the midst of a bacchanal. They were to be sorely disappointed.

Alex was having dinner alone with her dear friend, David Niven, Jr., the son of the quintessentially debonair English star and himself the debonair producer of such films as the hugely successful *That's Entertainment* anthologies. Answering a ring at the door, Niven found a policeman standing outside. First, he worried for Alex. But when the policeman told Niven that someone had done a hit-and-run on his classic Porsche, which was parked on the street, Niven worried for himself. Niven ran outside and saw that his Porsche was just fine. It had been a trap. He was slammed into handcuffs as the dozens of cops, guns drawn, descended on the house.

No commando force could have ever been more disappointed. There were no whores, no stars, no black books, no drugs. The only vaguely titillating items the cops found upon fine-tooth-combing the house were two scraps of paper bearing lists of names, a lone celebrity mentioned on each. One had Paul Newman, the other Lucille Ball, which made it difficult to leap to any sweeping generalizations. Nevertheless, the police arrested Alex, dismissing David Niven, Jr., without allowing him to come to her aid. He wasn't married, wasn't a politician. Only his surname would provide any shock value.

Alex was less fortunate. She was booked and arraigned for felony pandering and receiving stolen property. The *objets d'art* belonging to Dr. Bre were found, per the search warrant, at the Lloyd Place residence. Helena Roe, David Wells's roommate, was also arrested and charged with the grand theft of the artworks. Alex's bail was set at the gargantuan sum of $1 million, which was more appropriate for a serial killer like John Wayne Gacy or a fiscal master manipulator like Mike Milken than for a kindly maternal madam with a heart condition who was nearly sixty. The enormity of the situation was underscored by the presumptive fact that under the state penal code, the bail for pimping and pandering was $2,000, for grand theft, $1,500. The bail being asked was nearly three hundred times what was called for in the bail schedule. The police made their case that Alex was poised to flee the country. One rumor had it that some sheikh was sending his private 747 to spirit her away to Saudi Arabia. Another rumor had her decamping to Cannes. The reality was much less glamorous. Alex spent the next four nights in the hospital wing of the Sybil Brand Women's Correctional Facility having her heart and blood pressure monitored while her star criminal lawyer, Paul O'Hara, used all his legal skills to have bail reduced to $200,000. Alex had to put up her house as collateral for the bail bond.

While Alex was recuperating at home from the trauma of her arrest, and waiting for her trial, the L.A.P.D. was planning one more assault, just to have more evidence to make their case unassailable. Administrative Vice had been watching one of Alex's pets, a petite doll-like blonde from Woodland Hills named Tina Milano. On April 8, they had observed her go to the Four Seasons Hotel on Doheny and Burton Way to have sex with a visiting Oriental businessman there for two hours for $500. A week later, four vice officers stopped Tina as she was entering her new apartment. Among the officers were Patricia Corso and Alan Vanderpool, a one-eyed aging surfer type who was one of the standouts of his department and who had helped organize the last bust of Alex, in 1982, which had resulted in nothing more than the briefest probation.

Tina Milano was a classic overextended yuppie, wearing the right clothes, eating the right food, driving the right car, living at the right address. Except she didn't work in a bank, as yuppies are wont to do. She did have her problems with banks, though, and that's why the police were there. They immediately placed her under arrest for writing checks with insufficient funds in her account. She had just sold one BMW and was using the money from that sale to buy another, better one. Unfortunately, the $5,000 check she wrote to the Santa Monica BMW dealership was no good. Tina had written a number of other bad checks (which the police had with them), to the Westward Ho Market, to A & W German Auto, to Vera's boutique in Woodland Hills. Several years before, when Tina was eighteen, she had gone on an unauthorized shopping spree with her mother's credit card. She was convicted and spent seventeen days in jail on a sixty-day sentence with three years probation. Los Angeles was so tempting. She loved to shop, loved it so much that she went to work for Alex.

And now she was in handcuffs in her yuppie dream pad in Westwood. But the police gave her one final chance. They wanted to rig Tina up with a wire and give her $400 in marked bills, which she would bring to Alex as a payoff against money for tricks she had turned but still owed Alex 40 percent of. Cornered in her apartment by the police officers, Tina agonized for hours over playing Judas. By evening she decided that she should save herself, and she accepted the vice officers' proposition. They removed the handcuffs and installed the wire.

At 11:30 that evening, Tina arrived at Alex's Doheny Drive house and went into Alex's bedroom. She was desperately nervous, not only about the police but about facing Alex, of whom she was terribly afraid. She trembled at the prospect of Alex's reprisal, which could be as dire as anything the police could come up with. This is how Alan Vanderpool's affidavit described the encounter:

During Milano's conversation, [Alex] Adams told her that she still owed her $850 from the Aspen, Colorado trip, February 11th through 16th, 1988. Milano agreed, and gave Adams $400 that your affiant (Vanderpool) had given her previously. Adams had pieces of paper in her hands on the bed that she was sitting on, with female names and telephone numbers. Adams scratched an amount off of one of the pieces of paper, and told Milano that she owed a new amount, and not to let this happen again. Milano also mentioned to Adams that Claudio, a client of Adams, continues to telephone her. She said "all he wants is to fuck me, and he never pays me." Adams told her not to accept his calls, because he owes too much money that he will never pay. Adams told her that she should get the money first.

On the police transcript of Tina's wired conversation, Tina told Alex that she was supposed to go over to the house of the lead singer of a famous rock group. She asked Alex if she had any drugs she could take over there. Alex said she had nothing. Then Alex chided Tina for usually wearing too much makeup and noting that she wasn't now and "I think you look much better." "Yeah, that caked on look," Tina admitted. "I'm trying to get better. I'm not wearing that much cause it's summertime."

Alex offered Tina a glass of wine. Tina's statement for the upcoming trial gives some sense, albeit garbled, of what was transpiring between the two women:

> Well, she, I just know, I know her, I know when she looks at me, and I felt very bad doing this to her, and I just looked at her, and she just looked at me, and she said, like funny, I mean I could just see that, there was confusion, and she just said, so, I mean it was like, the things I was saying were things I would have never said before . . . I mean, I was a puppet. I was completely directed through everything with them. And I was not, I just wasn't myself, you know.

Tina chatted nervously to Alex, who gave her a look, a questioning look. The question was quickly answered. One of Alex's maids spotted police cars out front. Tina pretended they might be after her. Panic set in, but Alex was only worried about Tina, not herself. As per the transcript:

TINA: I wonder if they know that car was mine. I have a warrant.

ALEX: What?

TINA: I have a warrant, a traffic warrant. I'm a nervous wreck.

ALEX: Paul will take care of you. They will threaten you, bribe you, and do all kinds of shit.

TINA: They can't do anything to me?

ALEX: Nothing.

TINA: I just say I have nothing to say?

ALEX: "I have nothing to say, talk to my lawyer."

TINA: And Paul will help me?

ALEX: Yes, I'll make sure.

TINA: Let me go out right here.

ALEX: No, because they'll grab you, you better stay.

TINA: I'll just say I do errands for you. I'm a friend, I met you at the antique store.

ALEX: You're a receptionist for my doctor.

TINA: Which doctor, do you have a doctor friend?

ALEX: Yeah, named William Schwartz and he's at Century Park East. Suite 911 . . . You heard that I was having a problem breathing.

TINA: With your heart.

ALEX: And couldn't breathe.

TINA: Okay, and I came to see how you were.

ALEX: You were going to get me the medication.

TINA: All right.

ALEX: Just make up like you're a . . .

TINA: Receptionist.

ALEX: Receptionist.

TINA: Why would they come back again after they already got you? You want me to walk out the window and wait and stay here and then go to my car?

ALEX: No, honey, just stay here and be quiet. Do not say one word.

TINA: I won't.

ALEX: I'll kill you.

TINA: I won't, I won't, I won't!

ALEX: Just say, "Talk to my attorney."

TINA: Why would they come back, Alex? There was nobody behind me when I drove up here.

ALEX: Don't go anywhere, just stay here and be quiet. I know you got this probation shit.

TINA: It's over in three weeks but I never got arrested for prostitution or anything.

ALEX: Just say that you've never been a prostitute.

TINA: No, I never have. There's people standing out there.

Within a few minutes, the police, who had been taping Tina, swept down on the house and arrested Alex for one more count of felony pandering. A new bail was set at $100,000. From all indications, the game was over for Alex.

The People of the State of California v. *Elizabeth Adams* dragged on from 1988 through 1991. All Hollywood trembled at the prospect of Alex's client list coming out. It never did.

The big question at the trial was why the police wanted Alex so badly *now*, after nearly twenty years of tolerating, even sanctioning, her existence. They were clearly hell-bent to convict her, maybe too hell-bent, as her lawyers hammered at the police's crossing all borders of due process.

Alex had first assumed that the police action was somehow precipitated by Lissa and Nicky Kroll's having entrapped some high-level politician, with either Lissa herself or with drugs, to blackmail him into ridding them of their competition. Yet Alex could never prove this thesis. Lissa Trapp was as surprised by the police action as Alex herself. For Lissa, it was a windfall. Los Angeles still had to get laid, and Alex's arrest created the total power vacuum Lissa and Nicky had long dreamed about and had been conspiring to accomplish by their own violent means. Now the police had done it for them. Of course, the other madams were also vultures circling around the corpse of Alex's business, but Lissa believed she was ahead of the flock. Becoming Madam 90210 was her manifest destiny.

As stated by Pamela Ferraro, the deputy district attorney for the County of Los Angeles who filed the case, the rationale of the D.A.'s office was that Alex had gotten away with being a supermadam for too long.

> I had in front of me a file that had previously been handled by Organized Crime Division in which [Alex] had been a defendant.
>
> I noticed the file contained six felony counts filed against her and the resolution of the file that she had pled guilty to a misdemeanor for basically no time, no fine, no nothing.
>
> I wanted to know what had happened . . . I was not interested in filing a felony case against her that was going to end up in other than a misdemeanor plea. . . . The case was going to proceed as a felony. . . . Anything that had happened in the past was not going to happen again.

Much of the rest of the seemingly endless trial was devoted to a discussion of precisely what had "happened in the past": that Alex had not been prosecuted because she was one of the best informants the L.A.P.D. had ever known. The defense called a number of police officers to the stand to establish Alex's key position with the L.A.P.D. One of these was Daniel Lott, an officer in the Narcotics Group Major Violations Section and a twenty-seven-year veteran of the force. In the early 1970s, while still a detective at Administrative Vice, in the Organized Crime Division, Lott and his partner, Larry Corbitt, met Alex and put her to work for them:

> We considered Betty [Alex] as an under-agent working with us regarding other criminal activities within the city. . . . Betty's understanding was any time she came across anything involved in criminal activity, she would relay that. . . . Because of her endeavors, information that she received was a lot of times invaluable and also involved people involved in criminal activities. I couldn't get that type of information from a church person.

Questioned by one of Alex's attorneys, Anthony Brooklier, Officer Lott explained the procedure by which Alex would be protected for her efforts on the force's behalf.

BROOKLIER: You have been an officer with L.A.P.D. for in excess of 27 years. How would you place her [Alex] in terms of characterizing her value as an informant for the period of time you worked for her or she worked for you?

LOTT: She was the best informant I have ever met.

BROOKLIER: Why do you say that?

LOTT: The nature of the information that she gave us, the quality of the information, the quality of the arrests that were made. In all of the criminal areas, she was highly valuable. . . . She never lied to me.

BROOKLIER: Now, what would happen if she was ever arrested on prostitution activities as far as you were concerned?

LOTT: She had been several times . . . during my relationship with her as an agent. . . . If some other agency had arrested her, we would . . . try to go to bat for her as to provide a letter at the time of sentencing and try to make it a minimum sentencing situation. . . . If need be [we would] provide a letter from the Chief of Police on her behalf.

Lott's testimony was echoed by Sergeant Detective Glenn Souza, who had retired from the L.A.P.D. in 1984 after twenty-five years' service. Souza described Alex as "the most valuable informant that the department [Administrative Vice] had, assisting them in narcotics, firearms, thefts, assaults, every type of crime." Souza recounted that for her efforts for the L.A.P.D., Alex was often subject to threats and was once badly beaten and spent weeks in a hospital, requiring plastic surgery on her face. Souza said that Alex had even been revealed as a formal agent, complete with an agent's number, of the L.A.P.D. in connection with the U.S. Senate hearings investigating fugitive financier Robert Vesco, who had fled to Costa Rica. The reason Alex hadn't ever before been placed on probation, Souza explained, was that her madaming activities would have been limited by her probation officer to the extent that her utility as an informant would have been compromised. There was a "tacit understanding" at Administrative Vice that Alex would never be jailed for her prostitution activities. The material she delivered was far too good to lose. Of the department's two hundred to three hundred agents, Alex was at the top of the list.

Fred Clapp, a churchgoing family man who looked as if he should be leading tours at Knott's Berry Farm rather than leading raids on brothels, was one of the top detectives at Administrative Vice. For the last ten years he had been involved in well over one hundred major felony investigations in the so-called 3-P area (pimping, pandering, prostitution), and in over two hundred arrests. Clapp had first met Alex in 1979 at her home in Malibu as part of the Administrative Vice Division's "community outreach" service to ensure that Alex continued to provide useful information. He then spoke to her regularly by phone. By 1982, her information had slowed to a trickle. Alex needed a prod. Accordingly, Clapp, assisted by Officer Alan Vanderpool, organized an elaborate sting.

Clapp had a confidential informant, who used the name Roger Roydan, whom Clapp had caught at a brothel on St. Andrew's Place near Hancock Park that used underage girls. Roydan was married and worried. As a compulsive john, he had an equal compulsion to be an informant, as if to expiate his sexual addiction and somehow extirpate prostitution, if only to prevent himself from being able to use it. Clapp used Roydan as a front, giving him police money to have sex with call girls, after which Clapp would call the girls himself, pretending he was Roydan, and begin constructing his dragnet.

The process had begun in April 1982, when Roydan contacted Clapp and told him he had the telephone number of a new madam named Joan Pierce, a poor man's Alex, who lived on Sunset Avenue in Venice. Pierce had given Roydan a list of six girls to call, each of whom would have sex for $150. Clapp, pretending to be Roydan, made a tape-recorded call to Pierce. It was a long, chatty session, during which Clapp (as Roydan) told Pierce that he was in the auto-parts business, that he traveled extensively, and that he sometimes wanted girls with him, sometimes as far away as Italy. Pierce responded that she would send girls anywhere so long as the client paid the airfare. Clapp said that he had recently been in Rome. Pierce joked that there were no call-girl services there "because they're so Catholic."

Pierce pushed two "special" girls on Clapp. One was Maria Ricci, who had been a recent centerfold of *Penthouse*. The other, called Danielle, had been featured in *Hustler*. Both girls were billed as remarkably beautiful. Additionally, Pierce raved about Ricci's elegant apartment on Larrabee in Hollywood. Both girls sounded to Clapp like Alex material. Clapp located the back issues of *Penthouse* and *Hustler* and saw the naked pictures. Pierce had not been exaggerating. Clapp then called Roger Roydan and gave him $150 to find out more.

In June 1982, Roydan had his $150 session with Maria Ricci, a tall, statuesque brunet temptress. Ricci asked Roydan not to tell Pierce she had seen him, so that Ricci wouldn't have to pay Pierce her 40 percent cut. Ricci also gave Roydan Alex's number in case he wanted to see more girls of her caliber. Ricci told Roydan that he could use her name as a reference to get to Alex.

Clapp was thrilled at the easy networking. Again pretending to be Roydan, he called Alex (the conversation was taped), dropping Maria Ricci's name. Alex told Clapp that Maria operated on a much lower price scale than she did and that "my prices might be beyond you. I am a bit high." She quoted her 1982 scale, $300 for two hours, $500 for four, $1,000 a day, $2,000 out of town. Alex said to Clapp that "poor Maria" could be the darling of Alex's Arab princes but for her refusal to travel on dates out of the country. And besides, Alex added, ridiculing the $150 tricks Maria did for Joan Pierce, Maria had no idea how much she could *really* make.

Clapp told Alex he was in auto parts, lived in Chattanooga, Tennessee, and traveled all over.

Alex stated, "I can help you in London, Italy, Geneva, and I'm trying to establish a friend in Paris. I also have contacts in New York, Chicago, and Las Vegas." She gave him the number of "Scarlet" in London, who ran an out-call service, and told him to use her name and "that would be enough." Alex bragged about her Middle Eastern clientele, "the very top people in Saudi Arabia. They don't screw around when it comes to money. They spent it in big bushels if the girl is right. Maria could stay home six months [and do nothing] after a gig like that."

In July, Clapp (with Alan Vanderpool) flew to Chicago and checked into the Knickerbocker Hotel there under the name of Roger Roydan. He then called Alex, asking for the names of call girls. She gave him the names of two Chicago madams and told him that when he had first called, she "thought he might be the law," but that now she was no longer concerned. While in Chicago, Clapp sent "Roger Roydan"–signed postcards to Joan Pierce to confirm his identity as a traveler. He arranged to have other Roydan cards sent to her from Mexico and Italy.

When he returned from Chicago in late July, Clapp (again pretending to be Roydan) called Joan Pierce, taping the conversation. She welcomed him back and gave him more girls to call. She asked him if he had seen Maria Ricci. He lied and said he had not. That same day, Clapp (as Roydan) also called Alex, who connected him with a rangy model named Denise on Hammond Street in West Hollywood. Clapp then gave Roger Roydan three hundred dollars, which Roydan used for a two-hour sex session with Denise. Clapp (as Roydan) called Alex a few days later to thank him for Denise. Alex then suggested he call Denise's roommate Jade at the same number. "She's very pretty with dark hair and very big tits," Alex said. Clapp begged off, saying that he was uncomfortable seeing Jade in the bedroom she shared with Denise because of his recent visit there.

Clapp also called Maria Ricci again. All business, she told him that she knew he had seen a girl through Alex, and that if he wanted to see her, Maria, again, he would have to pay her at Alex's rate, which was double that of Joan Pierce. If Clapp had been a real customer, he might have been put out that what had seemed a generous introduction to Alex had merely been a way for Maria to raise her prices.

Clapp and Vanderpool also conducted a stakeout at Alex's mansion on Stone Canyon Road. They saw a striking twenty-year-old brunette driving a black Datsun 280-Z, with the personalized license plate JADED-A, talking to Alex in front of the house. When they checked the car with the Department of Motor Vehicles, they traced ownership to a girl whose number was on a list of call girls Alex had given to Clapp. The net was tightening.

On August 6, Clapp called Alex to tell her that he (that is to say, Roydan) was planning a party at his Malibu condo on August 11. He asked for seven girls, to be on duty from eight P.M. until one A.M. Alex said, "No problem. It should be six hundred dollars for each, but let's round it off to an even five hundred dollars." Then Clapp called Joan Pierce to ask for seven of her girls for the same party. Pierce quoted her price as $150 for each girl. Clapp placed the order and then got search warrants to raid both Alex's and Joan Pierce's homes the night of what was going to be the biggest deluxe prostitution bust in Los Angeles history.

The condo had a view of the black Pacific right outside the glass doors. It was romantic, there was good jazz on the stereo, there was endless booze. But Clapp/Roydan's guests seemed nervous, repressed, uptight. There was a good reason for it. They were all undercover cops, who had to be super-careful not to make any moves, physical or fiscal, that might be construed as entrapping the girls, inducing them to commit an act of prostitution. The girls had to ask for the money, the girls had to offer the sex. The cops had to remain passive or the bust of the decade would go up in the smoke of due process.

Joan Pierce's girls finally decided to liven things up. They began stripping off their clothes. They began kissing each other. They even began sixty-nining each other. The men watched politely. Too politely. Then Fred Clapp took charge. He announced to the group that the men were shy, and that they needed organization. The scene was too vague, too confusing. Everyone had to pair off. Like at a Sadie Hawkins Day dance, he announced a Ladies' Choice. The girls all lined up. Each was to announce her name and who sent her. Then each would pick a guy. Once they were together, she would quote her price, $500 or $150.

The matches were made. Some couples went into bedrooms, some went to the deck, some chose the bathrooms. One by one, the girls named their price and offered themselves.

Patricia Brown, using the name Penny, was a 5' 9", 115-pound, twenty-five-year-old redheaded model from Buffalo, New York. That night she was wearing a black minidress and metallic shoes. She told her chosen man, who was actually a Detective Spradley, that she would like to see the rest of the condo, and took him into a bedroom.

PENNY: Were you told of the arrangement?
SPRADLEY: No, should I have been?
PENNY: I guess not. It's five bills.
SPRADLEY: Five hundred sounds okay to me, I guess.
PENNY: It'll get you several hours of fun.
SPRADLEY: What kind of fun?
PENNY: How about a lay and some head?
SPRADLEY: Sounds good to me.
PENNY: Anything else you might like is okay too. Alex sent me here to satisfy.

Constance Gordon (whose nickname was Cat), one of Joan Pierce's girls, was a 5' 5", 110-pound twenty-year-old blond gemologist from Santa Monica. She was wearing green shorts and a white sweater. She lured her man, Alan Vanderpool, to the beach.

CAT: Why don't we get a towel and go on the beach?
VANDERPOOL: On the beach?
CAT: It is the best place to make love.
VANDERPOOL: Sounds okay to me.
CAT: You do know my fee is two hundred dollars.
VANDERPOOL: I do now.
CAT: Don't worry. I'll give you a head job you'll never forget.

At the end of each of these and other conversations, the men whipped out their . . . badges and arrested the girls, detaining them in plastic handcuffs. Only one girl resisted, kicking and hitting her officer and trying to stiletto her heels into his feet. She was charged with battery along with prostitution.

While the Malibu sting went down, simultaneous moves were being made across L.A. Another officer, Detective Carter, posing as the owner of a salvage business in Victorville, had used the Roger Roydan connection to set up a double date with two of Joan Pierce's girls, Marilyn Baker and Linda Lawrence, at Baker's apartment at 221 1/2 Kenmore, a rough area between Hancock Park and downtown. Baker was a former Santa Monica Police Department secretary who had switched to the other side of the law. Lawrence, who used the name Bridgette, was a tall, dark, slinky thirty-year-old aspiring songwriter from San Antonio. While Carter sat in Marilyn's living room, talking salvage, two other officers outside waited for the signal to come in and make the bust.

BRIDGETTE: Uh, Mike, we better get the business out of the way.

MARILYN: Yeah, after you're done and all tired it's tacky to talk about money.

CARTER: That's fine. Roger gave me all the money. Who gets what?

BRIDGETTE: We each get two hundred dollars. We don't get to keep it all. Joan gets to take some.

CARTER: I've never been with two women before.

BRIDGETTE: Oh, it's going to be fun. You'll enjoy it. We can do whatever you want. We can make love. Then we can trade off.

CARTER: Four hundred dollars is a lot of money to make love.

BRIDGETTE: Don't worry. It will be worth it.

CARTER: Oh, I'm sure it will be.

Carter reached into his wallet and gave the girls four hundred-dollar bills.

At this point the outside officers thought it was time to make their move. These officers, Detectives Harper and Oshynko, knocked on the front door. But Carter wasn't ready. Perhaps he thought he needed more for a prostitution charge to stick. Struck by Carter's hesitation to get up from the couch, Harper and Oshynko stated that they were there on a noise complaint. The cops told the girls to keep it down and left, waiting outside. But now the girls were scared.

MARILYN: That really put me off. I'm a little scared to do it here. We could go to a hotel.

BRIDGETTE: Yeah, but I've got another appointment at nine-thirty.

MARILYN: We'll just refund your money and give you our numbers and we can get together later.

The girls gave his bills back to Carter. He walked the two girls out to Bridgette's car.

BRIDGETTE *(to Marilyn):* Make sure you call Joan.

MARILYN: Yeah, I will.

Then Carter gave a signal and the other officers came out of the darkness and arrested the girls, Bridgette for prostitution, Marilyn for "keeping a house of ill fame."

Several miles west, on Larrabee, another friend of Roger Roydan's was about to do his thing with *Penthouse* Pet Maria Ricci, who, in the magazine, listed her occupation as "aerobic dancer." Maria hardly dressed for the glamorous call-girl part, in jeans, a faded gray T-shirt, tennis shoes, and no makeup.

Officer Nolan introduced himself as Joe. Maria didn't ask what he did. She didn't care. She had requested that he bring a bottle of white wine, over which she proudly showed him her *Penthouse* centerfold. Assuming he was appropriately aroused both by her looks and by her celebrity, she suggested they retire into her bedroom.

MARIA: But first we should get the business out of the way. Did Roger tell you I would cost six hundred dollars?

Alex had scolded Maria, who was only twenty, for being even greedier than she was lazy.

JOE: Isn't that just like Roger. He told me five hundred dollars.

MARIA: Isn't six hundred dollars okay?

It was. The undercover officer arrested Maria, just as other police were swooping down on Alex and Joan Pierce.

The entire entourage of madams and their whores was assembled downtown at the East Sixth Street station. Alex, who posted the fifteen-hundred-dollar bail for each of her girls, as well as Joan Pierce's, was shocked to find out that the Roger Roydan she knew was actually Fred Clapp—her friend Fred Clapp. "You should have called me," Clapp said, referring to the six months that had gone by without Alex's having contacted him with information on crimes or criminals that she might have gleaned.

Despite the military precision with which Clapp executed the bust, within a few days Alex and the girls were free. Her felony was reduced to a misdemeanor. There was no time, no probation, only a small fine. And it was business, big business, as usual. The reason? Alex started talking again, and talking fast.

As Clapp testified, "I made the decision, based on information that she was giving us about another criminal entity, that she greatly assisted us in the arrest of that criminal entity and that it was a trade-up situation [giving information on a bigger fish than she was], and that the reduction from felony to misdemeanor, no probation, was in the best interest of the police department."

The criminal entity in question was a group of multi-kilo drug dealers headquartered in a nightclub called the Candy Store on the corner of Sunset Boulevard and Laurel Canyon. The operation was run by a man named Rick Johnson, who was the front man for the owners, black mobsters from Detroit. Clapp was posing as a major drug dealer who had infiltrated the Candy Store by playing to the one pretension Hollywood has always been a sucker for: royalty. Clapp told Johnson he had an Ethiopian prince in town who wanted to see the L.A. high and low life, and asked for Johnson's assistance in giving the prince the grand tour. How could a mobster refuse a prince? Johnson rolled out the red carpet to Clapp and the prince, who was actually an undercover officer faking an African accent.

Borrowing a Rolls-Royce from another drug-dealer informant, Clapp

got fifty thousand dollars in cash from the L.A.P.D. and staged a big cocaine buy with another trusted informant in South Pasadena, with Johnson's henchmen observing the transaction. Still, doubts remained. This
was where Alex came in. Alex knew a Filipino bar girl at the Candy Store
named Tamara Lopez, to whom she chatted on occasion. Alex told
Lopez what big drug players Clapp and Vanderpool (who was now posing
as Clapp's drug partner) were, validating their cover, and Lopez, as expected, passed the validation on to Johnson, who then continued his
dealings with Clapp. In truth, Alex's cover saved Clapp's life and gave
him another big score. He was finally able to arrest Johnson and use him
as a stepping-stone to Stoney White, a major cocaine lord. White,
through Clapp's efforts, was put away for life. Clapp, then, owed part of
his life and his career to Alex. He remained her friend, and she remained
his valuable informant, for years. By 1987, however, Alex and Clapp
ceased to be in contact. Alex's informant file entry for July 1987 reads,
"No contact," "inactive," "should go to jail."

Other police testified how Alex had helped them in a major child-por-
nography case; in a big payola case in the record business, in which a
music mogul was accused of supplying prostitutes to radio and other recording executives as an incentive to play certain artists; and in numerous narcotics cases. All underscored how truthful and reliable Alex had
been. Even Alan Vanderpool, who had helped spearhead the current
bust, remembered that Alex had helped protect his life in the Candy
Store operation. Vanderpool rebutted the testimony of Helena Roe that
"Alex told her that if any of her girls ever turned against her, she would
. . . have them killed and dumped in the ocean." "Just the opposite,"
Vanderpool told the court, acknowledging that Alex had never harmed
any of her girls. Alex was a mother, not a gangster. Nevertheless, Vanderpool was evasive about why, after the L.A.P.D.'s long involvement with
Alex as their star informant, they would turn on her.

BROOKLIER: Let me ask you this: Let's say this is a hypothetical situation. You have a situation where there is an understanding, either ex-

pressed or tacit, between Ad[ministrative] Vice and an informant, and that understanding is the following:

That as long as the informant continues to give information, the informant will not be arrested for crimes, that Ad Vice knows that the informant is committing.

Given that situation, would it be the policy of Ad Vice to tell the person that "If you stop giving information, we are going to arrest you"?

VANDERPOOL: It is not a policy, no.

BROOKLIER: How do you, if you ever do, let the person know that if they stop giving information, they are going to be arrested?

VANDERPOOL: I can't say. I would have to have a particular incident to talk about it. Every situation is different.

BROOKLIER: Mr. Vanderpool, you told us that you knew she was a madam, right?

VANDERPOOL: Correct.

BROOKLIER: You didn't take any steps to investigate her or try to arrest her while she was giving information as a result of her madam activities, right?

VANDERPOOL: Correct.

BROOKLIER: So what I am saying is, let's say we have a situation where she just doesn't have any more information. Should she be arrested?

VANDERPOOL: In the circumstances surrounding her arrest, she should be arrested, should be investigated and then arrested.

BROOKLIER: Because she is inactive.

VANDERPOOL: Not because she is inactive in this case. An informant that had worked for her walked into [the] station and said, "I have a story to tell."

BROOKLIER: But you knew the story. You knew the story for years.

VANDERPOOL: Just because I know she is a madam, I can't put a case together on her just because she is sitting there like a pimp. You have to investigate. You have to get knowledge. You have to get arrests. You have to do undercover investigations.

There was never proof in this case, only theories, and then only out of court. Was David Wells really an outraged suitor, livid that his inamorata Helena Roe was working as a call girl? Or was it all a police setup just to squeeze Alex, as Fred Clapp had squeezed her into saving his life and his Candy Store case six years before? Were they after Alex's unbeatable defense lawyer Neil Grant, who had been the Clarence Darrow of dope cases, the bane of the D.A.'s office? Were there important people connected with the L.A.P.D., the courts, or city government that someone else was out to embarrass? Or was it simply that Administrative Vice needed some big publicity, a trophy case?

Alex, who had always assumed that she was protected by her friends on the force, was a sitting target, and a severely wounded one. She had had to sell her house to make bail, not to mention pay her attorneys. She had been in the hospital several times for diabetes and a heart condition that all the stress could only have exacerbated. She had no income. The best she could hope for was to stay out of prison, where she faced a minimum sentence of three years.

Alex was not without her sympathizers. Numerous pillars of the community—businessmen, doctors, and at least one well-known actress—wrote letters to the court in her behalf. Brenda Vaccaro's letter to Judge Candice Cooper proceeded thus:

> I have known Alex Adams 8 years now. She has always been a good friend.
>
> We began our friendship over books . . . I have an extensive library as well as she does and we would exchange books to read and then discuss them.
>
> The conversations we had when she invited me over to her home for tea were interesting and rewarding. She is a very intelligent and well-read person.
>
> Her Christmas and Thanksgiving dinners that I have attended with my husband were always gracious, elegant, and many important people were there so I always felt comfortable and entertained.
>
> We also share in common a love of cats and when the litter of kittens

were born from her Persian cats she very kindly gave me one as a pet. I am very grateful to her for her generosity as a friend, her insight, her patience, and her indomitable spirit.

I do hope you will see your way to be compassionate and lenient with this very special lady, Alex Adams.

Sincerely,

Brenda Vaccaro

In the end, Alex got the best she could hope for. After three years, five lawyers, and seven judges, on October 28, 1991, having bargained her case down to the single felony plea of "sale of a person for immoral purposes," Alex was sentenced to eighteen months' probation. There was, as in all of Alex's prior arrest, no fine, no time. "It was going to be messy and expensive," said Alex's lawyer Anthony Brooklier. "Both sides stood to lose something if this case went to trial." Alex's main line of defense, that because of her decades of service as an informant she ran her business with the approval of the L.A.P.D., was what brought the prosecution to the table with the deal. Deputy District Attorney Alan Carter had contended that Alex's relationship with the police was never authorized to the extent that she would enjoy immunity from prosecution, but he wasn't sure he could convince a jury of that. "Based on some of the testimony, there was some question about whether we'd be able to prevail," the D.A. said.

The other sword of Damocles was the feared client list. "Revelations, my dear," Alex told at least one reporter in a courthouse hallway. The paranoia, at least among the ruling classes, was fanned by a long 1989 *Vanity Fair* article. The prosecution denied vehemently that it made its deal to keep the clients—some of whom were whispered to be on the force, in the D.A.'s office, in City Hall, in Sacramento, in Washington—a secret. "It's not relevant to anything," District Attorney Carter said. "I have absolutely no idea who her clients are."

Or *were*. The day of the deal, Brooklier told the press that Alex now supported herself as a "Westside caterer." The following is from the report of the officer, Barry J. Nidorf, who approved Alex's probation.

Evaluation:

The defendant before the court is well-known in the community as the "Beverly Hills Madam," and she admits to running a highly sophisticated and internationally known prostitution organization. . . . It appears that she has been running a highly successful sexual service in the community as well as abroad.

The defendant appears to be honest, intelligent, sophisticated and very capable of benefitting from a grant of probation in regards to this matter. Throughout the investigation, the defendant was very co-operative, and she assured this officer that she has retired from her days as a madam, and that she is currently running a catering service.

The defendant's attitude toward the justice system and the probation department appears to be very good; and nothing in her expressed thoughts or feelings indicated that she was a danger to the community in the past or that she would be a danger to the community in the future.

However, the concerns of the community and the justice system appear to be valid, and it is this officer's opinion that she is in need of close probation supervision to insure that the defendant does not return to her former days as a madam.

Alex's probation terminated on April 30, 1993. She celebrated at home with several former celebrity clients, several new successful and/or happily married former call girls, her two maids, and her nine cats.

*L*issa Trapp's reign as the new Hollywood Madam was glorious but brief. In the first year following Alex's arrest, Lissa earned over half a million dollars as a beautiful vulture gobbling up the spoils of Alex's thwarted empire. Then the truly unexpected happened. Lissa fell in love. The man was a client, a young, brilliant workaholic Harvard lawyer from a Century City corporate firm who had no time for normal dating. It began as a five-hundred-dollar midnight quickie in the lawyer's office, a break from an all-nighter on an SEC registration statement.

The quickie became a weekly routine, first at the office, then at the lawyer's house in Rustic Canyon, a Frank Lloyd Wright Taliesin-style wood-and-glass tour de force that the lawyer used only to sleep in. There was a Modigliani, a live-in Chinese chef, a classic red Ferrari California convertible the lawyer never drove. Lissa was intrigued and entranced with the sheer ordered perfection of the lawyer's unused life. Then there were the business trips to Paris, where they stayed at the Bristol, and Tokyo, at the Okura, and the free rein Lissa had with his platinum AmEx. The lawyer was in negotiations all day; Lissa shopped. It was paradise—no ringing phones, no unruly girls, no cocaine *sturm und drang*. It was a holiday, and when the lawyer took Lissa completely by surprise by proposing, Lissa took herself completely by surprise by accepting. Her dreams of riches, luxury, and security had all come true without her having to work for them and with a little romance thrown in as well. Being a Beverly Hills Wife was even better than being a Beverly Hills Madam.

Nicky Kroll was devastated. While Lissa was on her honeymoon at the Cipriani in Venice, Nicky died of a drug-related heart attack in a private booth of the Show and Tell Party World adult-entertainment complex in Toluca Lake, trying to lure one of the "personal strippers" into his cocaine dreamland of Money for Nothing that Lissa had left behind.

The one-two punch of Alex's forced retirement and Lissa's surprise abdication created bedlam in the Hollywood deluxe sex trade that had enjoyed two decades of stability during Alex's long and forceful reign. This became the War of Sexual Succession, in which a coven of minor madams plunged into an internecine donnybrook of deception and betrayal, with drugs and stars as the trading cards, and delusional promises that would make even the most hardened William Morris agent blush. They all wanted to be recognized as the new Alex, the Queen of the Hills.

Out of this War of the Roses, which was all thorns, emerged a most unlikely champion, the twenty-something Heidi Fleiss, the personification of the decadently privileged Jewish American Princess who had fueled Lissa Trapp's gilded Beverly Hills dreams. Heidi was born with it all, but she wanted more. After dropping out of high school at seventeen, she honed her taste for more in the course of affairs with aging high-flying international financier and indicted fiscal manipulator Bernie Cornfeld, and with aging, high-flying television director and confessed bookmaker Ivan Nagy, who introduced Heidi to Alex. Heidi had an amazing network, not only through her lovers, but through her girl-friends, children of the stars like Victoria Sellers and Jennifer Young (daughter of Gig and celebrity super-realtor Elaine). Heidi dressed in the best clothes, ate in the trendiest restaurants, partied with the Brat Pack, the rock stars, not to mention the world's most famous DOMs (Dirty Old Men). The fact that Heidi Fleiss was a Hollywood insider with no need to be a madam was precisely what enabled her to rise out of the pack and make her mark. Like everything else in Hollywood, her connections were what really mattered.

The key part of the "more" that Heidi Fleiss wanted was to be famous. That most primal of all Hollywood desires was Heidi's hubris. While Alex's gospel was discretion, Heidi's was the time-honored Beverly Hills credo of shameless ostentation. She had it; she flaunted it. But in one instance it was too much. In June 1993, Sammy Lee, an undercover Beverly Hills cop who posed as a Honolulu businessman and drove a Ferrari Testarossa, had Heidi arrange dates—fifteen-hundred-dollar dates—at the Merv Griffin–owned Beverly Hilton with four Japanese business associates. The dates ended abruptly. The four girls were arrested by the businessmen—all undercover cops—on misdemeanor prostitution charges, which were quickly dropped. Heidi was arrested at her Benedict Canyon mansion on charges of prostitution, pandering, contributing to the delinquency of a minor (a seventeen-year-old girl was at the house), and possession of narcotics (thirteen grams of cocaine). In August, the police dropped the minor count and formally charged Heidi with five felonies—four for pandering, one for the cocaine. Facing over a dozen years in prison, she was held on $100,000 bail, a pittance compared to Alex's original bail of $1 million. Unlike the maternal Alex, Heidi, whose look was pure Beverly Hills (she came to her arraignment in a size-four Norma Kamali minidress and Oliver Peoples movie-star sunglasses), was a red-hot photo opportunity for the world press. The in-your-face image of the princess-gone-bad set off a mad media circus, transforming the secret reality that moguls and stars paid for sex into the most shocking of revelations.

In their respective relationships with the L.A.P.D., Alex had used her matrix of celebrities as a cross to a vampire; Heidi had used hers as a red cape to a bull. Heidi was taking high-class prostitution out of the closet. She was making it a cool fashion statement. The L.A.P.D. couldn't handle the change of style. They had no choice but to bring down Heidi Fleiss, just as they had brought down Alex Adams. However, in bringing Heidi down, the police unwittingly brought her up to the Mount Olympus of her desires. They gave Heidi her wildest dream, the Hollywood dream of the princess who has everything: They took the Hollywood Madam out of the shadows and they made her a Star.

ABOUT THE AUTHORS

ALEX ADAMS is, of course, Madam 90210.

WILLIAM STADIEM is a Harvard JD-MBA and former Wall Street lawyer who is the bestselling author of *Marilyn Monroe Confidential* and *Lullaby and Goodnight*. The Hollywood columnist for Andy Warhol's *Interview* and food critic for *Buzz*, he is also a screenwriter whose credits include *L.A. Law*, Franco Zeffirelli's *Young Toscanini*, and the upcoming *A Business Affair*, starring Christopher Walken. He interviewed over one hundred Hollywood call girls and a dozen rival madams for this book.